T0320310

CRITICAL PERSPECTIVES ON
RURAL CHANGE

Volume 1

RURAL RESTRUCTURING

RURAL RESTRUCTURING

Global Processes and
Their Responses

Edited by
**TERRY MARSDEN,
PHILIP LOWE
AND
SARAH WHATMORE**

Routledge
Taylor & Francis Group

LONDON AND NEW YORK

First published in 1990 by David Fulton Publishers Ltd.

This edition first published in 2023
by Routledge
4 Park Square, Milton Park, Abingdon, Oxon OX14 4RN

and by Routledge
605 Third Avenue, New York, NY 10158

Routledge is an imprint of the Taylor & Francis Group, an informa business

British Library Cataloguing in Publication Data
A catalogue record for this book is available from the British Library

ISBN: 978-1-032-49781-5 (Set)
ISBN: 978-1-032-49604-7 (Volume 1) (hbk)
ISBN: 978-1-032-49609-2 (Volume 1) (pbk)
ISBN: 978-1-003-39461-7 (Volume 1) (ebk)

DOI: 10.4324/9781003394617

Publisher's Note
The publisher has gone to great lengths to ensure the quality of this reprint but points out that some imperfections in the original copies may be apparent.

Disclaimer
The publisher has made every effort to trace copyright holders and would welcome correspondence from those they have been unable to trace.

CRITICAL PERSPECTIVES
ON
RURAL CHANGE SERIES

RURAL RESTRUCTURING

GLOBAL PROCESSES AND THEIR RESPONSES

EDITED BY

TERRY MARSDEN
PHILIP LOWE
SARAH WHATMORE

David Fulton Publishers
London

David Fulton Publishers Ltd
2 Barbon Close, Great Ormond Street, London WC1N 3JX

First published in Great Britain by
David Fulton Publishers 1990

British Library Cataloguing in Publication Data

Rural restructuring: global processes and their responses.
  – (Critical perspectives on rural change).
  1. Rural communities
  I. Marsden, Terry II.   Lowe, Philip
  III. Whatmore, Sarah   IV. Series.
  307.72

ISBN 1-85346-111-3

Typeset by Chapterhouse, Formby L37 3PX
Printed and bound in Great Britain by
Biddles Ltd, Guildford and King's Lynn

Contents

Contributors

Paul Cloke   Department of Geography
St. Davids College
University College of Lampeter
Lampeter
Wales

Patrick Commins   Agricultural Institute
Economics and Rural Welfare Centre
Hume House
Pembroke Road
Dublin 4
Ireland

Christina Gringeri   Department of Rural Sociology
College of Agricultural and Life Sciences
University of Wisconsin
350 Agriculture Hall
1450 Linden Drive
Madison
Wisconsin
USA

Francine Horton   Department of Rural Sociology
College of Agricultural and Life Sciences
University of Wisconsin
350 Agriculture Hall
1450 Linden Drive
Madison
Wisconsin
USA

Geoffrey Lawrence   Centre for Rural Welfare Research
Charles-Sturt University
Riverina Wagga-Wagga
New South Wales
Australia

Philip Lowe

Bartlett School of Architecture and Planning
University College London
22 Gordon Street
London WC1H 0QB
UK

Terry Marsden

Department of Planning, Housing and Development
South Bank Polytechnic London
Wandsworth Road
London SW8 2JZ
UK

Marc Mormont

Foundation Universitaire
Luxembourgeoise
Arlon
Belgium

Martin Peterson

Historiska Institutionen
Goteburg University
Sweden

Nanneke Redclift

Department of Social Anthropology
University College London
Gordon Square
London WC1
UK

Gene F. Summers

Department of Rural Sociology
College of Agricultural and Life Sciences
University of Wisconsin
350 Agriculture Hall
1450 Linden Drive
Madison
Wisconsin
USA

Nigel Thrift

Department of Geography
University of Bristol
University Road
Bristol BS8 1SS
UK

Sarah Whatmore

Department of Geography
University of Bristol
University Road
Bristol BS8 1SS
UK

Preface

Critical Perspectives on Rural Change

This series arises out of the increasing need for the international debate and dissemination of on-going empirical and theoretical research associated with rural areas in advanced societies. Rural areas, their residents and agencies, are now facing rapid social, economic and political change. The balance between production, amenity, mobility and development is readjusting as economic activities and their dependent relations become relocated. Similarly the values placed upon rural living and participation are subject to change. Local, national and international political forces have direct influence upon rural areas, not only for those concerned with agriculture but also with regard to rural development initiatives, overall economic and social policy and regional and fiscal arrangements. It is increasingly recognized that such changes demand a strong inter-disciplinary and critical perspective enabling a more holistic analysis to help our understanding. In particular this requires approaches that are more theoretically accommodating and capable of transcending traditional disciplinary boundaries as well as different spatial and institutional levels of analysis. This first volume in the series takes the broad theme of rural restructuring looking particularly at the nature of rural-related responses to global processes of change (see Introduction). Overall, the volumes are designed to attract a wide audience associated with international comparative research. They will provide reviews of current research taking as their focus, one major theme per volume. All the contributors are actively involved in research and committed to the development of international comparative research and able to provide current position statements about theoretical and empirical research in their particular fields of concern. It is intended that contributions should also be prospective in character, by identifying new research agenda and the likely consequences of contemporary changes in policy and economy. The overall focus upon 'rural change' should not encourage the 'ghettoization' of these particular strands of social scientific endeavour. The editors are committed to the use of this focus in providing a vehicle for the application of a wide range of social science approaches relating to theory and practice, and particularly, to exploring abstract social concepts and their 'grounding' through empirical research practice.

Terry Marsden
Philip Lowe
Sarah Whatmore
London 1990

Introduction: Questions of Rurality

Terry Marsden, Philip Lowe and Sarah Whatmore

Traditional rural sociology evolved during the 20th century largely around a common set of suppositions associated with the 'distinctiveness' of rural life. The essentially 'urban'-oriented nature of capitalist development and all its social and pathological consequences allowed rural sociologists to highlight aspects of 'traditional' society, focusing on a 'rural social system' that had its own internal norms and distinct patterns of stratification. Research tended to proceed along one of two complementary lines. The first involved the investigation of the internal mechanisms and procedures of traditional rural society. The second concerned the changes that occurred as rural societies became increasingly 'integrated' into national (or 'modern') society. These were studies of stability and change with the forces of stability being seen as intrinsic and those of change extrinsic. For the large part, rural society was also equated with agrarian society, with a central focus being placed on the roles, norms and changes associated with the farm family (see, for instance, Arensberg and Kimball, 1940; Rees, 1951; Haller, 1973).

Since the 1960s much of this research has been subjected to considerable challenge. Its strong *Gemeinschaft* orientation (Tonnies, 1957) emphasizing internal solidarity, kinship ties, generational continuity and traditional face-to-face society and its concentration on residual populations and the general absence of theoretical underpinning (see Bell and Newby, 1974) together led to a serious questioning of this research and, more generally, the status of a rural sociology in an increasingly 'urbanized' world. Moreover, the discovery of such putatively 'rural' characteristics such as strong kinship ties, the pre-eminence of face-to-face relationships and an emphasis on tradition in urban areas of Mexico (Lewis, 1949) and in Boston (Gans, 1968) but their virtual absence from Hertfordshire commuter villages (Pahl, 1964), eroded the conceptual power of the urban–rural dichotomy and challenged

1

the validity of a distinctive rural sociological method. Rural people and rural areas were not necessarily socially and economically apart or backward, nor were the sources of change or 'modernization' always exogenous. The post-war technological revolution in farming certainly altered its image as a traditional sector forming the bedrock of a stable rural world. Expanding patterns of counterurbanization and the urban–rural 'shift' in secondary and tertiary sector employment challenged the notions that rural areas were either detached or peripheral. These changes, along with sharply declining employment in a productivity-oriented agriculture, have tended more generally to decouple the fortunes of farming from the processes of rural development. At the same time, the expanded use of rural places for consumption-oriented activities – such as amenity, environmental protection, leisure and, above all, residence – rather than as areas dominated by primary production has led to a profound, if contested, shift in the images and societal definition of the rural (see Mormont, chapter 1).

Under these new conditions rural-based research and theorizing have pursued two distinct paths: one oriented to agrarian political economy, and the other to rural restructuring. Both directions emerged out of the extensive criticisms of traditional rural sociology that raged throughout the 1970s. Both, too, have been committed to a more theoretically informed approach relating rural problems more closely to mainstream social theory, while largely abandoning functionalist methods in the study of the rural community. In the following sections we trace the recent and divergent development of these two separate strands and point to the need for a new synthesis to address contemporary rural questions. This volume is the first in a series which seeks to reappraise rural change from a variety of challenging theoretical perspectives and thus to shape this new rural agenda.

Trends in agrarian political economy

Until the 1970s, rural sociology had largely ignored the body of agrarian theory established in the 19th century. Nothing less than a compensatory movement then took place, with the early classical approaches to agrarian development – such as those of Marx, Lenin, Kautsky and to a lesser extent Chayanov – being reapplied to contemporary questions (see Buttel and Newby, 1980; Bradley and Lowe, 1984). The 1980s were thus marked by attempts to establish a 'new' political economy of advanced agrarian systems. This intellectual thrust (see Freidland et al., 1981; Friedmann, 1982) has been both a reaction to the earlier empiricist orientation of established rural sociology and agricultural economics, and a search for a more holistic, and in some cases populist, agenda for coping with and understanding the farm and environmental crises (see Bradley, 1981; Buttel, 1982; Freidland, 1988; Goodman and Redclift, 1986). These changes were achieved in both the approach and the direction of agrarian research just at the time when mainstream sociology was subject to considerable theoretical disarray (Gouldner, 1970).

A central focus in this burgeoning literature was the conceptualization of agriculture as a distinct sphere of production that held particular obstacles to fully fledged capitalist development. In general terms theoretical and empirical work concentrated on four areas. These concerned, firstly, the ways in which capitalism sought to penetrate agriculture and the reasons why it was not always successful (Mouzelis, 1976); secondly, the nature of agrarian class structures and the role of rent in providing a theoretical underpinning for a comparative political economy of agrarian class structure (see Goss, Rodefield and Buttel, 1980); thirdly, the transformation and social patterns of resistance associated with the family labour farm in advanced capitalism; and finally a concentration upon the relations between agriculture and the state (see Buttel, 1982).

The distinctiveness of the rural community that was so apparent in the early rural sociological literature was now largely replaced by a focus on the distinctiveness of agriculture and its links with other parts of the agro-food complex. Arguments centred particularly on either the *integrative* or *exceptional* nature of agricultural production. This concerned two questions: firstly, how is agriculture integrated into the rest of the food system? and, secondly, why do the peculiarities of agricultural production present 'obstacles' to fully fledged capitalist development. Dominant in this literature was an exploration of the role of petty commodity production (i.e. market-oriented production reliant on family labour) as a persistent social formation in a world increasingly dominated by corporate capital (Friedmann, 1982), and a focus on the social mechanisms by which petty commodity producers reproduced themselves. The mode of production appears capable of successfully resisting the penetration and development of capitalism in agriculture. On the one hand, the ownership of land presents an obstacle to capitalism. On the other, the process of agricultural production remains largely dependent on biological phenomena that are incompletely mastered and still require the individual participation of the farmer to work them.

Since the mid-1980s, criticism has emerged of this earlier innovative work, mainly from authors seeking to build upon its central principles. The imperative has been to consolidate and extend political economy approaches, giving them more appeal across inter-disciplinary and national boundaries (Buttel and Goodman, 1989). It is necessary therefore to explore some of the ways in which the 'new' agrarian political economy is developing as well as to review several key weaknesses in its early phase of development.

In terms of approach and focus, there have been challenges to the over-deterministic nature of theoretical and empirical frameworks and the unilinear assumptions often implicit in the analysis of agrarian development. For several commentators (e.g. MacEwan-Scott, 1986; Long *et al.*, 1986), political economy interpretations have been too rigidly applied and economistically assessed. MacEwan-Scott sums up such problems by relating them to four basic questions:

> How to deal with variant and invariant manifestations of petty commodity production? Second, how to combine the economic with the political and the ideological in the analysis of structure? Third, how

to combine the elements of structure and agency into the analysis? And, finally, how to establish a form of causality that is neither functionalist, teleological nor tautological? (MacEwan-Scott, 1986, p. 20)

For McMichael and Buttel (1989) such problems are partly explained by the over-deductive approaches adopted and associated with a number of deeper problems that relate to the nature of explanation in structural Marxism (Benton, 1984). For instance, the inability to cope with variations in the forms of petty commodity production (see Friedmann, 1986) partly arises because of the orthodox assumption that all forms of petty commodity production *must* be explained by reference to a generalized law or model rather than to a series of historically specific factors (see Goodman and Redclift, 1986). Similarly, insufficient emphasis is given to the diverse forms of agrarian and production relations in the general development of the commodity form even though Lenin (1906) explicitly identified diverse forms of 'value relations', with 'wage labour' being only one form in the organization of labour under capitalism.

A further tension has been the primacy given to general economic 'laws' and the rendering of political and ideological factors as historically contingent (MacEwan-Scott, 1986). Explanation has largely proceeded in terms of the former, despite the fact that the latter factors are also causal and contribute to uneven development over time and space (see Smith, 1986). Such a tendency towards 'economism' has arisen because general 'laws' are usually distilled from economic relations alone. Hence, whereas Friedmann (1986) has more recently promoted the significance of the internal *social* processes of family farms as crucial in understanding their reproduction, the economistic framework within which the ideal type of petty commodity production is constructed does not allow her to proceed either in exploring these very issues or in assessing their variability. Such problems have encouraged some researchers to focus more specifically on the internal relations of households emphasizing the significance of power and ideological processes governing gender divisions of labour (see Redclift and Whatmore, chapter 7).

An associated shortcoming has been a reluctance to tackle the complex sets of relations concerned with 'convergence' in production forms on the one hand and the tendency towards uneven development and differentiation on the other (see Friedland and Pugleise, 1989). The relationship between unilinear tendencies and differential outcomes has attracted little comment or scrutiny. Nevertheless, it is this very issue – related, for instance, to the progressive spread of capitalist relations over peasant and family forms – that has so restrained the development of comparative analysis (see Buttel, 1982; Marsden *et al.*, 1987). As contributions to this volume illustrate, uneven development is an essential feature of and prerequisite to the maintenance of advanced capitalism, incorporating the opposing tendencies of the differentiation of capital penetration and the equalization of the conditions of production. Yet mainstream political economy approaches have tended to:

discount variation across time and space. That is, variation that does not conform to the tendencies deduced from the model is easily explained away – either because the model does not yet apply 'as a certain stage of development' has not yet arrived, or because some force exogenous to agriculture interferes with, or blocks, the process of transitions. ... What is deemed inappropriate is the reality to which the model is applied, rather than the methodological procedure of assuming models fit reality which (we stress) is problematic. (McMichael and Buttel, 1989, p. 13)

Such limitations have particularly affected the area of agricultural class analysis. Here, traditional Marxist class concepts have obvious limits when applied to agriculture given the persistence of millions of household farm enterprises. Nevertheless, through a process of marginalizing the 'historic peculiarities of nation, region and commodity organisation' (Friedland and Pugleise, 1989, p. 149) such concepts are applied at an international comparative level that does little to integrate features of uneven development into our analyses of capitalist development. For some (see van der Ploeg, 1986) this necessitates a reconceptualization of the commoditization *process* to focus on:

the matrix of commodity and non-commodity relations as they exist in particular concrete situations in which farming is embedded ... farm labour processes must be explored in order to determine the differential impact of relations. Finally, *farmers' responses* and their strategies should be acknowledged as being crucial to the formation of any concrete set of commodity relations. Indeed it is partly through the handling of these relations that farmers play their role in the struggle between direct producers and capital. (p. 54)

In response to such criticisms, work has begun to revise the agenda of agrarian political economy through a less deductivist approach and by tempering economistic analyses with an appreciation of how structural relationships are moulded by particular historical and social circumstances. This has become even more urgent given the tendency to reify agriculture in this literature during a period when agriculture itself is progressively losing its distinctive sectoral identity. Stressing the co-existence of simple commodity production can lead to the underestimation of the dependency relations that bind agriculture to the dominant mode of production. Similarly, if a characteristic of capitalism is to transform and restructure all that it encounters, then it is problematic to speak of the permanency of the petty commodity mode as this is already so altered through its longstanding involvement with the capitalist mode. In short, one insists on its permanence and co-existence when it may in fact be that the transformations and dependencies are more significant; including, for example, the gradual appropriation of the agricultural labour process by other sectors of the food system and its high degree of dependency on the provision of farm inputs and the processing of outputs (Goodman, Sorj and Wilkinson, 1987; see Commins and Peterson, chapters 2 and 3).

Such trends have encouraged the study of the changing role of agriculture within the food system. Much of the earlier work in this field was conducted in France originating initially from a concern with the complex financial and technological relationships farmers were entering into (Blanc and Lacombe, 1989). The study of the poultry chain, in particular, became an important focus for observing the integration of agriculture into the food processing industry. From such work emerged the concept of a food-production chain with its assumption that the type of economic structures prevailing at any point, from the production of agricultural raw materials at one end to the distribution of food products at the other, depends in part upon the immediately preceding and succeeding structures. The relationship between the various links in the chain are not only based upon the sale of products but also on the technology adopted. The nature and respective strengths of the economic structures in contact with one another thus influence both the manner in which the valorization of capital is distributed along the chain and the production methods at each point. Thus, any change affecting one link becomes transmitted along the entire chain.

The transnationalization of the food system means that food-production chains are increasingly international. The process is most advanced in North America where the most work has also been done on international food systems within the so-called 'commodity systems approach' (Freidland, 1988; Friedmann and McMichael, 1989). This involves the study of agricultural commodity production as 'a system in which technical and manufactured inputs are incorporated into a labour process in which commodities are produced, processed and marketed in distinctive industrial structures' (Buttel and Goodman, 1989, p. 87). In its most ambitious form this approach attempts to link together international commodity 'complexes' (such as the maize/soya/quality meat and fats–oils complexes) through the use of a world systems perspective (see Friedmann and McMichael, 1989; Sanderson, 1988).

If the current upsurge in work of this sort exhibits a gradual maturing of political economy approaches away from their deductivist and structuralist youth, the relative sparsity of research concerning links with other rural-based sectors and institutions tends only to re-emphasize the dominance of a focus on the agricultural and food sectors. The study of the agricultural has become divorced from the rural, and this has constrained a thorough examination of the influence of economic restructuring on the rural domain (see below). Whereas those pursuing a commodity systems approach have responded to the repeated calls not to view agriculture as autonomous, the consequence has not been a renewed understanding of rural economies but an emphasis, on the one hand on the increasingly residual character of land-based production and, on the other, on technologically induced change in the food system (Busch, Bonanno and Lacy, 1989).

The neglect by contemporary agrarian political economy of concepts and theories that attempt to explain the: 'massive upheavals in the national and international political economy . . . creating major changes in the economic systems, social relations and political balance of rural areas' (Bradley and

Lowe, 1984, p. 1) has led some commentators to announce the demise of the *agrarian question* (McMichael and Buttel, 1989). In that the fate of rural regions can no longer be characterized as a struggle between, say, capitalist and family-labour agriculture, this point must be conceded. However, whereas such a stance may appropriately reflect the declining salience of farming in the international food system, it offers little to illuminate the crises, dislocations and conflicts that accompany the progressive incorporation of rural areas into mainstream capitalist development. Here we must look to other social theory.

Restructuring rurality: global–local relations

A contemporaneous but largely separate body of literature has, during the 1980s, focused upon what is commonly termed the 'restructuring thesis'. This has been largely concerned with an urban or regional perspective despite its significance for our understanding of rural change (see Urry, 1984). Transgressing traditional disciplinary boundaries and applying a neo-Marxist critique to existing regional studies, this body of research developed rapidly during the 1980s based upon a critical analysis of the decline of Fordist industrial hegemony (see Cooke, 1988). In parallel with the agrarian political economists, however, a strong emphasis has been placed upon the consequences of the growing internationalization of industrial and financial capital and its consequences for nation-states and their regions. The collapse of the Bretton Woods Agreement in 1971, sharp oil price rises in 1973 and 1979, in addition to rapid acceleration of inflation in many advanced countries during the 1970s and 1980s, were all critical in terminating the post-war boom and establishing the conditions for the restructuring of economy and society. Whether this shift is seen to be associated with Kondratiev or Shumpeterian 'long waves' or as a secular change in the 'social structures of accumulation' (Gordon, 1980), there is a growing consensus in this literature that:

> across much of the world economy generally, it now seems that the individual, socio-political and spatial forms of economic organisation that constituted the basis of post-war development, are losing their former role as leading sources of growth and accumulation. Previously dominant industries, technologies, methods of production, skills, class divisions, state policies and even institutional arrangements are in rapid decline and are being superseded by new industries, new technologies, new production methods, new skills and class divisions and new policies and institutional configurations. Rather than simply marking a temporary inflexion of the economic trajectory of the post-war decades, the intense and wide-ranging reorganisation since the early 1970's would seem to herald a significant break from it. (Martin, 1989, p. 188)

Indeed, by the mid-1980s writers were discerning that the fundamental crisis of Fordism was associated with it reaching certain technical and human *limits*, which, in turn, were then engendering slowdowns and real falls in productivity. This necessitated the growth of new economic and social forms (e.g. flexible manufacturing systems, Just-in-Time delivery systems, more spatially concentrated small businesses/more flexible working practices); and demanded different sets of spatial priorities in terms of site location and degree of inter-firm linkage (see Summers, 1984). Also, as Clark (1989) and Green (1988) argue, this bundle of changes occurring at a global level promote new sets of dependent relations between finance and industrial capital such that individual firms (as well as their associated service-based activities) are increasingly prone to buy-outs and asset stripping based on complex credit relations. This produces increased instability and vulnerability both in the capital accumulation process and in terms of local labour markets, whether urban or rural. It engenders more reliance upon credit finance (i.e. geographically mobile capital) and the disassembly of previous industrial structures in order to ensure adequate returns and credit repayments. Nowhere has this been more evident than in the food manufacturing sectors. For instance, between 1983 and 1988 the multinational conglomerate, Unilever, sold 90 firms (worth £2.3 bn) and purchased another hundred (for £4.7 bn). Supported by merchant banks the companies overall borrowing limit exceed £14 bn because of its attempts to take control of firms with established markets in Europe. Clark also notes the case of RJR Nabisco where:

> symbolically and literally the leverage buy-out of RJR Nabisco by Kohlberg Kravis Roberts (KKR) for $23 billion reflects the geographical dominance of the arbitrage economy: as a merged conglomerate, the headquarters of RJR Nabisco had already been moved from Winston–Salem to Atlanta. With the leverage buy-out, the headquarters were moved from Atlanta to New York City. In essence the logic of centralised and decentralised production (so fundamental to text book treatments of the geography of corporate management) has been taken over: centralised control in other centres is now necessary for the efficient conversion of assets, and decentralised production networks are assets to be sold rather than managed. (Clark, 1989, p. 997)

How the current period of leveraged buy-outs, mergers and acquisitions will affect either the geography of the world economy or, more specifically, rural regions within it is yet to be understood. Whereas much was made, in the early 1980s, of the supposed urban–rural shift in manufacturing industries; it is now far less clear how rural regions are to fair in the post-Fordist international economy; or more specifically, how dependent rural localities will be on their regional and national economic contexts. Peripheral 'greenfield' locations may be seen as advantageous for inward international investment, enabling, at least, some rural localities to experience an economic 'windfall' (see Summers, 1984); and the spatial and social structures of rural areas may offer certain comparative advantages to the technologies and processes of flexible accumulation. Favoured and protected 'rural' areas in economically buoyant regions, such as East Anglia, Bavaria, Tuscany, Colorado and New England have lost their traditional image as economic backwaters based essentially on primary production and are projected as establishing proto-typical social and economic forms. As societies emerge out of the Fordist hegemony, however, combined with a reduction in state support for agriculture (see Lawrence, chapter 4 in this volume) some rural regions are set to bear a disproportionate burden of disinvestment and deregulation (see Falk and Lyson, 1989). Whereas, for instance, a common geographical assumption has been that:

> the geographical locus of capital accumulation has shifted to industralising rural areas such as the high technology-oriented company buoyant 'sunrise' and 'sunset' regions, such as the Southern states of the US, South-eastern parts of Britain and the Southern parts of France and Germany. (Martin, 1989, p. 188).

For critical analysts such processes are both highly uneven and shortlived. As Falk and Lyson point out with reference to rural America:

> Rural America is in trouble. It is losing jobs, it is losing people; it is losing its identity. After eight years of 'Reaganomics', record drought, a deluge of foreign imports, rural America finds itself in crisis. A key to rescuing this crisis is developing and nurturing a more diversified industrial and economic structure. (1989, p. 1)

The upsurge in research effort associated with these restructuring processes and the changing modes of state regulation to which they are tied (see Lipietz, 1985; Rustin, 1989) is now allowing the opportunity for a broader conceptualization of the *rural problematic* (see Bradley and Lowe, 1984; Rees, 1984; Urry, 1984; Mormont, chapter 1 in this volume). Not only is this being seen within the broader context of international restructuring and regulation (for instance, the current changes in GATT arrangements), but it is also allowing the application of mainstream social theory to research in the rural sphere. The contributions to this volume demonstrate this tendency. As Urry (1984) identifies, the centrality of the restructuring thesis holds important implications for what have been traditionally regarded as rural areas on the one hand and for political economy perspectives of rural sociology on the other. These contentions are worth developing briefly here.

First, the restructuring thesis (see Newby, 1986; Marsden *et al.*, 1987; Whatmore, Munton and Marsden, 1990) assumes the decreased significance of spatial criteria (particularly the urban–rural dichotomy). This is replaced by, as we have seen, an emphasis upon the ways in which capital accumulation (through active fractions of capital) seeks out exploitable spaces largely associated with the relative quality and costs of human labour power. Thus, the concept of the 'ruralization' of industry in North America and Western Europe is not so much a process caused by the geographical features of 'urban' and 'rural' places, but rather a consequence of; (i) the international and national restructuring of traditional capital, and (ii) the differential changes in the ease of exploitation between one area and another. As Urry argues:

> International capital has been transformed, first through an increasing spatial indifference, and second, by the fractionalising of its different global operations. Production plants are often relatively small (even if they are part of massive multi-nationals) and capital will be relatively indifferent as to where they are located. Hence labour power assumes a particular importance as to location – and this includes difference in costs, skill content and reproduction. Provided there is or could be sufficient labour in a 'rural' area then expansion may well take place in that (greenfield) site rather than in alternative areas. Cities have become relatively less distinctive entities, bypassed by various circuits of capital and labour power. (1984, p. 55)

Such economic forces are uneven and condition the 'time-space' structuring of regions and localities. The *historical conditions* of localities, including their particular economic and social legacies and cultural conditioning factors, affect new 'waves' of development (see Day, 1982; Rees, 1984; Marsden *et al.*, 1987). The outcome in contemporary capitalist societies cannot be usefully summarized in terms that are associated with urban or rural difference, or for that matter, of regions so identified conventionally (see Mormont, chapter 1 in this volume).

A second contention, but one which has so far been insufficiently developed, concerns the nature of relationships between the restructuring of capitalist production and of 'civil society' on the one hand, and the effects of these sets of relationships on 'local systems' of social stratification on the other. Considerable confusion exists concerning the role of stratification and class-based analyses of change in rural localities (see Cloke and Thrift, chapter 6 in this volume); and as Goodwin (1989) admits, the notion of civil society (Gramsci, 1971) is open to wide-ranging definition. Nevertheless, as Cooke (1989) outlines, locally based *action* often leads to the assertion of citizenship rights and thus tempers in some cases the inequalities of global structural change. Locality or the *local social system* is thus an 'expression of the conscious social base' (p. 248). Urry (1984) argues that one significant effect of the current rounds of spatial and economic restructuring is to heighten the socio-political significance of local systems. The period of restructuring in the 1980s has tended to undermine traditional notions of class and civil society that are now more prone to *local conditions* and the separate criteria associated with participation in a variety of markets. Hence:

> the stratification structure of any locality (whether formally urban or rural) is the interdependent effect of mutually modifying forms of structural determination especially of the complex overlap between diverse spatial divisions of labour. (Urry, 1984, p. 45)

A comprehensive understanding of power and class in rural localities and particularly the ways they may moderate structural change remains a significant gap in this literature. This may reflect both the undue emphasis given to structural and economistic principles in analyses. Nevertheless it is now increasingly recognized that the nature of global–local relations, and their specificity, need to be understood with reference to local social, economic and political action. This demands further abstract theorizing and the development of intermediate levels of analysis which attempt to ground these conceptualizations, linking local to macro-change (see Goodwin, 1989).

New rural questions

The 'new' rural sociology, since its emergence in the late 1970s, has made a number of achievements: it has successfully superceded the earlier behavioural orthodoxy and elaborated critical alternatives; it has dispelled the notion of the autarky of rural society and it has overcome the theoretical isolation of rural sociology. As we have seen, though, its development has become seriously bifurcated. On the one hand, agrarian political economists have been led upwards, following the vertical integration within the food system. On the other hand, those concerned with economic restructuring have been led outwards, following the horizontal disintegration and recombination of the spatial structure of society induced by the changing geography of capital accumulation. Few attempts (Bradley and Lowe, 1984; Newby, 1986) have been made within either perspective to focus upon rural questions; the researchers involved have simply looked in other directions. Indeed, under the centrifugal pull of these two diverging tendencies conventional rural categories are being deconstructed. Agrarian political economists, for their part, emphasize the diminishing role of agriculture in food commodity systems; industrial capitals' progressive appropriation of activities (once regarded as essential to farming); and the long-term tendency to eliminate a rural based (i.e. land-based) labour process. They thus portray farming as an economically residual, if not archaic, category (Goodman and Redclift, 1986). Meanwhile, the restructuring thesis challenges the specificity of rural localities arguing that their predominantly agrarian character was an outcome of past 'rounds' of investment and that present or future rounds may engender radically different spatial divisions of labour. Within this perspective, the 'rural' is largely dismissed as a 'chaotic conception', i.e. an historically-contingent, descriptive category lacking explanatory power (Urry, 1984).

Rural areas in the advanced capitalist societies (not to mention those elsewhere) are, indeed, currently experiencing diverse fortunes. Nevertheless, there are common experiences and identities that call for a more positive and coherent response from social scientists. Firstly, rural areas have in common an historical dominance by the social relations of agricultural production and this inevitably conditions the comparative advantages and disadvantages they offer to other fractions of capital as well as their responses to restructuring processes. Rural labour processes, for example, retain distinctive characteristics even though agriculture may have long ceased to be the dominant capital fraction (Bradley, 1984; Summers, Horton and Gringeri, chapter 5 in this volume). Secondly, farming remains an important social and ideological category still able to mould rural economic development through its politically entrenched position, as well as its monopoly control over rural land. Third, as the role of agricultural production diminishes, so the social function of rural space is being redefined to encompass other primary production (such as bio-mass) as well as distinctive consumption roles (such as residence, recreation, leisure and environmental conservation). This in turn creates new and locally specific accumulation opportunities, new identities and processes of social reproduction.

The problems associated with the transformation of rural areas thus need to be rescued from the conceptual hiatus to which they are increasingly assigned. Indeed it is imperative to respond, as recent research has singularly failed to do, to Newby's (1986) call for a holistic approach to the analysis of rural social relations. An appropriate starting point would be to reverse the respective telescopes of agrarian political economy and economic restructuring. In other words, to locate the contemporary predicament of rural areas at the intersection of the two major forces transforming them, the reorganization of the international food system and the social and economic restructuring of rural regions under the pressure of capitalist recombination.

The contributions to this volume explore this new rural agenda of theoretical and empirical issues that seeks to integrate the two separate strands of the 'new' rural sociology, in recognition of the multidimensionality of contemporary rural change. In doing so they deal, to varying degrees, with four key questions. These concern, firstly, what are the relationships between global processes and their outcomes at national and regional levels? Secondly, how is the uneven pattern of capitalist expansion altering at the international level and how do nation-states reproduce or moderate uneven patterns of rural development? Thirdly, how significant in affecting rural change is agriculture and shifts in state policy towards the sector? Finally, how is research adapting to the rate and direction of rural change and how can the analytical categories of social class, labour markets, household and livelihood assist this development.

Whereas such ambitious questions can never be sufficiently handled within the confines of one volume, the contributions start to point researchers in the direction of a more integrative and critical analysis. Subsequent volumes in the series will take up more specific themes. Together they will begin to expose novel rural questions by linking new theoretical insights to the changing realities of the 1990s.

Mormont (chapter 1 in this volume) starts by providing a re-examination of the 'sociology of the rural'. He traces the development of the specialism and, in particular, its conventional reliance upon established social divisions and sociological categories. The ways in which society defines and represents meanings confront the changing status of sociological theory. The history of sociological thought and its approaches are very much tied to the terms used to define the phenomena. Hence rural sociology has developed around an established set of cagetories distinguishing the urban from the rural. During the post-war period, having been created in a conservative and anti-urban mould it tended to redefine itself around a humanistic perspective whereby it defended and represented human values associated with rural living. These were largely measured by the degree of remoteness from the modern (urban, industrial) world. The underlying relationships between space and society, he argues, have now assumed a renewed interest given the current pace and direction of restructuring. Increasing mobility, new uses of the countryside and the 'use' of rural areas by urban residents mean that the relationship between the individual and space is defined less in terms of belonging to a particular place but has come to be associated more with the varying opportunities rural space affords. This demands a reorientation for the sociology of the rural founded on a *rurality* that is increasingly reliant upon the *social production of meanings* rather than on territorial space. Mormont demonstrates the ways in which rural sociology needs to accommodate the social, economic and political changes that are continuously redefining both the local and the rural.

Mormont's expansive discussion of the ways in which rural sociology needs to adjust to new circumstances is followed by three contributions that focus on the shifting significance of agriculture and agricultural policy as agents of change. Commins (chapter 2 in this volume) develops a conceptual framework with which to examine the original conditions, dynamics and outcomes of agricultural restructuring in modern western societies using evidence from the EC and Ireland. Agricultural restructuring has to be understood as a set of dynamic changes determined by (i) the macroeconomic forces of capitalist development; (ii) the nature of socioeconomic structures that condition the relative power of different interests to influence change; and (iii) by the activities of national and supra-national states to regulate change. Commins assembles a wide range of evidence that illustrates these structural trends and their outcomes in the transition from a 'productionist' to a 'post-productionist' policy framework for agriculture in the advanced economies. In Ireland, EC policy measures to restrain milk production (i.e. milk quotas) are tending to reinforce concentration tendencies in the sector facilitated by the new market in 'milk quota land'. This is doing little to diminish the impetus, supported by technological developments, for increased 'cost effectiveness' on fewer, larger farm holdings. The consequence is to consolidate the dualistic structure of modern agriculture whereby production is concentrated on a smaller number of specialized farms that coexist with a growing proportion of holdings practising varied forms of diversification. This is a highly uneven process, and it is difficult to correlate the EC's various agricultural measures with the problems of *local* farming communities and rural regions increasingly dependent on the European economy.

Peterson (chapter 3 in this volume) sets the current changes occurring in the political economy of agriculture in advanced societies in historical perspective by using the notion of a paradigmatic shift. He examines in detail the way that this shift has occurred in Sweden, and the contrasts this holds with current changes in the EC. Peterson traces the growth of a regulatory paradigm based upon corporatist interests, Keynesian welfare policies and the science-push of agricultural productivity. Whereas the Swedish regulatory model informed the development of the European Community's agricultural policy in the 1950s, Peterson argues that current deregulatory processes in Sweden may also have lessons for other Western economies. In the Swedish case deregulation is being positively supported as a means of introducing more flexibility into agricultural production as well as partly freeing farmers and rural communities from the technological treadmill. For Peterson, the move towards a new agrarian paradigm is associated with the battle of ideas and ideologies. Popular and official criticism concerning the degree of corporatist linkage between farmers' lobbies, political parties and agribusiness have intensified during the 1980s. Whether or not such criticism is merited, the internationalisation of economic relations as well as the specific problems of over production within the agrarian sector necessitate a new regulatory paradigm. This is stimulating the development of alternative, low-input production systems. In the Swedish case farmers' lobbies are actively promoting environmental conservation, alternative products and ecological farming, as well as an increased role for women in farming and its representative organizations.

These national and regionally-based initiatives need to be seen in the global context where radical changes are being canvassed by some of the major agricultural exporting countries under the auspices of the General Agreement on Trade and Tariffs (GATT). Any liberalization of the international regulatory order is likely to induce a different response in different countries although there are general pressures challenging state support and protection for agrarian production and trade. The example of Australia, the country that has led the campaign to liberalize world agricultural trade, certainly offers some striking contrasts with the Swedish experience. Lawrence (chapter 4 in this volume) focuses on the ways in which rural social change in Australia is presently being conditioned by the deregulation of agricultural policy, the application of new technologies, and the integration of the Australian economy into the Pacific Basin region. The process of deregulation began in the mid-1980s as part of a programme of national economic renewal. Following two centuries of export-based agricultural production dominated globally first by trade relations with Britain and then with America, Australia is now being progressively marginalized and de-industrialized as it is incorporated into the Pacific Basin largely as a supplier of raw materials. This has exposed the Australian economy, and its rural areas, to the full rigours of fluctuations in world commodity prices. Such vulnerabilities are enhanced by the increasing levels of protectionism and subsidized exporting promoted by other advanced countries, most notably Japan and the European Community. Such global conditions are promoting productivity-oriented technological development in agriculture, further reducing the demands for farm labour and redefining work roles and local labour conditions, with deleterious consequences for rural community life. The rationalization of social welfare provision based upon narrow definitions of cost and 'critical mass' are having a particular impact on the rural poor. Both the Government and farmers' unions are committed to the stimulation of agribusiness and technological development directed towards reducing production costs. Such strategies are running counter to the *local* needs for a sustainable and socially beneficial agriculture. Moreover, there seems to be no guarantee that 'high tech' (e.g. biotechnological) advances are likely to reassert Australia's previously strong position in world trade, given the stubborn protectionism of its world competitors and substitutionist strategies pursued by the traditional importers of food and fibre.

Lawrence provides an insight into the interactions between the increasingly turbulent global commodity markets, a state committed to exposing its national economy to these forces, and – through agricultural and technological change – the uncertain prospects for rural people.

In the next three contributions rural change is examined through a focus upon largely non-agrarian mechanisms. Summers, Horton and Gringeri (chapter 5) concentrate upon linking the theoretical and empirical interpretations of *rural labour markets* in the United States; Cloke and Thrift (chapter 6) assess the significance of *social class* and class cleavages as powerful means with which to assess economic restructuring and social recomposition in localities; and Redclift and Whatmore (chapter 7) review *livelihood* and *household* as important concepts in the analysis of rural change.

Summers, Horton and Gringeri critically review the extensive literature on rural labour markets in the United States and relate this to theoretical developments in the field. The food and fibre system is playing a decreasing role as a rural employer while the buoyancy of manufacturing employment – predominant in the 1970s – is also on the wane. Rural areas are becoming increasingly vulnerable to the instabilities of manufacturing and service sectors. Despite considerable theoretical debate neither labour economists nor sociologists has devoted much empirical attentions to these labour market trends. With the exception of studies of agricultural labour markets, there are significant gaps in our understanding of the segmentation and diversity of rural labour markets. The chapter outlines particular lines for future development given the new social and economic conditions emerging in rural areas.

Cloke and Thrift (chapter 6) review the nature and significance of class and class analysis in rural society with reference to Britain. They argue that until recently class analysis has remained largely descriptive in rural studies, with few attempts to link it either to the evolution of property and labour relations or to the wider processes of economic restructuring. For both theoretical and descriptive reasons it is necessary to focus upon the *dynamism* of class and class analysis and to examine how current rounds of economic restructuring are affecting class formation and consciousness. Although class is of central importance in understanding rural change we have to be aware of its multi-dimensionality both at the empirical and theoretical level. A focus upon class fractions is thus important, which the authors illustrate by reference to the role of the service class in rural Britain. This focus does not reduce the salience of class itself but reinforces the need to uncover the multiplicity of ways that class influences rural change including how class interests are organized and expressed.

Redclift and Whatmore (chapter 7) trace some of the main ways in which the concerns of household, consumption and livelihood are re-emerging as key issues in the analysis of rural restructuring. Their arguments draw upon the restructuring literature and feminist research, to provide a starting point for integrating class recomposition, deprivation and household production. Much of the research traditionally undertaken on these themes has uncritically accepted the mutually reinforcing ideologies of rurality and domesticity and ignored the centrality of gender relations. The authors offer an evaluation of the complex and contradictory relationships between the material changes taking place in rural areas and the concepts that have come to inform the related social and policy discourse.

Whereas the latter three contributions apply different conceptual frameworks to the analysis of rural changes, commonalities lie in several areas. Each of the chapters is directed to a fuller understanding of the diversity of rural life given the declining part played by agriculture. Each also is seeking an explanation of rural change and not simply a description. Finally, as with the earlier chapters all the authors attempt to integrate new developments in social theory – particularly associated with the restructuring debates – into the analysis of rural change. A focus upon global processes and their consequences for rural areas and people begins to redefine rural and agrarian questions. These are conditioned both by the increasing disorder of the global economy and policy frameworks and by the national and local contexts which mediate and contest these changes. The contributions expose the complexities of these new rural questions and provide a point from which to start to analyse them.

Bibliography

Aglietta, M. (1979) *A Theory of Capitalist Regulation: the US experience*, New Left Books, London.

Aglietta, M. (1982) World capitalism in the eighties, *New Left Review*, **136**, 5–42.

Arensburg, G. M. and Kimball, S. T. (1940) *Family and Community in Ireland*, Harvard University Press, Cambridge, Mass.

Benton, T. (1984) *The Rise and Fall of Structural Mannerism: Althusser and His Influence*, Macmillan, London.

Bell, C. and Newby, H. (1974) *Community Studies*, Allen & Unwin, London.

Blanc, M. and Lacombe, P. (1989) Quarante an d'économie rural. In Bodiguel, M. and Lowe, P. (eds) *Campagne Française, Campagne Britannique*, chapter II, L. Harmattan, Paris.

Bradley, T. (1981) Capitalism and the countryside: rural sociology as political economy, *International Journal of Labour and Regional Research*, **5**, 581–7.

Bradley, T. (1984) Segmentation in local labour markets. In Bradley and Lowe (eds), *Locality and Rurality: Economy and Society in Rural Regions*, Geobooks, Norwich.

Bradley, T. and Lowe P. (1984) *Locality and Rurality: Economy and Society in Rural Regions*, Geobooks, Norwich.

Busch, L., Bonanno, A. and Lace, W. B. (1989) Science, technology and the restructuring of agriculture, *Sociologia Ruralis*, 2, Vol. XXIX, 118-25.

Busch, L. and Lacy, W. B (1983) *Science Agriculture and the Politics of Research*, Westview Press, Boulder, Col.

Buttel, F. H. L. (1982) The political economy of agriculture in advanced industrial societies, *Current Perspectives in Social Theory*, 3, 27-55.

Buttel, F. H. L. and Goodman D. (1989) Class, state, technology and international food regimes, *Sociologia Ruralis*, 14 (2), 86-93.

Buttel, F. H. L. and Newby H. (eds) (1980) *The Rural Sociology of Advanced Societies*, Montclair, New Jersey, Allanheld, Osman and Co.

Clark, G. (1989) Remaking the map of corporate capitalism: the arbitrage economy of the 1990's, *Environment and Planning*, A, Sept.

Cooke, P. (1988) Flexible integration, scope economies and strategic alliances: social and spatial mediations, *Society and Space*, 3, 408-12.

Cooke, P. (1989) Critical cosmopolitanism: urban and regional studies into the 1990's, *Geoforum*, 20 (2), 241-52.

Day, G. (1982) Wales: the regional problem and development. In Rees, A. D. and Rees, G. (eds), *Poverty and Social Inequality in Wales*, Croom Helm, London.

Falk, W. and Lyson, T. (1989) Rural America and the industrial policy debate, unpublished paper, University of Maryland.

Freidland, W. H. (1988) Bologna aftermath, unpublished paper presented to members of the Rural Studies Research Centre, London, August 1988.

Freidland, W. H., Furnari, M. and Pugliese, E. (1981) The labour process and agriculture, paper presented at the working conference on the labour process, *University of California*, Santa Cruz.

Freidland, W. H. and Pugliese, E. (1989) Class formation and decomposition in modern capitalist agriculture: comparative perspectives, *Sociologia Ruralis*, 14, 86-92.

Friedmann, H. (1982) The family farm in advanced capitalism: outline of a theory of simple commodity production in agriculture, Conference paper to the American Sociological Association, Toronto.

Friedmann, H. (1986) Patriarchy and property: a reply to Goodman and Redclift, *Sociologia Ruralis*, XXVI (2).

Friedmann, H. (1989) Agrofood industries and export agriculture: the changing international division of labour 1945-1973, unpublished paper, University of Toronto.

Friedmann, H. and McMichael, P. (1989) Agriculture and the State system: the rise and decline of national agricultures, 1870 to the present, *Sociologia Ruralis*, 14, 93-118.

Gans, H. (1968) Urbanism and suburbanism as ways of life. In Pahl, R. E. *Readings in Urban Sociology*, Pergamon, Oxford.

18

Goodman, D. and Redclift, M. (1986) Capitalism, petty commodity production and the farm enterprise, *Sociologia Ruralis*, **XXV** (3/4).

Goodman, D., Sorj, D. and Wilkinson, J. (1987) *From Farming to Biotechnology*, Basil Blackwell, Oxford.

Goodwin, M. (1989) Uneven development and civil society in Western and Eastern Europe, *Geoforum*, **20** (2), 151-9.

Gordon, D. (1980) Stages of accumulation and long economic cycles. In Hopkins J. and Wallerstein, W. (eds), *Processes of the World System*, Sage, Calif.

Goss, E. F., Rodefield, R D. and Buttel, F. (1980) The political economy of class structure in US agriculture: a theoretical outline. In Buttel, F. H. L. and Newby, H. (eds), *The Rural Sociology of Advanced Societies*, Osman & Co., Montclair, Allenheld.

Gouldner, A. W. (1970) *The Coming Crisis of Western Sociology*, Avon, New York.

Gramsci, A. (1971) *Selections from the Prison Notebooks*, Lawrence & Wishart, London.

Green, G. (1988) *Finance Capital and Uneven Development*, Westview, New York.

Haller, A. O (1973) Review of seventy years of rural sociology in the United States. In Bertrand A. (Ed.), *Contemporary Sociology*, 3 (2), 138.

Hussain, A. and Tribe, K. (1983) *Marxism and the Agrarian Question*, Macmillan, London.

Kenney, M., Lobas, L. M., Curry, J. and Goe, W. R. (1989) Mid western agriculture in US Fordism, from the new deal to economic restructuring, *Sociologia Ruralis*, **XXIX** (2), 131-49.

Kloppenburg, J. (1988) *First the Seed*, Cambridge University Press, London.

Lenin, V. (1906) *The Development of Capitalism in Russia*, International Publishers, Moscow.

Lewis, D. (1949) *Life in a Mexican Village*, University of Illinois Press.

Lipietz, A. (1985) The world crisis: the globalisation of the general crisis of Fordism, *IDS Bulletin*, **16**, 6-11.

Lipietz, A. (1988) *Mirages and Miracles: the Crisis of Global Fordism*, Verso, London.

Long, N. and Van Der Ploeg, J. (1988) New challenges in the sociology of rural development: a rejoinder to Vandergeest, *Sociologia Ruralis*, **18**(1), 30-42.

Long, N., Van Der Ploeg, J., Curtin, C. and Box, L. (1986) The commoditisation debate: labour process, strategy and social networks, working paper, University of Wageningen.

MacEwan-Scott, A. M. (1986) Towards a rethinking of petty commodity production, *Social Analysis*, **20**, 1-25.

Mandel, E. (1978) *Late Capitalism*, Verso, London.

Marsden, T. (1989) Commoditisation of the labour process: farm households and British agriculture, Sociology of Agriculture (ISA), Working Paper No. 2.

Marsden, T. (1990) Key issues in the political economy of pluriactivity, *Journal of Rural Studies*, Special Issue 1990.

Marsden, T., Munton, R., Whatmore, S. and Little, J. (1986) Towards a political economy of agriculture: British perspective, *International Journal of Urban and Regional Research*, **10** (4), 498–521.

Marsden, T., Whatmore, S. Munton, R. and Little, J. (1987) Uneven development and the restructuring process in British agriculture: a preliminary exploration, *Journal of Rural Studies*, **3** (4), 297–308.

Martin, R. (1989), The reorganisation of regional theory: alternative perspectives on the changing capitalist space economy, *Geoforum*, **20** (2), 187–201.

Massey, D. (1984) *Spatial Divisions of Labour: Social Structures and the Geography of Production*, Macmillan, London.

McMichael P. and Buttel, F. (1989) New directions in the political economy of agriculture, unpublished paper, Cornell University.

Mouzelis, N. (1976) Capitalism and the development of agriculture, *Journal of Peasant Studies*, **7**, 483–92.

Newby, H. (1980) Rural sociology – a trend report, *Current Sociology*, **28**, 1–14.

Newby, H. (1986) Locality and rurality: the restructuring of rural social relations, *Regional Studies*, **20**, 209–16.

Newby, H., Bell, C., Rose, D. and Saunders, P. (1978) *Property, Paternalism and Power: Class and Control in Rural England*, Hutchinson, London.

Offe, C. (1985) *Disorganised Capitalism*, Polity Press, Cambridge.

Pahl, R. (1964) Urbs in Rure: the Metropolitan Fringe in Hertfordshire, LSE Geographical Papers No 2.

Rees, A. D. (1951) *Life in a Welsh Countryside*, University of Wales Press, Cardiff.

Rees, G. (1984) Rural regions in national and international economies. In Bradley and Lowe (eds), *Locality and Plurality*, GLS Books, London.

Rustin, M. (1989) The politics of post-Fordism: or, the trouble with 'new times', *New Left Review*, 55–77.

Sanderson, S. E. (1988) The emergence of the 'world steer': internationalisation and foreign domination in Latin American cattle production. In Tullis, F. L. and Holist, W. L. (eds) *Food, State and International Political Economy*, University of Nebraska Press, Lincoln.

Smith, C. (1986) Reconstructing the elements of petty commodity production, *Social Analysis*, No. 20, Dec., 50–67.

Summers, G. (ed.) (1984) *Technology and Social Change in Rural Areas*, Westview, Boulder, Col..

Tonnies, F. (1957) *Gemeinschaft Und Gesellschaft*, Harper Row, New York.

Urry, J. (1981) Localities, regions and social class, *International Journal of Urban and Regional Research*, **5**, 455–474.

Urry, J. (1984) Capitalist restructuring, recomposition and the regions. In Bradley and Lowe (eds), *Locality and Rurality*, Geobooks, London.

Van Der Ploeg, J. (1986) The agricultural labour process and commoditisation. In Long *et al.* (eds) *The Commoditisation Debate*, University of Wageningen.

Walker, M. and Storper, S. (1989) *The Capitalist Imperative: Territory, Technology and Industrial Growth*, Blackwell, Oxford.

20

Whatmore, S., Munton, R. and Marsden, T. (1990) The rural restructuring process: emerging divisions of agricultural property rights, *Regional Studies* following issue.

CHAPTER 1

Who Is Rural? or, How To Be Rural: Towards a Sociology of The Rural

Marc Mormont

When analysing social change, it is always important to distinguish between terrain, map and compass – that is, between object studied, models constructed and analytical tools employed. The distinction is particularly crucial in the case of rural change, where tools and model are themselves the products of their own history. Rural sociology, as a discipline, developed on the (more or less explicit) postulate that in modern (industrial) societies there was a significant division of the social domain into two relatively independent worlds, rural and urban. The approach could be supported by pointing to the obvious fact that the two worlds did indeed function differently, which could be ascribed, for instance, to the relative economic autarky of rural societies; to specific mechanisms in the political field; or to cultural differences. These factors were reflected in the very different reproduction mechanisms for city and country, with family, village and land looming very large in the latter. Not that rural societies had ever been independent of urban societies. The *raison d'être* of rural sociology was not that rural societies were independent of urban societies, but that they displayed a relative autonomy, albeit subject to external pressure.

Clearly, rural sociology should have devoted some of its efforts to studying how exactly rural societies have resisted the outside world; instead, most of its work has focused on the mechanisms for change, adaptation and integration in modern society. The result has been that rural dwellers' skills in withstanding pressure have only been revealed negatively. My prime concern, however, is the fact that the approach adopted implied that the urban–rural division reflected a social divide between two opposed groups – witness the large number of studies on contacts and conflicts between town and country dwellers. These two distinct social 'groups' were presumed, even though rural sociology never managed to adopt a clear terminology, to designate the nature of these sets (it is still wavering between terms such as rural society, rural environment and rural world). This lack of precision – theoretical, not terminological – has not stopped rural sociologists from carrying on with their work – not only because they have never been greatly exercised by theory, but also because the division of the social world was so obviously enshrined in the clearly visible spatial division between the cities and the countryside.

But is there today still such a thing as 'rural society'? And does the distinction between town and country still match that between rural and urban? Rural sociologists have to address these questions; yet traditional rural sociology, with its disinclination to theorize, scarcely provides them with the wherewithal for an answer. The problem has to be tackled at its roots by examining how rural sociology has evolved and what it has taken as its subject-matter – in short, by attempting a sociology of rural sociology. For, internal to the problem is the way rural sociology operates and the part it has played in legitimating a social definition of the 'rural', which is now a social (and scientific) obstacle to a true sociology of the rural.

Social divisions and sociological categories

A common feature of the categories used by sociologists studying the social world is that they also have popular currency (Bourdieu, 1980, 1981). Thus the categories that designate social classes, hierarchical strata or even socio-professional categories are used not only by sociologists (where they only acquire meaning within a theory) but also by individuals, groups and institutions to refer to each other. Obviously, the choice of terms used to designate a category is always determined by the relationship between the groups concerned, because the social recognition of a group (a particular category of workers, say) necessarily presupposes the existence of a category to designate it, with which individual members can identify and through which outsiders can perceive them as distinct.

My hypothesis is that a specific concept or category of the rural has evolved; this occurred in the 1920s and 1930s in a manner specific to each country, though in all cases there was an attempt to reformulate both the relationship between town and country and the definition of agriculture, as a result of the changes facing the countryside and its inhabitants. The concept of the rural evolved by distinguishing the rural and the agricultural, and by defining the rural in relation to the social and cultural context created by industrial development, now the dominant element of the social system.

The category that evolved was not only empirical or descriptive; but it also carried what I shall call a representation or set of meanings, in that it connoted a more or less explicit discourse ascribing a certain number of characteristics or attributes to those to whom it was applied. As any social category in ordinary use likewise implicitly ascribes properties to groups, the set of meanings underpinning it is necessarily linked to a representation of society overall. Thus the peasant has often been deemed to possess a kind of earthy wisdom rooted in tradition and work on the land. However, such attributions imply the existence of an abstract culture, especially a technical and scientific culture, associated with progress and innovation. Whenever anyone – peasant of otherwise – uses those terms, they perforce define their position *vis-à-vis* those criteria, either negatively – 'peasants don't understand technology: they are backward and hostile to progress'; or positively, emphasizing country wisdom in contrast to the baneful abstractions of 'urban' culture.

Such a category alludes not only to objective conditions, but also to social legitimation. Obviously, depending on its content, a social set of meanings will confer a greater or lesser degree of validity on each social group. Thus, if particular importance is attached to technical competence, those who possess the relevant skills are given licence to occupy dominant social and political positions. In simpler terms, the acknowledgement of this or that value necessarily implies the right of groups to exist, to be represented in social and political life, and to enjoy all the advantages that stem from legitimate representation.

Thus it is always the case that the history of a group is also the history of the terms used to designate it; that social history is also the history of those spontaneous representations that enable a society to contemplate itself; and that a social movement is also the action of transforming these representations[1] and a struggle to impose a different way of thinking about the social world and the groups that constitute it.

Sociological theory occupies a specific position in relation to everyday classifications and spontaneous notions of the social. Once sociology enjoys a certain degree of social legitimation, then understandably the categories that it produces may have social effects. The fact is that a particular group is the subject of sociological research contributes to that group's social visibility and its socio-political affirmation. Conversely, sociological theory borrows a considerable amount of its vocabulary of categories – and indeed of concepts – from everyday language, and defines itself in relation to that language.

The emergence of the rural and the development of rural sociology in Belgium[2]

The development of rural sociology was part of a dual[3] movement that characterized the 1920s and 1930s. On the one hand there was an (agricultural) modernization movement attempting to transform the structures of the rural world in order to integrate it technically and economically into the modern industralized world. On the other hand there was a (more ideological) movement of reaction against the social and political tensions of the age. It was that movement in particular that helped to define the concept of the rural. In the case of Belgium, elements in the Church played a crucial role, seeing the rural world as a fund of moral and social values – a potential model of harmony, compared with the conflicts that were tearing society apart.

The religious institution – here the Catholic Church – was itself experiencing the sociopolitical conflicts of the age. Not only was there a split between democrats and conservatives; but also the secularization of the State put in question all the social work that the Church performed – and sometimes monopolized – through a series of institutions in the fields of education, health and social assistance. Catholic Action, initially a movement with intellectual roots, defined itself in relation to that very problem: it sought to redefine religious action as the action to include the work of committed lay persons in secular institutions, and distanced itself from clerical institutions. It saw the Christian as a militant who worked in the sociopolitical world and endeavoured to transform it. At the same time, Catholic Action sought a model of social life that would resolve social and political conflict, and that would therefore transcend the dominant split between socialism and liberalism. The rural world was to serve as an important point of reference, not only because it continued, to a considerable extent, to bear the imprint of Catholic values, but also above all because it represented a world where social harmony seemingly overcame the social differences within communities.

The idea of the rural world as a sort of remedy to social tensions had begun to figure in Belgian politics during the 19th century. The State, for example, had organized the railway network in order to keep industrial workers in villages and rural areas; and similar sentiments had prompted the promoters of social housing to favour single family dwellings for the working class in rural or suburban locations.[4] Until the early 20th century, the social referents in promoting things rural were mainly farmers and peasants whose moral virtues and attachment to property were seen as a model to be set against the working-class world. From around 1925 onwards, however, the Belgian rural world was no longer mainly agricultural and the rural way of life itself became the reference.

Thus the rural came to be seen as a distinct category that furnished, implicitly, an alternative model for society, in which individuals' attachment to ethical values rendered social life not only possible, but indeed harmonious, despite differences in vocations and roles. What was involved was a social ethic ascribed to the village.

This was defined above all as a natural context for social life where, because everyone knew everyone else, and all contact was direct, social life was governed by values. That vision of the rural, which evolved gradually between 1925 and 1935, was first and foremost an abstract one; however, it was gradually given tangible shape in the popular movement that became very active in the year immediately following the war.

The development of popular movements in a rural environment derived from the encounter between these ideas concerning the social, and the experience of rural dwellers, particularly young people. Rural regions were indeed in crisis, though the main trigger for this was not economic difficulties, or depopulation (that had started back at the turn of the century); the crisis was a specific situation in which, as a result of technological, economic and social changes, the young had to make a choice, and to define their position in relation to traditional and new modes of behaviour. Farming methods, career decisons, leisure options, choosing a spouse – in all these spheres young rural dwellers were presented with a stark choice between the past and the future, between inherited customs and urban innovations, and each of these decisions obliged them to define their position *vis-à-vis* the traditional institutions of the rural world – family, parish and village. This was inevitably experienced as a moral crisis with the options seen in terms of loyalty to, or betrayal of familial, social and religious values that had held the local community together.

The discourse of Catholic Action found in these dilemmas the key to its effectiveness, because in emphasizing the value of the rural as a moral heritage it idealized it, and reassured rural people as to their essential identity. At the same time, through the type of outward-going action that it inaugurated, it enabled young rural dwellers to become active in new fields and in new ways. Thus, the value of village as an abstract ideal would be emphasized, but young people would be warned against the fruitlessness of trying to preserve actual villages as social backwaters. Efforts were made to preserve family farming too, but by encouraging young people to acquire the technical know-how they required. In this way, rural movements experienced considerable popular success once the war had ended, and became both the bearers of an idealized and moral vision of the rural world, and the vectors of moderate change – their main contribution, beyond a doubt, being to establish rural dwellers as the actors in these transformations. These developments had very strong parallels in France where a movement of young rural people formed a new generation of rural and farming leaders (Lagrave, 1987).

The category 'rural' that was then evolving was a social category of a very particular kind. 'Rural' clearly designated a set of people, a subset of the population; it was thus a social category, but not *ipso facto* a class, because 'rural' comprised a variety of different socioeconomic categories, and was not a category whose interests were defined against those of others. The rural–urban distinction thus represented a division, but not of the kind that divides social classes. Ruralists were much less concerned to show what divided rural dwellers from the rest than to show what their particular characteristics were. This enabled them to point out the contribution made by those specific characteristics to society as a whole. Whether the contribution to society took the form of a social ethic that makes for a well-balanced society (the 1920s and 1930s version), or of a way of living in society that guaranteed respect for the individual and the participation of all, the rural was legitimated by its sociopolitical role. Hence if 'rural' is a social category, it is not so much a category contrasting rural dwellers with others in terms of economic interests, but rather one which defines a world of (primarily moral, but also cultural) values in which rural dwellers participate.[5] Ruralists see economic or material interests (or for that matter political ones) only as ways of preserving and promoting that world of values, and not necessarily as what distinguishes the rural from other categories.

Rural sociology: the repressed question of identity

The emergence of sociology marked a shift in the mode of legitimation of the category 'rural' and of rural movements, from the religious to the scientific. The developing rural sociology abandoned the moralizing attitude formerly predominant. It considered the rural world to be a social world or a form of civilization – a rural civilization[6] – differing from urban civilization in its distinctive values and social organization. Inspired by American functionalism and cultural studies, it saw the rural as a kind of specific sociocultural system within society. That system was characterized less by the existence of different economic functions than by having a differing system of values expressed through separate institutions (mainly the village) and by different social relationships. Central to this view is the assertion that the rural world's organization in small local communities implies that its social life is made up of personal relationships; hence everyone is necessarily involved in social life, as no collective organizations stand between the individual and 'society'. This form of social life preserves the individual and above all maintains the priority of human values, whereas the city requires large organizations that take precedence over the individual. Rural organization also prefers compromise to conflict as a means for dealing with social tension. This view of the rural world, in the pre-war years, embodied a position that was clearly anti-urban and anti-working-class (i.e. opposed to workers' associations), and hence conservative. During the post-war years, it was also critical of the importance given to economic factors in the development of rural areas. Ruralists and rural sociologists were of the opinion that country planning and agricultural development should not be based on abstract economic criteria alone (giving rise, for example, to concentrated infrastructure and population), but should be carried out in such a way as to preserve village communities and everyone's participation in the management of collective infrastructure.[7] The 'ruralists' opposed the creation of 'intercommunal development companies' not subject to local control and attempted to establish voluntary umbrella groups between communes, directly controlled by locally elected aldermen. This illustrates how rural sociology, having been created in a conservative and anti-urban mould, gradually redefined itself in a humanistic perspective which, while accepting technological and economic progress, defended the human values (notably participation) inherent to the rural world. It was sociology that provided the tools to observe and study social change in the rural environment. For example, a large number of empirical studies showed that rural people do have different mores and lifestyles; even industrial workers living in a rural environment have a different outlook from other workers regarding their work and their families. Moreover, sociology frequently argued that the State should subsidize rural needs for social and cultural amenities. Thus, rural sociology proclaimed itself a sociology focusing on the advancement of a category of citizens – a sociology intended to serve a cause.

Yet rural sociology had ceased to address the question of the global identity of the rural, and the hopes that rural movements pinned on the creation of a rural movement. In the event, rural sociology came to follow two dominant and, I think, distinct orientations. On the one hand it developed towards being a sociology of agriculture of Marxist or liberal orientation, always intent on ways of integrating that sector and that social group more fully within the national social structure;[8] on the other, it developed towards an ethnography of rural communities, assuming that it was possible to understand development and rural structures while confining oneself to a monographical approach. The rural now ceased to have any particular unifying criterion; not really constituting a specific social category, it was only defined inclusively as a multiplicity of local communities. Put more simply, it represented a set of communities that were all small, having their own structures or institutions still dealing with certain aspects of daily life, but with the formal economy hardly represented at all.

The trajectory of rural sociology has thus been ambiguous![9] battening on to the crisis of the rural world, it has proclaimed the rural to be an independent reality, while promptly rejecting it as a social category. Indeed, it broke with the rural movements attempting to create a true social identity, and came to view the rural simply as a field of study, characterized by its concern with local communities.

A crucial factor in the development of rural sociology from the early 1960s was the gradual decline of popular rural movements. There were many reasons for this, including their political weakness, their lack of economic organization and the fact that the standard of living of rural populations improved (more jobs, growth of the farming sector, improved public services), thus reducing the necessity for collective promotional action. Rural sociology, having developed as a science not only legitimating the rural but also legitimated by services rendered to the rural world, went into decline.[10]

It survived in part by performing other functions: rather than contributing to the emergence of a rural social identity[11] (as it did between 1950 and 1960). It evolved gradually into a sociology of social change, where the characteristics of the rural were only studied in terms of responses of rural systems (perforce defined as traditional systems) to the technological, economic and other changes brought about by the modern world. The rural was measured solely by its remoteness from the modern world. In short, rural sociology transformed an emergent social set of meanings of the rural based on a social division into a set of meanings attaching particular importance to the temporal dimension, and defining the rural in relation to the diverse changes wrought by external factors, and often misleadingly lumped together under the rubric 'modernization'. The rural was seen as a world in flux, and an amalgam of imposed changes and instances of resistance and adaptation – all, however, local in nature.

What rural sociology studied were space-times remote (in social, economic, technical or cultural terms) from arenas of growth. Overall, that view dominated the period from 1960 to 1975. The trajectory of rural sociology thus reveals gradual neglect of a central question at the very root of its own development, the question or rural identity in the social field. Viewed thus, the term 'rural' can only be a descriptive one – theory means agricultural theory, or the theory of local communities. At the end of the day, what legitimated sociological research in this period was not so much the idea that the rural had a specific function in the social field (only agriculture had such a function, as a food-producer) as the idea that social progress implied a gradual integration of rural regions and populations in economic and industrial development. If there was a risk of disequilibrium, the danger was that some regions might remain too remote from progress and unable to catch up. What this reveals is that behind the gradual development of research work, there had been a radical shift in the process of legitimating rural sociology, which no longer had to worry about the specificity of its subject. It was taken for granted that its subject was the least developed regions and least integrated areas.

What makes rural sociology possible

I am not concerned here to develop a scientific critique of the bias of rural sociology towards the angle of the local community or village – a bias encouraged by ethnography and geography.[12] On the contrary, I wish to identify the conditions under which such a representation of the rural occurred. It seems to me that the term 'rural' has never been thought through by rural sociologists because it was built on two palpably evident facts. The first was that this category corresponded to a spatial cleavage between city and countryside giving social content to what seemed a matter of common sense and geography. Secondly, it was indeed possible to divide the social field into two worlds between which the relations were not clearly defined, the rural world's cohesion deriving precisely from certain types of relationships between space and society. My thesis is that this set of meanings although completely underestimating some aspects of reality (such as political relations), was only viable for a limited period. The period when country life, hitherto effectively organized locally, was being turned upside down by changes at every level, and was increasingly losing a large degree of its autonomy.

This is a sociological paradox, and one which needs to be emphasized. In a pre-industrial society there is no rural identity in the sense of a common set of meanings, shared by all the population and expressed in representative organizations; each community has its own identity and its own relationshps with the wider society, mediated by local notables and important landowners. Within the rural, however, there are also identities specific to the family and property relationships between individuals within the local system, the latter comprising a common social and cultural set of values guaranteeing the cohesion and homogeneity of each community. With the subsequent changes, especially in the period to which I refer, socioeconomic position became less and less linked to local position, and increasingly dependent on relationships to external markets and institutions. The eventual consequence was increasing heterogeneity, but initially, internal differences became less meaningful and important in response to the much greater differences that emerged between the villagers as a whole and the outside world, or between the town – now familiar and accessible – and the village. That state of affairs was further reinforced by the fact that the changes imposed were the same for all social categories and for all villages. Technological change appeared as an ubiquitous threat to artisan, farmer and trader alike, whereas village priest and children's father often felt that their authority was being challenged and supplanted by the education system. This homogenizing effect and the reaction to it were significant in producing the strong rural movement of the 1950s.

It was as if the rural had been meaningful because change had forced all rural dwellers to define their position afresh, and had for the first time compelled them to see themselves in a broader context; as if the rural only existed as a common reaction to those changes at a particular point in time – a reaction highlighting the problems common to all rural dwellers rather than those problems that were specific to each category. To put it another way, in the 1950s, rural identity was only a homogeneous and common reaction of different local communities to a series of changes imposed on them.

Finally, it is possible to deduce from this analysis what the fundamental conditions are that make it possible for there to be rural sociology, and a category 'rural' as a socially and scientifically legitimate notion.

What first justifies the existence of rural sociology is the rural–urban distinction – a distinction that is accepted because it corresponds not only to a self-evident territorial division but also to a social problem which makes it meaningful. Whether the issue is how to restore a lost social balance (with the rural representing ethical capital) or how to achieve socioeconomic modernization (the rural being the terrain where it is implemented), one is dealing with a sociospatial whole (the countryside) that is relatively homogeneous with respect to the issue.

However, at the same time rural sociology has a vast field of specific issues to study because it uses a theoretical and methodological framework that constructs its subject-matter in terms of specific local communities. By defining its object in such specific terms it effectively gives itself a multiplicity of apparently real subjects to study, all of them specific social spaces, the frameworks in which real groups and group life exist. The bulk of rural studies work, and most monographs, deal with the adaptation and the transformation of local communities following technological and economic changes. Rural sociology is thus a sociology of the localized effects of social change more than a sociology of space.

My hypothesis is that as long as the relationship between local situations and the changes induced in the countryside remained relatively similar, rural sociology was able to operate in the same manner. Though there was a considerable diversity of 'rural societies', in terms of social composition, economic structure, history and culture, it was nonetheless meaningful to study them in parallel as long as they were having to determine their position in relation to the same force for change, and the same series of transformations – all of which fall within the *rubric* of technological and economic modernization. Though everyone readily emphasized how diverse these 'rural societies' were, they nonetheless constituted a single whole by virtue of the relationship established between them and the forces of modernization. What gave rural sociology a certain unity (though not real specificity) was the fact of studying the various types of transformation of multiple local space-times under the impact and influence of modernizing change. Thus 'rural societies' shared a number of common properties (more formal than substantive), including the following:

    (i) they were small-scale communities whose social control was based on personal relationships in a restricted space (what could be called an ecologically-based social control);

    (ii) their particular cultural characteristics were rooted in their history, hence in a tradition;

    (iii) they had local institutions or forms of economic cohesion[13] of varying degrees of strength.

These characteristics might represent entities that were relatively comparable either in the way they operated or in their reaction to externally-generated change. Thus what characterized rural societies was much less their intrinsic properties than their relationship to change. What made them a homogeneous whole was an unquestioned relationship to time, and what defined their specificity was the uniqueness of each community living in its own local space.

Relationship to space and social position

This raises what is today the crucial question of the relationship between space and society – a relationship that can no longer by conceived of according to traditional paradigms involving a division between rural and urban space, or towns and countryside, or between local communitites and the outside social world. These paradigms are predicated on a series of hypotheses, which, I believe, have been completely overtaken by events.

The criticisms that may be levelled at this view are relatively well known and lead to a radical revision of the concept of locality. Let us review them briefly with reference to the situation of the countryside:

    (i) The increased mobility of persons, goods and messages is such that no local community can now be regarded as autonomous, nor do local communities still have their own institutions in most social fields, particularly in the field of the socialization of individuals.

    (ii) As a result of the delocalization of activities, it is no longer possible to define homogeneous regions even at the economic level: the separation between place of residence and place of work, the shifting of some production to peripheral areas, indeed the spatial diversity of different periods of daily life mean that it is no longer possible to define any given area as industrial, agricultural or tertiary.

    (iii) The new uses of the countryside and the specialization of spaces (the tourist industry, natural parks, development zones, etc.) have the effect of creating a network of relationships specific to each area, trying it to a given field of activity or social institution, the various agents of which are no longer 'local'.

(iv) One consequence is that, in determining the 'population' to be taken into account in order to study a given rural area one now has to include agents who only reside there on a temporary basis, or who act from the outside (owners of second homes, naturalists' organizations, etc.).

(v) The emergence of the term 'rural space', which is beginning to be used to refer to functions performed by the countryside for non-rural users and characterized by the fact that they exist independently of the action of rural populations (i.e. no rural agent – and above all, no rural community – is necessarily implied in this usage of rural space).

The relationship between the individual and space is defined less in terms of belonging to a particular space than in terms of the opportunities enjoyed by the individual of participating in a variety of networks of relations – what one might term the multiple locality phenomenon.

Consequences for space

Does this mean that physical or geographical space has become an insignificant component of social life? Not at all. Geographical space continues to play a crucial role in social relations, though in ways that differ from the territorial model that has dominated rural sociology to date.

Why is this so? The first point to make is that increased mobility ought logically to be conducive to an increase in spatial uniformity, mobility tending to cancel out the differences between geographical locations in terms of access to goods, social interaction and information. Such is the dream of those who believe that telecommunications could enable rural regions to enjoy a fresh period of development by eliminating the handicap of their remoteness from centres of activity. Taken to the extreme, that line of reasoning would lead to the very concept of centres being superseded, a development conceivable in geographic, but meaningless in sociological terms. For if there are flows of information (technological flows, for example), then there must be a producer of those flows, whatever their geographical location. It is of course, possible to conceive of a space in which producers are located in many different geographical locations, but is nonetheless obvious that, in social terms, not all information has the same value. Producers exist within hierarchies and structures, the hierarchies being reflected in gradations in the social (and hence, perhaps, also economic) value of the information produced, which in turn will create degrees of rarity. Spatial uniformity, as a trend, is thus a sociological illusion, despite the equalization in the spatial conditions for communication.

That is why increased mobility will not lead to a homogenization of space. Indeed, it will bring about a new hierarchy of space, based on the value on any market that each space manages to attain. The increasing accessibility of all parts of any territory therefore tends to endow each 'region' thereof with particular characteristics. The best example of this is the fact that increased mobility tends to reduce the value of leisure areas that are close at hand and relatively ordinary, and increase that of specific leisure areas and tourist regions so designated precisely because they are not ordinary and are out of the way. The same happens in the economic field, where mobility enables firms to divide up the production process and locate each component in the area best suited to that particular phase; for example, R&D in areas with good scientific infrastructure and where highly skilled staff would find it pleasant to live; decision-making centres close to the corridors of power where contacts are often informal; routine production activities in areas where labour is plentiful or cheap; activities that generate pollution in areas where the negative externalities are least costly; and so forth.

This rationale – which, it should be borne in mind, concerns trends rather than the present situation – thus does not destroy the specific characteristics of local spaces; what it does is to create a new type of locality, which, in any given area, is the result of the interaction of the various forces that operate, from a variety of fields, to confer value on that space. Thus in future, a local space will have to be understood, not in terms of its constituent elements, but in terms of the possible combinations of externally determined forces able to confer value on it. This also gives fresh content to what is commonly called local politics, the role of which is now not so much that of representing a local population to the central power (though that is still, in part, the case, depending on the political system and the extent to which the State makes its presence felt). Local politics is increasingly coming to mean the local harmonization of external forces, and of strategies for enhancing the value of the territory concerned. After all, the economic, environmental, tourist or other value of a local space can only be maintained by the concerted action of a number of agents acting on the territory concerned. Thus a space that is attractive to high-technology industries and industrial research centres will have value in terms of the local trade it generates, and the public services it provides – a university, perhaps – and in terms of the living conditions it offers to those employed in that sector. Each of these elements is a joint product, and the role of local politics is increasingly to enable these assets to be created and maintained, without their being threatened by other forms of intervention. This is giving new significance to local administration and planning, and making it a domain where interests clash.

Social effects

There has also been a change in the relationship between social actors and space. To describe the new relationship being established between the individual and geographical space metaphorically, one might speak of a general tendency towards the nomadic, or rather multiple-locality. Relationships to space are coming to be defined more by mobility than by belonging somewhere, and security derives more from the ability to communicate than from having one's own enclosed space.

Moreover, each field of social and economic activity has its own projection in space, and thus its own spatial hierarchy. To understand this one only needs to compare the geography of tourism with the geography of traditional industry: one is virtually the mirror image of the other. In relation to any given social field, each local space occupies a position on a continuum between the extremes of 'hub' and 'limbo'.

Thus, for an individual, localization will always be a factor that *defines* his or her position in relation to different social fields, and mobility one way of moving from one position to another within the same field, or from one field to another. There are also trajectories of daily life that are specific to each social position; indeed, there is a case for a geography of the modal movements of each social class. In other words, space remains a form of social classification.

One effect of this contemporary way of relating to space is that it is probably no longer relevant to use a local identity to denote any individual's or social group's relationship to space. It is only for certain groups who are subject precisely to a lesser degree of mobility, that a geographical localization still has any meaning. Conversely, degrees of mobility and quality of spaces frequented would today doubtless be a good indicator of a group's social position.

Finally, and because I started with the question of identity, it must be emphasized that the relationship between identity and space has undergone a profound change. Apart from the case of certain powerless groups who are indeed tied to one particular space, one can no longer think in terms of identifying persons or groups as belonging to a single space. Each space is governed by a specific order (or possibly by several concurrent orders), and by a criterion for defining legitimate uses, whereby agents occupying it are classified or ranked in a hierarchy. What counts is the extent to which a social actor is able to realize an aspect of his identity across all the locations where he is present, and to do this in all the arenas that are important to his or her position or social strategy. Such an analytical principle could make it possible to understand the different ways in which group or class identity can be expressed in our society, depending on the spaces where this occurs, just as it would enable on to understand the range of alliances that could be forged within one space between categories that in other fields are separate or even in opposition – for instance, the alliance between middle-class second-home owners and small farmers against major tourist developments, one party defending local amenity, and the other their economic interests, with, perhaps, both parties speaking in the same terms of protecting the environment. Space thus retains its essential function of underpinning social identities, but the function is broken down into a large number of sub-identities, and no doubt, the higher a person's position in this social hierachy, the more this is the case.

Rurality and social relations

These phenomena have both spatial and social consequences for the countryside. The spatial effect is to introduce a distinction between rural space qua physical space, lending itself to a variety of functions, and rural space qua locus of social relations. The phenomenon is a general one, albeit often masked by the signs of revitalization in local spaces or territories. It derives from the 'urban' roles of the countryside – performing ecological functions and providing open spaces, scenic beauty or other assets – which place the countryside within a framework of relations in which rural actors have little or no involvement. Managing the countryside is once again becoming an important issue, but it does not necessarily involve local actors. This happens, for instance, with parks, that display all the characteristics of territorial units (this is what they are, in geographical terms), and they may even look like local communities (because there is an institution running them). In fact these are social actors in a particular social field (conservation, say, or tourism, or some other field, depending on the circumstances of the case), and governed by considerations, and social forces, operating at the level of society as a whole. Moreover, these territorial units are rarely, if ever, demarcated in a way which corresponds to any sense of geographical identity on the part of the inhabitants of the regions concerned, but rather on the basis of scenic, ecological or tourist considerations not directly linked to any sort of local social habits.

Increasingly, therefore, one is dealing with abstract spaces that may overlap or be interlinked – a country area might belong to a regional nature park; it might be a disadvantaged agricultural area, or an industrial development zone, or a district protected because of its architectural heritage. There is no longer one single space, but a multiplicity of social spaces for one and the same geographical area, each of them having its own logic, its own institution, as well as its own network of actors – users, administrators, etc. – which are specific and not local. Moreover, because problems occur in the management and coordination of public intervention, one is now justified in talking in terms of 'integrated' or 'total development'. Indeed, the very use of such terms, with the implication that policies do require 'coordination', demonstrates the extent to which geographical space is now fragmented, and the extent to which the local territorial unit is in fact multiple and heteronomous (i.e. ruled from outside), no longer belonging to a single actor, the local community.

Thus, the question of who is rural has to be addressed in new terms. In brief, the question is rather how each occupant of rural space feels – or becomes – rural.

In descriptive terms, one would have to start by describing the various categories of users of rural space according to whether they are there on a temporary or permanent basis, how they use their space and what local relationships they establish with other users. That approach yields a number of criteria that can serve to classify these categories in terms of their attachment to the space concerned. Of course, there is an economic hierarchy, extending from landowners who use their land to temporary occupants; but there is also a social hierarchy, ranging from those who have most of their network of social relations in the place concerned to those for whom it is merely a geographical space interchangeable with any other.

Finally, there is a cultural or symbolic hierarchy according to the importance of the place in the constitution of a person's body of knowledge, or sense of identity. These various hierarchies are not necessarily convergent inasmuch as, for example, modern-minded farmers with a considerable amount of local capital may have scant interest in enhancing the cultural value of the countryside, an aim defended above all by those categories for whom rural space is essentially a place of recreation.

It is no longer possible for the rural sociologist to plump axiomatically for one criterion rather than another in order to classify these categories as rural or otherwise; and that what is essential to analyse is what precisely the meaning of the term rural is for each of these categories, and to what extent they are able to mobilize resources and deploy social alliances in support of their own definition of what is rural. In other words, what is central in this approach is the symbolic battle over rurality – that is, the legitimate definition of the term 'rural'. The symbolic conflict obviously has practical, economic and political effects, as can be seen clearly in the conflicts, both open and secret, which have emerged since the beginning of the 1970s in regard to a number of development projects for rural regions – tourist projects, plans for nature parks, indeed, even major infrastructural developments. What is at stake in the creation of a nature park, for instance, is the institutionalization, inter alia, at a legal level, of a certain number of criteria dictating what the territory concerned should become. Priorities clash: cost-effective economic production (particularly agricultural) versus residential amenity, versus the tourist potential of the local scenery, perhaps even of the local folklore. And each of these properties of the space, however 'authentic' or 'local' or 'natural' it may be asserted to be, is in fact only valid in relation to a particular market (the market for tourist, farm, or 'natural' products) that is now no longer local, but national, or event international. It is quite possible that the choice of a particular priority might accommodate not only the symbolic but also the economic and political needs of a given category of inhabitants. Some farmers might take advantage of an opportunity to market higher-value-added products by means of the 'natural' label, whereas others might see an obstacle to their plans for more intensive farming. The question of whether agricultural land should be 'set aside', possibly entailing a shift in agricultural policy, might very well prompt new alliances, and new definitions of the term 'rural', incorporating ecological, economic and social priorities of very diverse origins.

From an analytical point of view, one aspect merits particular attention: the agents who design and implement local planning and local development projects, and who thereby manipulate the definitions of legitimate rurality. They are the multiple location pundits who see to it that information flows between headquarters and site; as often as not, they are of above-average cultural and professional aptitude, and are thus attuned to middle-class desiderata. They tend to set themselves up as a body of specialists performing the role of intermediaries with society as a whole. They are the vectors of a new set of meanings of rurality, as well as being the people who stand to gain the most – in symbolic and economic terms – from having that new set of meanings recognized and legitimated, indeed, even institutionalized.

Hence the question of how to redefine contemporary rurality involves asking both whether those intermediaries are able to produce a legitimate definition, and whether it will be possible for that definition to match the diversity of local actors and strategies, all of them situated in heterogeneous spaces and different social fields. There is today a tendency to replace concrete terms – the rural world, the rural environment, the rural class, even – with an abstract one: rurality.[14] This is because it is today no longer possible to redefine rurality other than in terms which are abstract and general enough to be able to be 'applied' to a very wide range of specific strategies and situations. Probably many rural sociologists will be tempted to launch their own definition of rurality on this market of representations, based on their own affinities with a particular social field or class fraction, thereby avoiding an analysis of their own role.

If that were to happen, there would be a danger of rural sociology fragmenting into as many polemical disputes and narrow research areas as there are implicit definitions of the term rural, which would effectively put an end to any communication between the sub-domains of rural sociology.

Towards a sociology of the rural

The foregoing analysis may seem purely negative, if not downright destructive, and indeed its effect is to deny any substantive content to rural sociology, lacking as it does any specific subject-matter. For the fact that rurality is not a thing or a territorial unit, but derives from the social production of a set of meanings, leads to the rural being reincorporated as one of the possible subjects of a general sociology that examines the production of the social, and of spaces, groups and identities. No one would dream of suggesting that there could still be a sociology of the worker separate from the sociology of class relations. The same holds true of the rural – it can no longer be separated from a sociology of space, extending to cover both urban and rural space, the space of international relations and the space of particular localities.

I should like to demonstrate in conclusion that the sociological analysis of the rural is significant, not as a separate subject, but because rurality is a significant area, albeit often a secondary one, for general social and ideological conflicts. These, I believe, constitute the real dynamics behind rural change.

To do this, I shall make two working hypotheses. The first concerns space as an element underpinning identity: it is that social identity exists primarily in *relation* to space – this is because it is by the practical apprehension of a structured space that the individual first becomes aware of the world and learns to define his or her position within it. The second is that identity (perhaps an infelicitous term) is not a whole, but a number of acknowledged characteristics valid in a particular context, and a particular field of relationships. There is consequently no point in defining an identity without defining a field of relationships, and an individual may very well belong to several types, or registers, of identity as his or her social life evolves. If one considers both the relative autonomy of the fields of social relations, and also the proliferation of spaces that is partly associated with that, one can understand that the question of identity is a far more complex question, and that the 'rural', or more precisely, rural space (which itself is differentiated) is an area where a number of partial identities may be realized.

The place of the rural within class relations is certainly no longer defined by contrasting it with the urban. I would venture the hypothesis that rural space impinges on class relations, being the arena where strategies of symbolic significance can be implemented. Compared with other spaces – urban, or periurban – rural space has a number of features that make it particularly suitable now as an arena where social actors can express and display value systems for which there are far fewer opportunities to express at work, or in daily life in the cities, or in big public or private organizations.

Structural properties of rural space

Rural regions derive from their socioeconomic history certain characteristics that I shall call structural in order to indicate that they are the characteristics that define the position of the rural within systems of meaning. Their incorporation in the logic of technological and scientific progress has been late and incomplete, and there are still many social spaces which are not – or not fully – subject to technological management and market forces. They thus display characteristics that define them as being remote from the 'values' or 'paradigms' that are deemed to regulate social life. For a long time this remoteness was seen, not least by sociologists, in temporal terms: they lagged behind traditional patterns of behaviour. However, this remoteness may also fire criticism to the effect that solutions do not necessarily require technological artefacts, and uses of nature and techniques other than those proffered by progress are available (e.g. alternative modes of energy production). In more general terms, therefore, the rural is a space symbolizing difference – a difference that may be interpreted in a variety of ways.

These features represent opportunities for symbolic expression; I shall mention some of them. First, there is the opportunity to have a greater amount of space, which is also less structured, for family or other social activities. Thus, to cite but one example, the second home can become the main focus for a freely-chosen social life – where one entertains one's chosen friends, say – in contrast to the relationships imposed by work and the conventions that predominate in the cities. That function is, moreover, reinforced by the fact that it is easier to establish one's frontiers, to fence off the outside world, than is the case in the urban environment. For other categories, the second home can also be a place to recreate a social life similar to that in working-class urban areas, where hobbies are pursued, or games played, in a group. With tourism developing as it is, rural space could well become the main space outside the world of work in which social groups express their own system of values, in short, their own private lifestyle.

Moreover, the fact that the countryside contains far more objects and artefacts from the past – architecture, the relics of agricultural activities, folklore in general – means that there is a wealth of elements that can be reinterpreted according to one's own vision of the world or of social time. Thus even small-scale, peasant farming can be seen as an amazing denial of the modern age, or, alternatively, as the prefiguration of an ideal relationship with nature. And nature itself, especially now that farmers are releasing vast tracts of land, offers an immense area for the pursuit of activities both economic and symbolic, where every subculture can express itself – both the dynamic, all-conquering man, eager to meet challenges to the prowess of his body or the machinery at his command, and the man who is at one with the cosmos and the beneficent forces of nature.

What is more, because they were late in being incorporated in the dominant economic system, rural regions were the last to internalize the culture of technical and economic progress, and it is probable that their élites still share a strong belief in salvation through incorporation. The structural properties of the rural are thus not necessarily the cultural characteristics of their élites; it follows that the main conflict in rural regions today is precisely a conflict between those élites (and their set of meanings) and the groups who bring with them new conceptions of the rural, and new uses for rural space.

The rural and partial identities

The general principle underlying these uses of rural space would seem to be a dual one. The rural is where values are expressed (whereas the town is defined as a space governed by constraints); both group and individual values can be manifested. It is therefore a space for identification, inasmuch as spatial differentiation provides a framework for different identities.

It is possible to distinguish several possible relationships between identity and the rural. Identity is not monolithic or homogeneous, particularly in a social system characterized by the relative autonomy of social fields, by a complex division of space, and by a proliferation of different lifestyles. There is a multiplicity, or at least a diversity of possible identifications, based on the way the day is divided up, or on the history of an individual life, or on the multiple-locality phenomenon,[15] which reflects in part the autonomy of the countryside.

This means that a whole series of studies undertaken in recent years on what have been termed the urban uses of rural space need reappraising in a global perspective, doing away with the artifical and glib distinction between urban uses (which are anything but homogeneous) and 'rural' uses. The aim should be to create a typology of social uses of space related to the identifications underpinning them. This would also mean analysing the conflicts over the legitimate definition of rural space – that is to say, what activities are permitted, and which criteria are used to define legitimate users.

A study currently being carried out shows that the opposition between town and country now has hardly any social meaning for the majority of inhabitants. From within an area that is mainly strongly urbanized, country life is perceived above all as having residential advantages (quiet, pleasant surroundings) and disadvantages (more difficult access to services, to shops), but no longer as life in a different social world. The differences remaining apparent are social differences in so far as class identity reveals different requirements: the well-educated find social and cultural advantages in the city, whereas the less-educated see mainly the economical and practical advantages in terms of job-opportunities, infrastructure and transport facilities. For the latter, the countryside is above all cheaper and less polluted, whereas the former see that it offers more space and quiet. This analysis tends to show that people do not feel themselves to be rural as a result of social differences with city dwellers, but that each category of rural population perceives and uses the countryside differently.

There is, however, a very strong attachment to local space for temporal relationships, i.e. it is belonging to a local group (via family, marriage and village sociability) that has meaning. This establishes within the rural population a series of subtle splits. There are those who are deeply rooted in the village, those who have returned after having lived in the city, those who are there temporarily and there are immigrants from the city. These splits combine with local forms of sociability: neighbourliness, participation in associations and local activities. Within a relatively uniform perception of the city and the countryside, there are numerous possible forms of local rural life, and of tension between those who favour the physical surroundings, or social activities, or for whom farming and cottage industries are important (and who tolerate their nuisances), etc.

Does this approach entirely negate the theory that local populations (or particular fractions within local populations) identify with 'their' space, 'their' district or 'their' region?

Regional identities?

This analysis does not deny that local identities may evolve, on anything from the village to the regional scale – witness, for example, the re-emergence of the various 'pays' in France a decade or so ago. However, the type of 'region' involved does not derive at all, in my view, from a process specific to the local space, in the sense of their being local issues at stake which are embodied locally.[16] A region may rediscover meaning through processes such as the marketing of local space (e.g. tourist areas, 'appellations' for products, brand images or a folklore tags) or devolution giving rise to new career opportunities.

This is the case for 'farming development' groups seeking to promote products 'labelled' on the basis of the region's brand image. This may also be the case for tourist development agents attempting to attract more clients. Such action tends to recreate or create 'images' of the region that have a meaning within a specific market and that may agree or disagree with the requirements of certain rural populations depending on the advantages they may hope to gain. The fact that a given space is recognized as an area of tourist interest may well meet the interest of some to protect the landscape (from which they benefit as residents) or provide scope for an improved transport network. Regional identity therefore results from concurring local social demand and from strategies for local development.

Strategic issues in rural-space management

Finally, there is a third dynamic to be analysed; which is of fundamental importance. It concerns the management of a number of issues that arise at the strategic level and that require rural space to be managed inasmuch as it is a reservoir holding a number of resources valued by society at large. The simplest instances are of the management of the environment: the quality of water available depends on the proper functioning of the water cycle, which occurs for the most part in the countryside, and consequently makes it necessary to enforce protective measures concerning water use – or, more generally, the water table – in certain areas; or indeed to restrict some activities by means of regulations, taxes or charges. It is not clear that in all cases the rural populations are involved in this management process other than as intermediaries. Very often, indeed, the principal actors are public or private actors who operate at a national, and sometimes international level (cf. European regulations), without local populations or their representatives being able to intervene in the transactions.

Environmental disputes are not specific to the urban or rural domain. They are general conflicts, expressed in a specific way in each type of social space. The same could be said of agricultural policy disputes involving both consumers and producers in deciding what and how to produce and for whom. Thus the conflicts concern either collective assets (which is what most environmental assets are) or the role of rural space in the general context of a particular production process.

The impact of these conflicts is not only to give social importance to the rural – as a space and a resource more than as a social universe – but also to make the representation of the rural – a resource to be exploited or an asset to be preserved – a symbolic issue.

Conclusion

The rural is a category of thought. It was constructed at a time when peasant societies were being integrated into society as a whole. However, although it served to define a field of sociological research, to elaborate a discipline, it is not essentially a product of sociological research. In a sense, the rural is perceived similarly to traditional Third World societies. Is not the aim once again to define a field of research pertaining to a gradual and forced integration into the prevailing socioeconomic universe, to define a manner of considering scientifically the relationship between peoples formerly called 'primitive' and the society absorbing them? It is of fundamental importance to realize that the classification that delimits the field of rural sociology is based on a representation of the social, on a social mythology that sees both peasant and village as the opposite of the predominant social world:

positively, where the aim is to promote the moral and social values of rural civilization, and negatively, where the aim is to ensure integration into the socioeconomic world. The history of rural sociology illustrates how these two oversimplified extremes were combined and coexisted.

The integration of peasant societies is now virtually complete in developed and urbanized countries such as Belgium. This deprives rural sociology of the essence of its traditional object. However, the opposition between city and countryside remains, and may now take on new social significances depending on the ideological or cultural frame of reference to which the agents refer: natural universe vs. urban artefact; a world of sociability vs. the abstraction of large organizations; a world of skills vs. the alienation of industrial work. Different versions of the rural–urban opposition are currently being constructed, with different ideological references, various social foundations and some reinterpretation of traditional representations. Hence there are different ways of considering oneself to be rural, of identifying with 'rurality'. This makes it difficult to delimit the scope of rural sociology, and virtually impossible to define the rural world as a distinct social group or even to contrast it with the urban world. Rural identity is manifold and heterogeneous.

In the world of rural sociologists, there are several possible responses to this state of affairs. The first would be to consider that the traditional rural–urban opposition is obsolete and that rural sociology as such has no real object. This view would imply that there are now only urbanized populations and forms of differentiated land use: countryside and cities. The other extreme is for rural sociologists to identify with one or other redefinition of the rural, as in the case of a sociology of the rural refounded on the concept of environment and equating the rural world with forms of adaptation of the social to the constraints of the biophysical environment.

The benefit of a history of rural sociology – yet to be established on the international scale – would be to start from the hypothesis that the rural–urban opposition is socially constructed and that the rural exists primarily as a representation serving to analyse both the social and space – or rather to analyse the social while defining space – borne and interpreted by social agents. The fact that it is a constructed representation and not an ascertained reality does not deplete a sociology of the rural of subject. Its subject may be defined as the set of processes through which agents construct a vision of the rural suited to their circumstances, define themselves in relation to prevailing social cleavages, and thereby find identity, and through identity, make common cause.

It is plausible to assume then that the differences between the city and the countryside are a reality which is ascertained, but is reinterpreted by each society; that in view of this, the rural is a category that each society takes and reconstructs, and that this social construction, with all its implications, defines the object of a sociology of the rural.

42

Notes

1. Or as A. Touraine (1984), puts it: 'a social movement is a conflictual action by which cultural orientations and the historical field are converted into socio-organizational forms, these being ruled by general cultural norms and by power relations'.
2. It is not possible to give here more than a summarized historical research; see C. Mougenot and M. Mormont (1988).
3. The importance of these two trends is probably very different from one country to another, and this factor might in part account for the different trends in rural sociology still apparent today in Europe.
4. On this issue, see especially Mougenot, C. (1988a; 1988b).
5. This probably explains why rural sociologists liked to think of the rural in terms of degrees or a (rural–urban) continuum: when considering values, it is normal to think of gradual change, whereas a social cleavage implies something like conflicting interests or strict criteria.
6. The most important works of this period were: Laloux, J. (1956) and Hoyois, G. (1967). Hoyois was also the driving force behind a periodical: *Les Cahiers Ruraux*. Hoyois and Laloux were behind the creation of the European Society for Rural Sociology in 1958.
7. Rural movements gradually came to criticize the type of development and especially of country planning proposed to them, on the grounds of giving priority to promoting all rurals, in the same way that the urban movements criticized functionalist urbanization in the name of the defence of neighbourhood social life. In Belgium, a large proportion of urban movements have the same ideological foundation (within Catholic Action) as the rural movements.
8. This was a dominant feature of German and even Dutch rural sociology, which were mainly developing in agricultural education and extension, whereas in France, for instance, the social and overall political weight of farmers and rural voters was a significant concern.
9. I do not wish to analyse the history of rural sociology here, as this would involve describing specific national trends. For an overview of French rural studies see *Bulletin de l'Association des Ruralistes Français* (1988). For Belgium, see C. Mougenot and M. Mormont (1988).
10. The periodical founded by Hoyois (*Les Cahiers Ruraux*) disappeared with his death in 1969; the 'Centre for Rural Studies' that he directed was closed and its staff split up. It is also significant that economic geography was to become the most influential discipline in country planning (Mougenot, 1986).
11. In France two books are significant of this shift: Mendras, H. (1967) and Morin, E. (1967). Both are concerned with social change more than with analysing specific rural features. In Belgium the same trend can be found in Remy and Voye (1974), which is not focused on the rural but on the process of urbanization of the countryside.
12. The best critique of the monographic approach was written in 1974 by Champagne (1975).

13. When studying forms of local cohesion among rural industrial workers (Jollivet and Mendras, 1971), it is really difficult to determine how these forms differ from those observed in a traditional popular dwelling, except that these rural workers were staying in 'their' village. The really interesting sociological problem would be to compare various forms of worker's solidarity in everyday life and in different kinds of social space (Weber, 1989). By ascribing the observed forms to 'rurality', the observer tends to 'explain' social forms on the basis of past structures more than socioeconomic position. The theoretical and methodological framework was to induce the interpretation.

14. One of the concepts underlying this abstraction is 'banalization', a polysemous term (ecological, architectural, cultural) used in various fields of discourse: it enables one to define a general opposition between town and country, giving an artificially unified perception of the rural.

15. One could illustrate this process with the case of hunting (Bozon, Chamboredon and Fabiani, 1981).

16. 'This is the end of a world where the principle of local village hierarchy to be found locally (land ownership), where conflicts originating largely in local issues were disputed locally: this was doubtless a long-standing process' (Chamboredon, 1985).

References

Bourdieu, P. (1980) L'identité et la représentation: éléments pour réflexion critique sur l'idée de région, *Actes de la Recherche en Sciences Sociales*, No. 35, 63–72.

Bourdieu, P. (1981) Décrire et prescrire: note sur les conditions de possibilité et les limites de l'efficacité politique, *Actes de la Recherche en Sciences Sociales*, No. 38, 69–73.

Bozon, M. Chamboredon, J. C. and Fabiani, J. L. (1981) Les usages sociaux du cadre naturel: elaboration sociale et conflit des modes de consommation de la campagne: l'exemple de la chasse. In *Des Forêts et des hommes*, Le Paradou: Actes-Sud, p. 273-9.

Bulletin de l'Association des Ruralistes Français (1988) Les études rurales sont-elles en crise? Numéro spécial, **41–42**, pp. 81.

Chamboredon, J. C. (1985) Nouvelles formes de l'opposition ville-campagne. In *Histoire de la France Urbaine*, Seuil, Paris, pp. 557–73.

Champagne, P. (1975) La restructuration de l'espace villageois, *Actes de la Recherche en Sciences Sociales*, **3**, 43–67.

Hoyois, G. (1967) *Sociologie Rurale*, Editions Universitaires, Bruxelles.

Jollivet, M. and Mendras, H. (eds) (1971) *Les collectivités rurales en France* Armand Colin, Paris.

Lagrave, R. M., (ed.) (1987) *Celles de la terre. Agricultrice: l'invention politique d'une profession*, Editions de l'Ecole des Hautes Etudes en Sciences Sociales, Paris.

Laloux, J. (1956) *Problèmes actuels du monde rural*, La Pensée Catholique, and Paris, Office Général du Livre, Brussels.

Mendras, H. (1967) *La fin des paysans, innovation et changements dans l'agriculture française*, SEDEIS, Paris.

Morin, E. (1967) *Commune en France, la métamorphose de Plovézet*, Fayard, Paris.

Mougenot, C. (1986) Les populations rurales: évolution et perceptions, *Espaces Populations Sociétés*, **3**, 11-18.

Mougenot, C. (1988a) Promoting the single-family house in Belgium – the social making of a model, *International Journal of Urban and Regional Research*, **12**, (4), 531-49.

Mougenot, C. (1988b) 'Building a house or a social universe', in D. Canter, M. Krampen and D. Stea (eds), *Ethnoscapes, vol. 1, Environmental Perspectives*, Aldershot: Avebury.

Mougenot, C. and Mormont, M. (1988) *L'invention du rural: l'héritage des mouvements ruraux*, Bruxelles: Editions Vie Ouvrière, Brussels, pp. 1288.

Remy, J. and Voye, L. (1974) *La ville et l'urbanisation*, Duculot, Gembloux.

Touraine, A. (1984) *Le retour de l'acteur*, Fayard, Paris.

Weber, F. (1989) *Le travail à côté. Etude d'ethnographie ouvrière*. INRA and Editions de l'Ecole des Hautes Etudes en Sciences Sociales, Paris.

CHAPTER 2

Restructuring Agriculture in Advanced Societies: Transformation, Crisis and Responses

Patrick Commins

Introduction

Since World War II the agricultural sectors in the advanced economies have been dramatically altered by a complex of transformative forces. Whereas the composition, scale and impact of the changes show variations from one country to another their common features are unmistakeable. In particular capital-intensive technologies have progressively replaced human labour and raised production and productivity. Farm activities have come under the influence of agri-industrial systems that supply an increasing range of farm inputs and create new products and processes beyond the farm gate. Production has become concentrated in fewer and larger units as well as showing greater commodity and territorial specialization. With the growth in the trade of agricultural products and the transferability of scientific knowledge and technological innovations, modern farming sectors are now part of an international agricultural and food system. Surplus production of farm commodities is a central concern of agricultural policy and budgetary management. Rapid technical progress has induced and has been accentuated by state intervention in all aspects of agricultural product and factor markets (Goodman *et al.*, 1987: 13). Indeed the growing prevalence of public policies in agriculture is one of the most extensive and sociologically significant forms of intervention of the modern state (Havens and Newby, 1986: 291).

Despite the universality of these structural trends rural sociologists, it has been argued (Havens and Newby, 1986), have shown little interest in, or understanding of, the broader structural features of the contemporary

45

farming system or of the economic forces that have changed agricultural production and rural society in all advanced capitalist countries over the past few decades. Havens and Newby add that rural sociologists have traditionally looked to agricultural economists to provide them with an understanding of those economic factors that affect the organization of rural society. However, these authors claim, agricultural economists have also been slow to provide the kind of macroeconomic institutional analysis – or broadly-based political economy – that would meet the needs of sociologists. Instead the general tendency within agricultural economics has been to reduce analysis of issues to narrowly-focused technocratic predictive models, based on unreal assumptions.

Mindful of these strictures this chapter seeks to elucidate the originating conditions, dynamics and outcomes of agricultural restructuring in modern western societies. The first parts set out the main elements of an interpretive framework that we have adopted to conceptualize the restructuring process. Subsequent sections provide an empirical analysis of key features of the motion and consequences of agricultural transformation; what we are concerned with here are the dynamics and outcomes of the productionist paradigm of agricultural development as these have manifested themselves particularly, but not exclusively, in EC countries in recent decades. The final sections discuss the current options being considered by EC policy-makers as they attempt to respond to the problems created by the agricultural revolution of modern times.

Our main thesis is that, conceptually, agricultural restructuring has to be understood as a set of dynamic changes determined by the reciprocal relationships among (i) the macroeconomic forces of capitalist development, (ii) the nature of socioeconomic structure that conditions the relative power of different interests to influence change, and (iii) the role of government intervention. Empirically, the analysis examines several structural trends and their outcomes in the transition from a 'productionist' to a 'post-productionist' agriculture in developed countries. A general conclusion is that current policy responses to the problems of agricultural restructuring will consolidate the distinction between farms that produce quality food efficiently and those farms that will serve other functions for modern society.

Main elements of an interpretative framework

To conceptualize the determinants and dynamics of structural change in agriculture we draw eclectically from several theoretical sources. These offer insights, which, we believe, can be productively linked together in a coherent framework. Our starting point is Hayami and Ruttan's (1971) model of the manner in which technological and institutional changes are 'induced' in the process of agricultural development. Basically their approach is grounded in neoclassical theory and posits that: (i) the capacity to develop technology consistent with environmental and economic conditions is the single most important factor explaining the growth of agricultural productivity; (ii) technological changes are induced by economic forces; and (iii) cultural, political and economic institutions are adapted to realize the growth potential opened up by new technical alternatives. The pattern of technical change is a function of the market mechanism; changes in relative factor scarcities determine changes in relative factor prices and these changes lead to the development of cost-minimizing technologies with a bias towards saving on the most expensive factor of production. The achievement of rapid technical progress in agriculture is considered to depend on the 'socialization' of much agricultural research for the generation of a stream of technical innovations, on the innovative efforts of private enterprise, and on the development of non-agricultural sector capable of transmitting increased productivity to agriculture (e.g. through developments in mechanical or chemical engineering). This stream of technical inputs is then supported by institutional investments, such as in education or credit. The induced innovation model hypothesises that, in response to market signals, there is effective interaction between agricultural producers, public research institutions and private enterprise.

Whereas this model has proved useful in explaining the emergence of, and balance between particular kinds of technologies its several limitations have been pointed out, especially by de Janvry (1977) and by de Janvry and Dethier (1985). Principally, the Hayami and Ruttan model does not make sufficient distinction or linkage between economic forces (such as market price determination and resource allocation/use) and socioeconomic structure (social group organization based on differential access to resources). Because of its neoclassical provenance it regards the market as a self-correcting mechanism, thus tending to confine the role of the state to that of smoothing out 'imperfections' in the market. Most importantly, the model is simplistically linear in which the causal influence is from technological to institutional change.

Critics of the neoclassical view suggest a complementary or 'structuralist' theory that conceptualizes the generation of technological and institutional innovations as a recursive process of causation (de Janvry, 1977: 553–4). In this process of reciprocal relationships non-market forces (social and political or institutional forces) can 'distort' market forces and influence the rate and nature of technological innovations, and of institutional change itself (de Janvry and Dethier, 1985: 7–8). In particular the socioeconomic structure and the politicobureaucratic structure are given explicit roles. In brief, social groups with different sources of power will pressure the politicoadministrative structure for public goods to be (or not to be) generated, depending on the pay-offs such groups expect to receive. The relative power of a group over other groups and over the politicobureaucratic structure influences the extent to which a group's demands will be satisfied. In turn the acquisition of gains by particular groups place such groups in an advantageous position for demanding, or capitalizing on further benefits.

This view is also in line with the approach of Havens and Newby (1986) to the study of state intervention in agriculture in advanced capitalist societies. Their model recognizes that the causes of structural change in agricultural centre on the nature of the market economy *and* the role of the state in defining and promoting the public interest. In this role the state, while pursuing its own view of the public interest, is drawn into negotiations with policy influentials – with different abilities to mobilize politically. The resultant policies set down the conditions of agricultural production but these conditions favour some groups of producers more than others. This, in turn, has downstream effects on the structuring of the agricultural sector and sets the context for a further round of changes in the socioeconomic conditions for agricultural production (Havens and Newby, 1986: 296–8).

These various ideas are illustrated schematically in Figure 2.1. The dynamics of agricultural restructuring (H) are influenced by both market and non-market forces (G and F). Non-market forces are generated by the state (B) through public sector innovations and policies (D). State intervention is influenced in turn by the socioeconomic structure (A), i.e. the configuration of organized interests and their degrees of power. Market forces derive from the innovative efforts (E) of entrepreneurs–farmers, agri-business or possibly the state itself – in response to economic forces and opportunities (C). The inclusion of two other elements in the scheme, outcomes including crises (I), and response (J), is intended to take account of the specific EC context where the contemporary problems of restructuring under the influence of the Common Agricultural Policy (CAP) have led to the adoption of reformist measures, some of which are based on renewed reliance on market forces while others rely on non-market mechanisms. Following de Janvry and Dethier (1985: 7–10) these are referred to respectively as the neoclassical and structuralist or institutional response, and illustrated as recursive loops in the diagram.

It will be helpful to elaborate further on each of the three main sets of determinant forces suggested by this interpretative framework.

Economic forces and conditions

The induced development model suggests that agricultural production and productivity growth is a dynamic process of adjustment to original resource endowments and product demand, as these are reflected in factor and product markets (Hayami and Ruttan, 1971: 4, 59). The general progress of science and technology also influences technical change in farming and the supply of agricultural products. Innovations in the non-agricultural sectors transmit increased productivity in the form of cheap sources of inputs or new knowledge about producing food (Hayami and Ruttan, 1971: 4). However, much empirical evidence for developed countries indicates that the demand for food is not very responsive to changes in price or increases in income, although the composition of the food demanded may vary (Commins and Higgins, 1987: 16–31).

At a more general level we may say that in advanced societies agricultural transformation is affected by the dominant forces of the capitalist economy. The most important element in the maintenance and reproduction of capitalism is accumulation, an activity that is ensured through earning

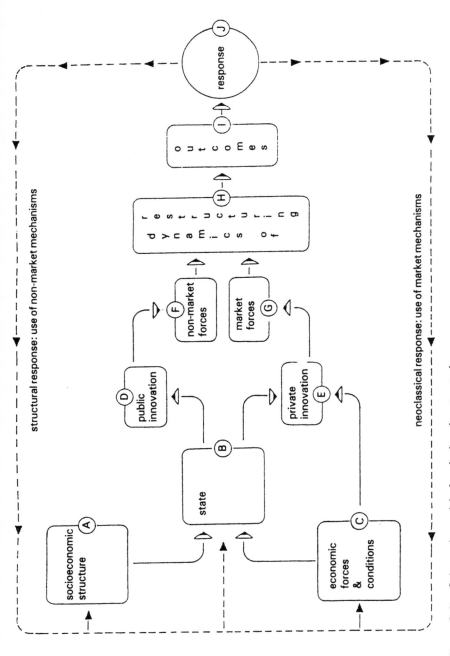

Figure 2.1. Schematic model of agricultural restructuring

sufficient revenues to cover production costs and provide adequate funds for the purchase of additional means of production (Bonanno, 1987: 132). Thus accumulation is also a fundamental task for capitalist agriculture, which is characterized by efforts to increase returns for units of capital, land and labour.

In recent decades the farm sectors in advanced societies have greatly increased the supply of agricultural products but given the conditions of inelastic demand, there has been little change, in real terms, in the total revenue earned (CEC, 1987a: 40, 119; OECD, 1987: 201). As a consequence returns per worker have been maintained only by the continuous outflow of labour from farms and its replacement by labour-saving technology. The absorbtion of the surplus labour has been facilitated by developments in the non-agricultural economy.

In considering the role of capitalist penetration into agriculture a distinction must be made here between *farming* and the totality of the *agriculture sector*, i.e. including the production and marketing of inputs to farming and the processing and marketing of farm outputs. Except in special cases (such as intensive production of poultry and livestock) farming activities have been comparatively immune to capitalist penetration compared to the rest of the agricultural sector (Lewontin and Berlan, 1986). This relative failure of capital to extend accumulation to on-farm production has been ascribed to a combination of factors that centre around the unique features of the production process in primary agriculture (Kloppenburg and Kenney, 1983; Lewontin and Berlan, 1986; Goodman *et al.*, 1987). Goodman *et al.* argue that this uniqueness of farming lies in its subservience to nature, extensiveness in space and the biological cycles in crop and animal production. Unable to overcome the constraints involved – and thus unable to devise a unified production process as in a branch of industrial production – industrial capitals have responded by taking over selective elements of the production chain and transforming them into industrial activities, e.g. as when fertilization with animal manure is replaced by chemical fertilizers. Similarly, Goodman and colleagues argue, the utilization of the products of agriculture poses unique problems for industrial production. Food products cannot be readily displaced by other industrial products. Nevertheless, they note that the industrialization of agricultural products is taking place and accounts for a steadily rising proportion of value added to farm products. Furthermore, commodities produced on farms are being replaced by non-agricultural raw materials or industrial substitutes for food and fibres. Thus whereas farmers occupy a physically indispensible link in the chain of production the control of the conditions of production has moved towards external capital (Lewontin and Berlan, 1986: 26). In this way primary agriculture becomes integrated into an agri-industrial complex.

Socioeconomic structure

In the induced development model the market system is regarded as a self-correcting mechanism, with the state intervening only in a facilitating role, i.e. to iron out market 'imperfections'. We need to extend this view to take account of the politically determined nature of the way the state acts in forming policy. Policies may be viewed not so much as *solutions* to problems but as the *outcomes* of an overtly political bargaining process among diverse interests with unequal influence, including especially farmers' organizations, agencies of state, agri-business corporations and consumers (Petit, 1985; Havens and Newby, 1986: 290).

This approach to understanding policy-making does not exclude some form of bureaucratic 'rationality'. The state benefits from a certain degree of autonomy relative to civil society (de Janvry and Dethier, 1985: 12). This is because in order to generate its own resources the state (i) must ensure the reproduction of capital accumulation and surplus creation in general rather than protect the interests of any individual capital (any specific social group), and (ii) it must ensure an operable degree of political consensus and control over possibly antagonistic pressure groups (Bonanno, 1988).

Following de Janvry and Dethier we may refer to this relatively autonomous role of the state as 'the state acting from above', and the appropriation of the policy-making capacity of the state by interest groups as 'the state activated from below'.

Generally in advanced societies the agricultural sectors have been able to command a considerable degree of political influence (see, e.g. Hathaway, 1963; Neville-Rolfe, 1984; Bowler, 1985; Petit *et al.*, 1987; Tracy, 1989). Bowler (p. 43) describes the network of lobbying and consultations in EC agricultural policy-making that allows close contacts to be developed among government ministers, Commission officials, and leaders of pressure groups. Compared to consumers farmers, despite their differences, are more easily organized into interest groups[1]. However, national farm groups are led by the larger, more economically better-off members. National tendencies are reinforced at the European level where, as Averyt (1977) notes, farm policy is such a labyrinth that only farmers with large amounts of resources – wealth, time and knowledge – are able to understand the decision-making process sufficiently to influence its output. Tracy (1989: 333) argues that the tardiness in dealing with the problems of the EC's CAP (i.e. over-production and over-expenditure on agricultural support) during the 1970s and 1980s was due to the tendency for many EC agriculture ministers to be overly concerned with short-term considerations such as political survival and the need to curry favour with the farm electorate. Brown (1989: 53) shows how CAP benefits converged on a minority of larger farms, those who were most able to lobby and capture gains.

The state

The concern here is with the 'state acting from above', under the influence of bureaucratic or political élites. In this role, typified by Keynesian policies, the state ensures both the general conditions for capital accumulation and the reproduction of the social order (de Janvry and Dethier, 1985: 12). Intervention on this basis may be based on practical measures and/or on the creation of ideologies in support of capital accumulation or the creation of political consensus. As a result of the overriding concern with food procurement the state has been long involved in agriculture, providing research and extension systems, as well as instituting land reforms, and establishing marketing and credit facilities.

An important factor in the development of the EC's CAP has been the leadership provided by the Directorate-General for Agriculture although, given the other interests involved, its right of initiative is not exclusive (Bowler, 1985:20). In a review of the policy process leading up to the compromises reached on the EC's agricultural budget crisis in 1984, Petit *et al.* (1987:116) found that the Directorate-General was a 'highly effective actor' in terms of technical competence. They also reported that although individual Commissioners of the EC are sensitive to national interests, the Commission as an institution acted as guardian of the Community's fundamental principles.

Goodman *et al.* (1987) illustrate the thin line that can exist between the managerial/technocratic functions of state management 'from above' and the role of organized interests mobilized 'from below'. Whereas historically the application of scientific principles to agriculture was promoted by non-state organizations (e.g. the Royal Agricultural Society) state research in Europe and the US was justified in those areas of agricultural production not susceptible to industrial organization. That is, natural processes such as those inherent in biological cycles and requiring long-term and costly experimentation were considered to belong to the domain of public sector research. However, Goodman and colleagues note that the success of state research in controlling the biological components of production, which had eluded private capitals, paradoxically created the conditions for capital accumulation by sectors of agribusiness. As biological knowledge has become an industrial property public research priorities have been realigned to avoid conflict with opportunities for private profit-making (Goodman *et al.* 1987:161). Currently, with the advances in biotechnology private spending for agricultural research is growing at a faster rate in the public sector but the two sectors are regarded as complementary. Private firms engage primarily in projects that yield immediate or near-term commercial application, but without the knowledge from publicly funded basic research applied results would 'dry up' (USDA, 1988). Thus agricultural research, whereas ostensibly serving farmers and consumers, is moulded by the expansionist needs of capital in the input-supply industries, with decisive influences on the nature of farming (Goodman *et al.*, 1987; Lewontin and Berlan, 1986).

The productionist paradigm: dynamics of change

In this and the next section we analyse how the main determinant forces already discussed manifest themselves through the dynamics of change in the agricultural sector, and through the outcomes that have ensued from the transformations occurring. The time scale of relevance is roughly from the mid-1960s to mid-1980s. Under several headings common trends are identified for the EC and US but at some points these are also illustrated by reference to the Republic of Ireland.

Technology: trajectories and impacts

It requires little reflection to accept that the generation and diffusion of technology has been one of the most powerful economic forces dictating the rate and shape of agricultural adjustment. 'Technology' here encompasses several types: (i) mechanical, (ii) biological–chemical, (iii) information technology, and (iv) organizational techniques (e.g. management systems and structures). Each of these has its own impact on the course of structural change but the interactions among them and their synergetic effects are also of significance.

Mechanical innovations in general have tended to be scale-related, being more adapted to large production units. Moreover, as mechanization becomes more complex it tends to be introduced in systemic fashion. For example, if a component of an operation is to be efficiently engineered mechanically it may be necessary to introduce complementary changes in related components. Thus, it is easier to mechanize manure handling if animals are kept in slatted housing. Mechanical innovations have substituted for labour but this has also meant the substitution of land for labour, as higher output per worker through mechanization allows a larger land base per unit of labour.

Between 1955 and 1982 the average application of nitrogenous fertilizer per hectare in the EC-12 rose from 15.5 kg to 73.5 kg – an increase of 374 per cent (Agra Europe, 1989: E/4). Biological and chemical technologies facilitate the substitution of capital and labour inputs for land. Whereas biotech innovations are intrinsically scale-neutral their successful adoption may call for levels of knowledge, skills and managerial ability that tend to be distributed in favour of the larger units. Furthermore, such innovations may be 'packaged' with other less scale-neutral developments, a point amplified below.

In its general sense biotechnology includes several component technologies and processes. These are principally genetic manipulation (or 'recombinant DNA'), cellular manipulation (e.g. tissue culture to allow genetically manipulated organisms to grow and express desirable traits), and fermentative and enzyme technologies that are essential for the mass production and conversion of many substances (e.g. hormones, feed additives). Internationally, developments in biotechnology and related areas have increased the participation of commercial organizations in the generation of agricultural technology. In the US, for example, biotechnology firms multiplied in virtually every field of endeavour following a Supreme Court decision that resolved the uncertainties about getting patent rights for laboratory creations (Cunningham, 1984).

Corporate involvement in the generation of farm technology has been precipitated by developments in the electronics and computer industries. A new generation of machines constitute not only as an advance in mechanical power but also a complex of information technology for farm and agribusiness management. Micro-computer applications at farm level serve several functions including record-keeping, production control, forecasting the market outcomes of alternative production strategies, and identification of optimum use of resources. Information and organization technologies tend to meet the needs of larger production units or the more capital-intensive operations.

In effect, then, the diffusion of modern agricultural technology has not been a random process but differentiated between small and large producers. Public sector extension services, which originated on the assumption that the transfer of technology was largely a matter of transmitting sufficient information to farmers, have not eliminated the differential adoption pattern. This is because the take-up of technology is generated by a set of socioeconomic structural factors, or 'access conditions' (cell A in Figure 2.1) which determine that all potential adopters do not have equal opportunity to benefit from new developments. Comprehensive European research on the adoption of technology is difficult to find but Irish and US evidence shows clearly that, compared to others, early adopters are better educated, more 'rational', more specialized in their farm operations, and tend to have greater resources (see e.g. Frawley, 1985; Rogers, 1983; 241–70). Furthermore, the 'social distance' between these types of farmers and research/extension personnel is much shorter than for other farmers. The high adopters are those with greater access to research extension and services both directly and through the political and representative process. As resources have become more limited extension services have pursued a 'progressive farmer strategy', concentrating efforts where the prospects of results were greatest. In Ireland, for example, recent policy decisions to charge farmers for extension services raises the possibilities of directing these services more selectively towards high-income categories. Other implications of the policy are noted in the penultimate section of this chapter.

A further aspect of technological diffusion arises from the increased involvement of private capital in agricultural research, and from structural change in the agribusiness sector. Companies producing a variety of inputs now tend to sell complete input packages to farmers, including advice on management and production. In this event the focus will be towards the more capitalized farms. Chemical companies, for example, have recognized the possibilities for developing 'market pairs' of inputs such as seeds and herbicides (Hueth and Just, 1987). Kloppenburg (1984) refers to the dominant position of the petrochemical and pharmaceutical companies in this context and cites cases of firms that propose to develop plants and other products in such a way that they are complemented by, or even require, the application of chemicals.

Thus, farmers have become increasingly enmeshed in economic relationships dominated by industrial capital, factor and product markets. Their conditions of production are therefore affected by the restructuring processes taking place in agri-industry. Before identifying other features of structural change beyond the farm gate it will be useful to consider the changing composition of purchased inputs on modern farms.

Farm inputs and factor substitution

Technical progress in agriculture has had a distinct bias towards saving labour while using machinery and other purchased inputs (feedingstuffs, fertilizers, pesticides, energy and services). Between 1960 and 1980 the average annual percentage growth in the capital/labour ratio in advanced countries generally ranged from 4 to 9 per cent (OECD, 1987: 190). In the EC the use of purchased inputs rose very significantly between 1966 and 1984, whereas as far as fixed asset formation is concerned the level of investment in EC farming has been higher than in the overall economy (CEC, 1987a: 22).

One consequence of factor substitution in the US is that retained farming earnings are less able to meet the capital requirements of modern agriculture, with the result that increased debt – and persistently high interest rates – have precipitated a cash crisis in many US farms (Green, 1986: 417–18). Another consequence of the growing importance of purchased inputs is that the farm sector and especially net farm incomes are increasingly vulnerable to economic forces which can affect the variability of costs and revenues (OECD, 1987: 199).

Agri-industrial integration

There are other trends besides the changing factor composition on farms that integrate agricultural production into the industrial economy. As we have noted advanced technologies tend to dissolve the distinction between 'agriculture' and 'industry'. Different aspects of agricultural production become transformed into types of industrial activity whereas industrial processes account for a steadily rising proportion of value-added, or agricultural products are replaced by non-agricultural components (Goodman et al., 1987: 2, 58).

Producers no longer supply traditional markets but must meet industrial-processing requirements. These in turn are tailored to meet carefully determined specifications regarding quality, delivery dates, presentation and health requirements. One way in which the functions of farms and agri-industry have been linked is through forms of vertical integration. By making contractual arrangements farmers can share managerial decisions, as well as risks in production and marketing, with one or more related businesses – supplier, processor or distributor. Most US food is produced on contract arrangements. Contract integration between processors and farmers is now quite common in Europe and is likely to increase (Higgins, 1988: 26–7).

Apart from risking-sharing the advantages of contract integration to producers include firm prices and access to technical advice and to capital. However, where contracts specify comprehensive production terms the farmer is virtually relegated to the role of a semi-autonomous employee or pieceworker for agribusiness (Roy, 1972). Furthermore, contracts between farmers and processors are contracts between unequal partners unless there is vigorous competition among firms wishing to enter contracts. The more usual case, though, is one in which processors are in a monopsony or near-monopsony position in regional markets (Higgins, 1988:28).

As an alternative to entering contracts agribusiness firms may take on the functions of production directly. Data on vertical integration through production ownership in European agriculture are not readily available but evidence from the US suggests that agribusinesses have made substantial investments in on-farm production facilities, accounting for about 6 per cent of US farm sales in 1981 (Knutson *et al.*, 1983). Whereas this overall total is not significant the proportion is much higher for individual products – over one-third for eggs, fresh vegetables, vegetables for processing, citrus fruit and potatoes (Marion, 1985:5).

Economic forces in the agribusiness complex

Because of these various upstream and downstream linkages production agriculture is affected by the organization and restructuring strategies being pursued in the agribusiness complex. The predominant trends are towards greater concentration, oligopolistic structures, internationalization of business and diversification of activities by large-scale organizations. From a review of the available literature Higgins (1988) concluded that large multinational firms now dominate the European tractor, fertilizer, agrichemical and pharmaceutical industries. As the development of mechanical technology is dominated by US-owned multinationals their products are unlikely to be ideally suited to many EC farming situations where production scale is much smaller than in the US. Economic concentration among input suppliers is a cause of rising production costs for farmers. The picture emerging in the US is that of a large number of independent producers sandwiched between an oligopoly-controlled input sector and an oligopoly-controlled output sector (Havens, 1986:45).

Concentration is also evident in food manufacturing, especially in secondary processing (consumer products), whereas the advent of large multiple stores has concentrated food distribution (Higgins, 1988). In the UK, for example, over two-thirds of the sales of several food items originate from three firms; a similar situation obtains in France (Dawson *et al.*, 1986). The food industries in Ireland tend to follow the trends in other advanced countries and, currently, further amalgamations among large dairy cooperatives are considered necessary to maintain competitiveness in international markets. Ireland has also followed the European trends towards fewer food outlets, with the number of grocery stores declining by 46 per cent during 1966–83 (Higgins, 1988:6).

The significance of concentration in food distribution is that large multiples can oblige manufacturers to produce to their specifications; they can exert pressure on manufacturers' profit margins, which, indirectly, squeezes the returns available to farmers who have the least market power in the food production chain. Goodman *et al.* (1987: 54–5) note how the importance of production agriculture has fallen at an accelerating rate in recent decades, 'caught in a vice between input industries and downstream processing and distribution activities'. In this situation, a declining share of the consumer's bill goes to farmers.

Rising production and productivity

Perhaps the most significant feature of modern agricultural restructuring over the past 20 years has been the steady rise in productivity and production. In 1966–86 the volume of farm production increased annually by 1.9 per cent in the six original Member-States of the EC whereas the annual growth rate during 1973–85 in EC-10 was 1.8 per cent. Comparative indices of agricultural production for 1966–84 suggest that output in the industrialized world expanded at virtually the same rate as in the Community (CEC, 1987: 18–9).

Because of changes in technology and input composition farm yields increased substantially in Europe over the past 35 years. Annual growth rates in yields from the major crops ranged from 1.6 per cent to 3.0 per cent. Milk yields per cow have been increasing by 1.8 per cent per annum over the past 25 years but for the shorter period of 1975–83 those yields rose to 2.4 per cent per annum (Commins and Higgins, 1987). For the US index values of farm productivity rose from 61 to 116 during 1950–85 on a 1977 base of 100 (Wimberley, 1986: 40).

Specialization

Traditionally, farmers diversified production in order to reduce risks and income variability. Price policies have modified this variability and so diversification in farm management is less important than formerly. Moreover, technological change has different consequences for different enterprises, especially in regard to economies of scale. These factors dispose farmers to specialize in a smaller number of crop and livestock enterprises in order to benefit from price security and size economies.

This trend is illustrated – though indirectly – in EC agriculture where the percentages of holdings having various enterprises have declined while there has been a general increase in the average area of crops grown or livestock maintained per farm (Table 2.1).

Scale enlargement and concentration of production

Farming has not only become more specialized but also there is a long-term tendency toward increasing the size of the individual production unit. Between the early 1960s and mid-1980s the average size of a farm in EC-9 increased by over 50 per cent – from 12 to 18 hectares. Area size, however, does not allow for distinctions between extensive and intensive systems of farming. For this purpose the concept of economic size unit (ESU) is used in

Table 2.1 Summary of the trends of change in cropping and livestock 1975–85
(+ = increase, − = decline, 0 = no change, n.d. = no data)

A = percentage of farms with each crop or type of livestock							B = change in average area grown, or size of herd/flock, per farm[1]	
	Cereals		Potatoes		Sugar beet		Roots	
Country	A	B	A	B	A	B	A	B
Belgium	−	+	−	+	+	+	−	+
Denmark	−	+	−	+	−	+	−	+
Germany	−	+	−	+	−	+	−	0
France	−	+	−	+	0	0	−	−
Ireland	−	+	−	+	−	+	−	+
Italy	−	+	−	0	−	+	−	+
Luxembourg	−	+	−	+	n.d.	n.d.	−	+
Netherlands	−	+	−	+	−	+	−	+
UK	−	+	−	+	−	+	−	+

	Cattle		Dairy cows		Other cows		Sheep		Sows	
Country	A	B	A	B	A	B	A	B	A	B
Belgium	0	+	−	+	+	+	+	+	−	+
Denmark	−	+	−	+	−	0	+	−	−	+
Germany	−	+	−	+	+	+	+	0	−	+
France	−	+	−	+	+	+	+	+	−	+
Ireland	−	+	−	+	−	0	−	+	−	+
Italy	−	+	−	+	−	+	−	+	−	+
Luxembourg	−	+	−	+	+	+	+	−	−	+
Netherlands	−	+	−	+	n.d.	n.d.	+	+	−	+
UK	−	+	−	+	−	0	+	+	−	+

Note: [1]Base is the number of farms having each particular crop or livestock.
Source: Author's analysis of Eurostat data in CEC (1987b) *Farm Structure – 1985 Survey: Main Results.*

order to give a better measure of the volume of farm business. Using this measure Table 2.2 shows the rate of scale enlargement in EC-10 and Ireland during 1975–83.

Not only is the proportion of large farms increasing but also those at the top end of the scale account for more than their proportionate share of total farm output. This trend towards concentration of production is a common feature of agricultural restructuring. In the EC the percentages of producers with large livestock enterprises are increasing (based on 1973–85 figures) and these represent a growing proportion of total animal production. The most dramatic changes occur in those enterprises that are less dependent on land, like pig farming. For the EC-10 the percentage of pig farmers with more than 400 animals increased from 0.8 to 3.9 per cent during 1973–85, whereas the proportion of all pigs on such farms rose from 24 per cent to 58 per cent (Commins and Higgins, 1987). In general about 80 per cent of all EC-12 farm

Table 2.2 Percentages of holdings in economic size units (ESUs)

	EC–10		Ireland	
Scale size in ESUs	1975	1983	1975	1983
		Per cent		
Small (2 or less)	44.0	36.6	42.5	29.9
Medium (2 to 8)	31.2	31.0	43.6	40.3
Large (Over 8)	24.8	32.4	13.9	29.8

Source: CEC (1987a), *The Agricultural Situation in the Community: 1986 Report*, p. 30.

production comes from 20 per cent of holdings. In the US 4 per cent of farms, operating 22 per cent of the land, sell nearly half of all agricultural products (Wilkening and Gilbert, 1987: 281). This last figure is expected to increase to three-quarters in the year 2000 (OTA, 1986: 9).

Scale enlargement and concentration make for increasing socioeconomic and spatial differentiation within the farm sector. This process can be illustrated with reference to Ireland where livestock and livestock products account for 87 per cent of farm output and there has been substantial restructuring in animal enterprises. Firstly, in the context of liberal farm price supports milk production has become concentrated on fewer but larger farms (Table 2.3), these being predominantly in the eastern part of the Republic. Secondly, during the 1950s and 1960s the small farm economy of the western region experienced considerable outmigration and consequent debilitation of the demographic structure. Associated with this was a trend away from labour intensive enterprises such as dairying and towards a low-input, low-output pattern of drystock cattle production. For example in Connacht – the western province – dairy cow numbers declined by 27 per cent during 1960–80 whereas they increased by 33 per cent in the rest of the country. Thirdly, these trends are reflected in contemporary farm survey data which show clear socioeconomic differences among categories of farms,

Table 2.3 Percentages of milk suppliers and milk supplies[1] in Ireland, 1966–86

	Percentage of supplies			Percentage of suppliers		
Level of supply (000 gallons)	1966	1976	1986	1966	1976	1986
Under 5	76.8	49.4	24.9	40.7	13.1	3.7
5–10	16.1	22.6	21.0	30.1	19.3	8.5
10–20	6.2	17.8	23.4	22.9	28.9	18.4
Over 20	0.9	10.2	30.7	5.3	38.7	69.4
No. of suppliers (000s)	110.5	74.7	54.0			
Average supply (gallons)				3,683.0	9,033.0	18,215.0

Note: [1]Data refer to milk delivered creameries for manufacture.
Source: Fingleton (1983; 1989).

depending on region, scale of operation and system. The basic contrast is between part-time farms, defined as those requiring less than 0.75 standard labour units to operate, and the remainder. Part-time farms account for almost two-thirds of the holdings in the country; they are located predominantly in the west region; they occupy two-fifths of the country's utilized agricultural area but produce less than one-fifth of gross output; and their system of farming is based almost exclusively on low-income livestock production rather than on the higher income dairy enterprise (Table 2.4).

Table 2.4 Selected socioeconomic characteristics of Irish farms, 1987

	East region		West region	
	Full-time[1]	Part-time[2]	Full-time[1]	Part-time[2]
Percentage of the state's				
Total number of farms	23.2	16.5	13.4	46.9
Gross farm output	64.4	0.7	20.1	14.8
Family farm income	56.4	5.7	20.8	17.1
Utilized agric. area	41.1	10.9	19.3	28.7
Economic size units	59.2	7.0	19.3	14.5
Dairy cows	66.5	1.8	26.5	5.2
Other cattle (livestock units)	42.5	15.0	14.9	27.6
Labour units on farms[3]	32.5	13.0	17.6	36.9
Standard man days (SMDs)[4]	54.2	6.4	21.1	18.3
Average values				
Gross farm output (Ir. £)	44,206.0	7,076.0	23,810.0	5,044.0
Family farm income (Ir. £)	14,253.0	2,026.0	8,988.0	2,135.0
Utilized agric. area (ha)	46.0	17.2	37.4	15.9
Economic size units	22.1	3.7	12.5	2.7
Dairy cows	25.9	1.0	17.8	1.0
Other cattle (livestock units)	31.1	15.5	18.8	10.0
Labour units on farms[3]	1.6	0.9	1.5	0.9
Standard man days (SMDs)[4]	1.8	0.3	1.2	0.3

Notes: [1] Full-time farms are those requiring at least 0.75 standard labour units to operate on a standard man-day basis.
[2] Part-time farms require less than 0.75 standard labour units.
[3] Labour on farms converted to standard adult equivalents.
[4] An SMD is 8 hours of work by a person over 18 years old; the number of SMDs required per hectare for different crops or per head for various categories of livestock are used to derive the total number of SMDs required by a farm.

Source: Author's calculations derived from Power *et al.* (1989), *National Farm Survey 1987*.

The 'cost-price squeeze' and declining farm incomes

One of the remarkable features of the modern agricultural transformation is that despite the aspirations to maintain parity of income with the rest of the economy and the massive subsidies provided for this purpose, the relative income position of the farm sector has remained virtually unchanged in most of the OECD countries since the 1960s (OECD, 1987: 201). For EC-10 during 1975–87 aggregate real income in farming (in value-added terms) declined steadily but because labour moved out of farming the income per work unit, in real terms, remained relatively constant over the 12 year period (Table 2.5). Although agricultural production expanded a fall in net value-added occurred despite the productivity of farm inputs. The explanation lies in the steady deterioration in the ratio of farmgate prices to input prices, i.e. the cost of inputs rose more rapidly than the price obtained for products sold (CEC, 1987a: 120). Of course, these general trends conceal variations between farm size groups and regions. Those less adversely affected are the larger farm categories in the northern European countries.

Table 2.5 Trends in agricultural income, EC–10 (100 = average for 1979/81)

	1975	1987
Volume of final production	88	109
Ratio of farmgate to input prices	102	98
Net value-added of the sector (real)	115	99
Farm labour-work units	115	87
Net value added (real) per work unit	103	100

Source: CEC (1987a), *The Agricultural Situation in the Community: 1986 Report*, p. 120; CEC (1989), *The Agricultural Situation in the Community: 1988 Report*, p. 53.

Labour outflow and disguised unemployment

Decline in the farm labour force is a universal feature of modern agricultural restructuring. In EC-10 total numbers of working on the land were halved during 1965–85, implying a reduction rate of 3 per cent per annum. For the later decade of this period the rate of decline slackened off somewhat due to a more unfavourable employment situation outside of agriculture. Similarly in the US total farm employment was halved between 1960 and 1985 (Wimberley, 1986: 40).

Labour adjustment in agriculture is also marked by two other features: disguised unemployment and a trend towards part-time farming. The latter has been observed in many industrial countries (Abercrombie, 1985). During 1975–85 most EC-10 countries showed a decline in the proportion of landholders working full-time on their holdings. However, the proportions of landholders devoting all of their normal working time to farming now range widely, from 12 per cent in Italy and Greece to over 70 per cent in Luxembourg and the Netherlands. Yet not all of the others have a gainful activity outside of farming. The overall position for the EC-10 (summarized in Table 2.6) shows that whereas 71 per cent of all landholders worked less than full-time on their holdings 61 per cent of these (i.e. 43 per cent of 71) had no other gainful economic activity. This is an indication of the level of hidden unemployment. The problem is not so severe in Ireland.

Table 2.6 Landholders in EC–10 and in Ireland classified by proportion of normal working time on the farm, with and without outside gainful activity, 1985

%	0–50		50–100		100+		Total
	A	B	A	B	A	B	
EC–10	24	30	4	13	3	26	100
Ireland	21	8	9	17	4	41	100

Notes: A = with outside gainful activities; B = without outside gainful activities.
Source: Derived from CEC (1989), *The Agricultural Situation in the Community: 1988 Report*, pp. T/102–T/103.

The rising costs of state supports

State interventions especially in the form of commodity price supports have been a very influential element in agricultural restructuring. A comprehensive analysis of the origins, aims and instruments of agricultural policy (OECD, 1987) has shown how concern for low farm incomes and the presumed inefficiencies of agricultural markets have resulted in a progressively broader range of measures being brought to bear on the agricultural sector, to the point where policies impinge on virtually every aspect of the agricultural economy. In consequence, the volume of resources devoted to policy objectives has increased enormously. In the US, for example, average annual net public outlays for price support and related programmes were 70 per cent greater (at constant prices) in the 1981–85 period than in 1965–69. The expenditure on the EC's CAP was seven times greater in 1988 than in 1973.

The main trends in the US and the EC in the 1980s are shown in Table 2.7. As countries subsidize their farmers in different ways the OECD has applied the concept of the Producer Subsidy Equivalent (PSE) to measure the degree of agricultural supports on a common basis. The PSE represents the total payment that would be required to compensate farmers for loss of income if policies were removed. It measures both direct supports (e.g. market subsidies) and indirect assistance (e.g. advisory services). Expressed as a percentage the PSE shows the ratio of assistance to producer incomes.

Reflecting the data in Table 2.7, PSEs have risen sharply in the US, the annual figure going from about 16 per cent in 1979–81 to 35 per cent in 1986. In the EC, PSEs increased from 37 per cent in 1979–81 to about 50 per cent in 1988. For OECD countries in general the PSE rose from 30 to 47 per cent in the same period (OECD, 1988: 18). In the main these shifts represent increased support for market prices. Generally, in the major developed societies the total costs borne by taxpayers and consumers for supporting agricultural commodities almost doubled in the period 1979–81 to 1984–86 (OECD, 1988: 18).

Budgetary data understate the costs of agricultural income support policies because they omit the part of the costs borne by consumers – through paying higher prices for food products. OECD estimates of the relative magnitudes of the financial contributions made by taxpayers and consumers

Table 2.7 Pubic expenditure related to agricultural policy

	1979	1981	1983	1985
Expenditure per capita ($)				
EC–9	95	105	122	140
US	98	119	203	238
Share of government spending (%)				
EC–9	2.7	2.3	2.3	2.3
US	2.9	2.7	4.0	4.1
Share of nominal value added in agriculture (%)				
EC–9	30.3	31.2	32.2	36.6
US	28.5	32.6	71.7	67.3

Source: OECD (1987), *Structural Adjustment and Economic Performance*, p. 187.

to financing agricultural policies indicate that in the EC consumers carry a relatively heavy share of the burden – 63 per cent as compared with 27 per cent in the US and 36 per cent in Canada (OECD, 1987: 189). In Ireland, for the period 1975 to 1981 consumer losses in terms of domestic transfers under the CAP were around Ir. £250 m but producer gains amounted to Ir. £950 m (O'Connor *et al.*, 1983: xvi).

Transfers to agriculture are comparatively large when placed against the size of the sector itself. Again, for several of the advanced countries OECD estimates imply that, for 1979–81, consumers and taxpayers together spent on agricultural policies an amount equivalent to 68 per cent of the sector's value-added, with the EC being among the high levels (OECD, 1987: 189).

Shifting balance of agriculture expenditures

As well as rising sharply in recent years the balance of overall budgetary expenditures has changed. The objective of increasing agricultural incomes has become progressively more important, absorbing to a considerable extent the other objectives of policy (OECD, 1987: 188). Short-term income maintenance, as distinct from income distribution, has marked the direction of policy measures. Price supports increasingly insulated producers from the effects of the operation of the market, i.e. price declines in conditions of over-production and consequent disincentives to further production.

The shifting balance of price and non-price support in agricultural expenditure is revealed clearly in the EC's financing of the CAP. The Agricultural Guidance and Guarantee Fund (EAGGF) has two sections: the guarantee section which finances expenditures under market organization and the guidance section that covers expenditure on improving farm structures. When the EAGGF was established in 1962 it was intended that one-third of appropriations would go to the guidance sector. This ratio was soon abandoned and eventually whittled down to less than 5 per cent as market expenditure soared. One reason for this is that the Community provides only partial funding of relevant guidance schemes; Member-States and beneficiaries – farmers or agribusiness – contribute the remainder. Understandably, the income transparency of higher prices for commodities produced and the 100 per cent funding of price supports had far greater appeal to farmers' organizations and political leaders than schemes that partly funded improvements at farm level. The EAGGF also included a series of structural measures in support of farming in specified regions. However, as Tracy (1989: 329) observes, some of these were introduced as political strategems, 'hastily concocted as make-weights' during difficult price bargaining, to enable particular ministers to accept a more comprehensive package agreement.

The impacts of CAP price supports vary by type of commodity produced, although the effect is conditional on size of farm. In 1984–86, gains for EC farms over 40 economic size units were 15 times larger than those accruing to farms of less than 6 economic size units (Brown, 1989: 34). Within most size categories dairy farms obtain more benefit than other types; overall in 1984–86 dairy farms obtained gains at least 50 per cent higher than for other farm types (Brown, 1989: 7). Brown's data for Ireland show that on a per farm basis dairy farmers received over two-and-a-half times the benefits accruing to drystock producers.

Outcomes: benefits, problems and crisis

Benefits

The beneficial outcomes of the highly-capitalized, productionist model of agricultural development are undeniable. In the case of the EC, for example, the food shortages of the early post-war years were eliminated and consumers have been guaranteed an expanded range of products, much improved in terms of quantity and quality. Whereas food prices have risen the rate of increase has been somewhat lower than for disposable income, or for consumer prices as a whole (CEC, 1987c: 27). The guaranteeing of fixed prices sheltered farmers from fluctuations in world market prices and ensured a regularity of supply for consumers. Europe's food producers gained new market outlets as the Community became a leading world exporter of food and agricultural products. Although the EC once consumed far more than it produced there is no longer any major commodity suitable for widespread production within and Community in which there is a structural deficit (CEC, 1987a: 118). On the contrary, with demand within and outside the Community increasing only very slowly, surpluses have built up that cannot be disposed of at economic prices. This pattern is replicated in other advanced countries.

Problems

Problems have arisen because of the self-driven dynamic towards over-production that is built into price support programmes backed up by technological change. Support prices are sought to enable the 'average' farmer to stay in business but the bulk of output is produced on large farms where unit costs are lower than average. Studies by OECD (1987a: 191) illustrate the Catch-22 situation. In 1980–82 60 per cent of US farms made a loss, implying that prices were below cost of production for the average farmer; however, because 94 per cent of total farm output came from the 40 per cent that had positive net incomes farm prices were in fact below production costs for only 6 per cent of output. Such disparities in profitability would not be as great in the EC because of the lower concentration of output but the general tendency is similar. That is, at prices that result in a loss for most farmers (hence creating political pressure for price supports) larger farmers have strong incentives to increase output. The problem is exacerbated when profits are capitalized into land values, as happens when price guarantees reduce market uncertainties (OECD, 1987a: 191, Wilkening and Gilbert, 1987: 279). The increased price of land and other costs become the basis of a renewed claim for further commodity price supports. In this spiral process the gains accrue to those who own the greater share of productive assets – not to those with below average incomes. In the US, for example, in 1984 15 per cent of farms producing three-quarters of the output obtained 70 per cent of direct government payments (Ahern, 1986: 87). In the EC transfers reward the agricultural sectors that increase production rather than change structures. In 1984–86 the one-third of farms with the highest agricultural incomes per labour unit received almost two-thirds of all CAP benefits (Brown, 1989: 7). Because Member-States bear the marginal costs of rising support prices according to their VAT valuation[2] and not on the basis of their marginal contribution to these costs an incentive exists to favour higher agricultural support prices (Koester, 1977: Runge and von Witzke, 1987: 218)[3].

Inevitably, then, the disparities between social groups and regions are widened. Variations in farm incomes are significant within the EC although several factors, besides price supports and technology, account for these. At EC-10 level the gap between economic size groups (ESU categories) in 1984 was 1 to 7.8, but if account is taken of both Member–State and economic size effects this ratio increased to 1:20, and extended to 1:40 if sub-national regional variations are also considered (CEC, 1985a). Regional income differences have increased during the course of agricultural development (Weinschenck and Kemper, 1981) and whereas some regionalization of EC policies has taken place these have not significantly altered the regional disparity gaps.

The changes in farm production in northern Europe since the end of World War II – and now increasingly in southern Europe – have been a decisive factor in transforming agricultural ecosystems. Many animal and plant species have been endangered or destroyed entirely (von Meyer, 1988: 17; Nature Conservancy Council, 1982). Modern production systems involve significant environmental costs that are externalized – borne by society. In the US monocultural production – a feature of specialization – is a major contributing factor to soil erosion, reduced levels of soil organic matter, and to greater use of pesticides. Similarly, the separation of crop and livestock production reduces the potential application of organic wastes to improve soil composition and creates pollution problems associated with large livestock enterprises (Buttel, 1984: 94).

Simultaneously with these concerns in advanced economies the long established 'policy community' of exclusively agricultural interests was being challenged in the construction of the agricultural policy agenda. New interests began to assert their influence in favour of the environment, and in support of consumers, and of food carrying less health risks. The European Parliament has shown itself to be more sensitive to the interests of consumers and taxpayers. In the US advocacy groups have expanded public concern over the hazards of certain technologies (Hadwiger, 1982: 150–68). Although agricultural leaders and research agencies had initially discouraged researchers from studying environmental hazards and other externalities they were eventually pressed to seek alternatives to some existing technology and to pay attention to the unwanted side effects of existing systems.

Critical turning points

What has generally been referred to as a 'crisis' in advanced society agriculture during the 1980s was not in fact some sudden and unexpected happening but a predictable stage 'in an essentially evolutionary process' (McInerney, 1987: 12). In the US the genesis and particulars of the crisis were somewhat different than in Europe; it was triggered by federal monetary policy that resulted in increased interest rates, deflation of land values, overvaluation of the dollar and decline in export markets (Wilkening and Gilbert, 1987: 285). The crisis of the EC CAP manifested itself in (i) the high cost of storing products, (ii) the high cost of export subsidies and the related tensions in international relations concerning export supports, (iii) political aversion (e.g. by the UK) to high consumer costs, and (iv) the budgetary limits of the CAP. The really critical point was reached when CAP spending threatened to exceed budgetary resources – a politically intolerable situation for the Community's integrity as an alliance. Faced with this prospect the Council of Agricultural Ministers and their main constituencies at national level – the farmers' organizations – had to accept the inevitability of reform in the CAP. As Winters (1987: 292) observed: major policy change became possible only in time of crisis when everybody agreed that 'something must be done'.

The EC also had to take several other factors into account. One was the reality that the 80 per cent of Community farmers who produced 20 per cent of output did not obtain very much support from legislation that distributed resources so regressively. Furthermore, a shadow hung over the European labour market where the outlook for reducing the high unemployment rate (12 per cent or 17 million job-seekers) remained dismal. Consequently, restructuring of agriculture through increased exodus from farming offered rather limited prospects for the immediate future. At the same time it was clear that given the likelihood of little change in food demand the growth rate in total agricultural production would have to be curbed.[4]

Overriding these various considerations in the early 1980s was the intention to establish the Single European Market by 1992. Central to this proposal was the creation of a common market permitting the free movement of capital, good and services within the Community. The idea was grounded in the theory positing links between free trade and economic prosperity, with hopes that the European economy could be revitalized in a single and larger market that would expand demand, facilitate economies of size, allow regional specialization based on comparative advantage and enhance productivity. It was considered that with this economic boost the EC could compete more effectively with its main rivals, Japan and the US.

Parallel with these European trends of the 1980s was a more generalized critique of agricultural policies that sheltered farmers from market forces. The OECD made a strong appeal for the return of farming to a freer market (OCED, 1987a: 185). In the US the high cost and selective impact of price supports, as well as the institutions and policies constructed over previous decades, came increasingly under question. Some saw this juncture as an economic and political opportunity to reactivate a comprehensive programme of rural development (de Janvry *et al.*, 1989).

Policy responses

By the early to mid-1980s, then, EC policy-makers faced two main challenges. The first was to create an internal market as a basis for increased prosperity and to adapt to keener competitive conditions emerging in world markets. In this context European agriculture would have to improve its own competitiveness and achieve a better balance between product supply and demand. The second challenge was the need to counter possible disaffection and further economic marginalization that such reforms could induce among the Community's less-favoured producers. Since their inception the CAP commodity support programmes were intended to achieve both economic objectives (e.g. adequate food supplies) and social objectives (e.g. the maintenance of a fair standard of living for farmers). They did not do so because of the skewed distribution of CAP benefits and the limited impacts of a watered-down sociostructural policy (Tracy, 1989: 332). Consequently, a new policy menu has been prepared in which the aim is to 'decouple' income supports to farmers from supports that increase prices or add to the volume of agricultural production. In the terms of the schematic model outlined in Figure 2.1 the effect would be to make clearer distinctions between the two recurved loops, J-ABC and J-BCA. Moreover, as a supplementary strategy the Community wants to diversify agricultural activity from surplus production to products that are currently under-produced (such as timber), and also to support programmes for rural development.

In their practical application policy measures can serve more than one function in either a manifest or latent manner. Cash incentives to farmers to retire from agricultural activity are an income support but their effects may also help in farm enlargement or the adjustment of supply and demand for a commodities. Thus, in classifying current perspectives and measures on EC agricultural policy we describe them in respect of their primary orientations:

whether they are directed mainly towards agricultural restructuring on free market economy principles, or on lines that give more explicit recognition to certain social objectives of the EC and its CAP (Table 2.8).

Table 2.8 Contemporary EC policy perspectives and measures as types of response to CAP crisis

Type of response	
Neoclassical	Structural/Institutional
Main orientation	
Towards a market economy model of restructuring	Towards an agrisocial model of restructuring
General aims and policy concerns	
Contain CAP crisis	Contain possible disaffection
Balance supply and demand	among marginalized groups
Increase competitiveness	Maintain solidarity with 'less
Improve quality of produce	-favoured' regions
Maintain entreprensurship[1]	Preserve 'rural social fabric'
Diversify production into non-	Protect environment
Surplus lines	
Main measures	
Reducation of price supports	Special schemes, such as
Quotas on production	compensatory allowances, to
Stabilizers – limited guarantee	support farm incomes in 'less
payments beyond certain	-favoured' areas despite
production limits	adding modest contributions to
Incentives to allow land to	output
lie fallow, or reduce output	Direct payments to low-income
Use most modern technology	farmers
Upgrade education/training	Early retirement of farmers
	Management agreements with
	farmers to protect environment
	Promotion of pluriactivity

Note: [1] According to the EC Commission the role of the public authorities is not to substitute for the advantages and risk of the entrepreneur (CEC, 1985b).

Responses in Ireland

The main operational aspects of these policy orientations may be exemplified with reference to Ireland. It is generally accepted that although commodity price supports continue the liberal price increases of former years – often announced triumphantly by agricultural ministers returning from Brussels – are no longer possible. Quota limits on milk output and incentives to dairy farmers to transfer to other farm enterprises have speeded up the restructuring of milk production. Prior to the quota significant declines took place among small dairy herds – those with fewer than 20 cows. Since the quota was introduced all herd sizes up to 40 cows show a net decline but the smaller herds are going out of milk production at an even faster rate than the pre-quota era. Thus the pre-quota trend whereby milk production was being concentrated in the hands of fewer, but larger, producers has intensified under the quota regime (Fingleton, 1989).

Milk producers may sell their allocated production quotas provided they also sell the land to which the quota is attached. There is a high demand for such 'milk quota land' and, correspondingly, prices are bid higher than for comparable land. Those in the best position to buy are predominantly well-established dairy farmers who built a strong financial base in the post-EC years of liberal milk price supports and can now capitalize on their earlier benefits.

Over the longer term, however, the producers' response to quota restrictions is expected to be on the lines of increasing efficiency of production, and reaching quota limits with fewer cows. In this context cost-reducing technology becomes important. Currently, as elsewhere in Europe there is a strong Irish lobby in favour of allowing the use of bovine somatotropin or BST - a synthetic growth hormone available through advances in biotechnology - which could increase milk yields substantially. Whereas BST is expected to be available to US milk producers in 1990 the EC has made no decision to remove its ban on the hormone, pending more detailed information on the possible effects of its use.

Renewed emphasis on managerial efficiency has highlighted the need for comprehensive education and training programmes for young and adult farmers. Ireland receives considerable support from the European Social Fund for such programmes. Concerning extension services we have already noted that domestic budgetary restrictions have obliged the Irish agricultural extension service to charge farmers for technical information and advice that were formerly freely available. One effect of this measure is to push extension work in the direction of a privatized service. Fee-paying farmers will be selective and avail themselves of private consultants whereas those state service advisers who can earn high fees have an incentive to leave the public service and establish themselves in private practice. Fee-based extension services also tend to sharpen the distinction between the more commercial farmers and others. Compared to the position prior to charging fees, when the generalized promotion of agricultural development and increased agricultural production were important elements in the mission of extension work, the current orientation of the service is towards responding to specific technical problems on a delimited category of farms - those disposed to pay for the services provided.

Ireland has a plethora of structural reform measures that could be described as conforming to the establishment of an agrisocial model of agriculture. In 1986, in accordance with EC regulations, a revised programme of investment aid for farm improvements was introduced. By comparison with the restrictive eligibility criteria of its predecessor, which disadvantaged smaller farmers, this new programme excluded virtually no full-time low income farmer whereas precluding larger commercial farmers from dominating the scheme. However, the conditions attaching to the type of investment fund stipulated that farm improvements should be in line with market requirements, while reducing costs and improving living and working conditions. In effect, the programme has been used by small holders for small-scale infrastructural and labour-saving improvements that simply help to maintain existing production levels (O'Hara, 1986).

Of more significance to Ireland are the EC's measures in favour of specified 'less-favoured areas'. As a result of the importance of livestock the country has benefited in particular from the compensatory allowances or 'headage payments' – based on the number of livestock per farm irrespective of quality. The current National Development Plan (Government of Ireland, 1989) regards these as having 'a vital role in supporting family farm viability and in preserving the social fabric in less-favoured areas'. Together with the state's own smallholders' assistance scheme these subsidies make the difference between survival and extinction on many small western farms.

An EC Commission proposal to provide direct payments to low-income farmers has not yet been accepted by the Council of Ministers. Such a proposal would tie the level of benefit to the income circumstances of individual farms and make it difficult for larger producers to receive the 'hidden' benefits obtainable under commodity price supports.

An element of the agrisocial model is 'staged farming', whereby farming is supported not for reasons of basic commodity production but ro preserve particular environments, such as wildlife habitats (Newby, 1989: 48). Policies promoting this type of agriculture have not yet been introduced in Ireland but grants are made available to farmers to control pollution from farming activities.

The move towards the completion of the single internal market has brought more urgency to the need to achieve greater economic and social cohesion in the EC. In this context the Community proposes (i) to double the amounts of its Structural Funds[5] by 1993, and (ii) to give priority status to, *inter alia*, the development of less-developed regions, the adjustment of agricultural structures and the promotion of rural development. Under this arrangement the Irish government have sought support for a set of measures designed to maximize rural job and wealth creation and to stabilize the rural population. Apart from the absolute increases the changing balance among the Structural Funds is of significance. In 1986–87 the European Regional Development Fund accounted for 27 per cent of total Structural Fund allocations to Ireland; but the proportion will rise to 48 per cent of the aggregate amount for 1989–93.

Concluding comment

The concern of this chapter has been to trace the origins, direction, dynamics and outcomes of agricultural restructuring in modern economies. Particular attention was paid to the situations in the EC and the US, with illustrative reference to the Republic of Ireland. The processes of transformation were considered to derive from a complex of interactions involving three main factors. Firstly, macroeconomic and technological forces, including those affecting agri-industry, exert determining impacts on the pattern of farm production. Secondly, the interventionist role of the state, especially when exercised through policies supporting agricultural commodity prices, has resulted in a skewed distribution of costs and benefits among producers and between producers and consumers. Thirdly, state intervention in turn is conditioned by the differential abilities of interest groups to organize and pursue collective action in their favour. Over the past three decades these various influences have combined to create a paradigm of agricultural restructuring that could be described as expansionary and 'productionist'. The longer-term trajectory of change reached a crisis point in the 1980s when the dominant pattern of increasing output, unquestioned productivity growth, technological development, and a supportive structure of price supports could no longer be sustained (see Peterson, chapter 3 in this volume). In Europe, the earlier needs for periodic adjustment had given way to the necessity for more basic reforms. In discussing these the contemporary profile of EC agricultural and related policy measures was represented in terms of two broad orientations: those directed towards re-establishing the norms of the market economy in agriculture, and measures that attribute to agriculture other societal functions besides food production.

Following Bonanno (1987; 1988) we may interpret the implications of this critical juncture in agricultural restructuring as the need for the state to strike a new balance between the continuing requirements of capital accumulation in agriculture and the necessity of maintaining the social conditions – minimum levels of political consensus and quiescence – under which accumulation in general can occur. In the EC's case the compromise involves, on the one hand, a general appeal to productive efficiency within restrictive output limits and diversification of surplus productive capacity in new directions and, on the other hand, the greater institutionalization of the social or legitimate functions of 'non-productive' farming in modern society. One effect of the resultant policy profile is to consolidate the dualistic structure of modern agriculture whereby a category of productive farms co-exists with a growing proportion of holdings that must be 'allocated other roles' in the rural economy. A corps of quality food producers is more sharply segregated from other rural 'resource managers' or occupiers. In this interpretation the persistence of 'unproductive' farms is inevitable – even desirable.

Based on the interpretative framework adopted (see Figure 2.1) we may expect that the outcomes of, and policy responses to, the productionist paradigm of the past few decades will reconfigure the determinants of future agricultural restructuring. Analysis of past CAP benefits reveals not only where gains have accrued but where resistance to change will be greatest (Brown, 1989: 54). Although production quotas are a restraint on output they will be of least disadvantage to those producers who have already high output levels. These will tend to lobby for the maintenance of price supports in the context of production limitations. Where quotas are tradable they are likely to be acquired by those who have already achieved the stronger resource base. Rents arising from the high support prices of the past are capitalized into the value of tradable quota rights and the regressive impact of policy shifts from the distribution of income to the distribution of wealth (OECD, 1987:200). These points have particular relevance for Ireland where, mainly due to the CAP, dairying has become strongly associated with the top income levels in farming.

Although some categories of the farm population are more favourably circumstanced than others to benefit from new or proposed agricultural policies it seems likely that the disproportionately large political influence exerted by agricultural interests as a whole will not be maintained. Whereas 20 years ago the hazards of technology were the concern of committed but isolated critics, there now exist networks of scientific, environmental and consumer groups playing the roles of permanent watchdogs (Mazur, 1983:32). Bowler (1985:37) notes several trends such as the decline in the farm vote, by which non-agricultural interests are becoming more influential in the formation of agricultural policy. An example is the fact that, acting largely in response to consumer pressure, the EC has banned the sale of meat from animals treated with hormones.

As a final remark, it could be argued that some of the recent EC reform measures (see Table 2.8) are conceived more in terms of political expedients rather than as intrinsically desirable measures in themselves. That is to say, the protection of the environment, the maintenance of farm incomes or the promotion of rural development have emerged as responses to the problems of productionist agriculture – and the CAP specifically – or as an inducement to subscribe to the idea of the Single European Market. An alternative policy thrust and rationale could be derived from a consideration of the problems of local rural communities and regions in a European and global economy, rather than from agriculture's particular restructuring difficulties. This view suggests the need for more comprehensive EC fiscal, economic and social policies as offering prospects for more balanced and equitable forms of development.

Notes

1. Some reasons for this are advanced by Senior Nello (1984).
2. EEC revenues are subject to a budget ceiling set primarily by the fact that contributions from Member-States are limited to a fixed percentage of value-added taxes.
3. This is known as the 'restaurant bill' effect. When a group agrees to share a bill for a meal there is an incentive for individuals to order expensively (Runge and von Witzke, 1987:218).
4. EC-10 the average degree of self-sufficiency had increased from 97 per cent in 1974 to 112 per cent in 1984. If production trends and demand growth were to remain unchanged the overall volume of surpluses would double within another decade. (Henrichsmeyer and Ostermeyer-Schloder 1988:146).
5. These are the guidance section of EAGGF, the European Social Fund (ESF) and the European Regional Development Fund (ERDF).

References

Abercrombie, K. (1985) *Part-time Farming in the Rural Development of Industrialised Countries*, Arkleton Trust, Langholm, Scotland.

Agra Europe (1989) EC curbs within 4 years on fertiliser and manure usage, January 13, E/3–E/4.

Ahern, Mary (1986) An income comparison of farm and non-farm people, Joint Economic Committee, Congress of the US, *New Dimensions in Rural Policy: Building Upon Our Heritage*, US Government Printing Office, Washington, DC, pp. 79–88.

Averyt, W. F. (1977) *Agropolitics in the European Community*, Praeger, New York.

Bonanno, A. (1987) *Small Farms: Persistence with Legitimation*, Westview Press, Boulder, Col.

Bonanno, A. (1988) The state and agricultural policies in advanced capitalist societies, paper to VII World Congress of Rural Sociology, Bologna, Italy.

Bowler, I. R. (1985) *Agriculture under the Common Agricultural Policy*, Manchester University Press.

Brown, C. (1989), *Distribution of CAP Price Support*, Jordbrugsokonomiske Institut, Kobenhaven.

Buttel, F. H. (1984) Socioeconomic equity and environmental quality in North American agriculture: alternative trajectories for future development. In Douglas, G. W. (ed.), *Agricultural Sustainability in a Changing World Order*, Westview Press, Boulder, Col. pp. 89–106.

CEC (Commission of the European Communities) (1985a) *The Agricultural Situation in the Community: 1984 Report*, CEC, Brussels.

CEC (Commission of the European Communities) (1985b) *Perspectives for the Common Agricultural Policy*, CEC, Brussels.

CEC (Commission of the European Communities) (1987a) *The Agricultural Situation in the Community: 1986 Report*, CEC, Brussels.

CEC (Commission of the European Communities) (1987b) *Farm Structure – 1985 Survey: Main Results*, Eurostat, CEC, Brussels.

CEC (Commission of the European Communities) (1987c) *The Common Agricultural Policy and Its Reforms*, CEC, Brussels.

CEC (Commission of the European Communities) (1989) *The Agricultural Situation in the Community: 1988 Report*, CEC, Brussels.

Commins, P. and Higgins, J. V. (eds) (1987) Towards the year 2000: longer-run trends in agriculture. In *The Re-structuring of the Agricultural and Rural Economy*, An Foras Taluntais, Dublin, pp. 1–38.

Cunningham, E. P. (1984) Agriculture, raw materials and the Irish context, paper to Royal Irish Academy, Dublin.

Dawson, J. A. *et al.* (1986) *Structural Change and Public Policy in the European Food Industry*. FAST occasional paper No. 115, EEC/DGXII, Brussels.

de Janvry, A. (1977) Inducement of technological and institutional innovations: an interpretative framework. In Arndt T. M (ed.) *Resource Allocation and Productivity in National and International Agricultural Research*, University of Minnesota Press, pp. 551–63.

de Janvry, A. and Dethier, J. J. (1985) *Technological Innovation in Agriculture*, The World Bank, Washington.

de Janvry, A. *et al.* (1989) Towards a rural development program for the United States: a proposal. In Sumers, G. F. (ed) *Agriculture and Beyond*, University of Wisconsin.

Fingleton, W. A. (1983) Dairying-changing structure and performance. In *Adjustment and Structural Problems in the Agricultural Sector*, An Foras Taluntais, Dublin.

Fingleton, W. A. (1989), *The Economics of Milk Production*, Teagasc, Dublin.

Frawley, J. (1985) Technological development and change on Irish farms. In *The Challenge Facing Agriculture in Difficult Times*, An Foras Taluntais, Dublin, pp. 31-60.

Goodman, D. *et al.* (1987) *From Farming to Biotechnology*, Basil Blackwell, Oxford.

Government of Ireland (1989) *National Development Plan 1989-1993: Summary*, Government Publications, Dublin.

Green, G. (1986) Credit and development, In Joint Economic Committee, Congress of the US, *New Dimensions in Rural Policy: Building Upon Our Heritage*, US Government Printing Office, Washington, pp. 415-21.

Hadwiger, D. F. (1982) *The Politics of Agricultural Research*, University of Nebraska Press.

Hathaway, D. E. (1963) *Government and Agriculture*, Macmillan, New York.

Havens, A. E. (1986) Capitalist development in the United States: state accumulation and agricultural production systems. In Havens S. A. E. *et al.* (eds), *Studies in the Transformation of U.S. Agriculture*, Westview Press, Boulder, Col. pp. 26-59.

Havens, A. E. and Newby, H. (1986) Agriculture and the state: an analytical approach. In Havens A. E. *et al.* (eds), *Studies in the Transformation of U.S. Agriculture*, Westview Press, Boulder, Col. pp. 287-303.

Hayami, Y. and Ruttan, V. W. (1971) *Agricultural Development: an International Perspective*, John Hopkins Press, Baltimore.

Henrichsmeyer, W. and Ostermeyer-Schloder, A. (1988), Production growth and factor adjustment in EC agriculture, *European Review of Agricultural Economics*, **15**, 137-54.

Higgins, J. (1988), Structural changes in the agri-industrial complex, paper to Agricultural Economics Society of Ireland.

Hueth, D. L. and Just R. (1987) Policy implications of biotechnology, *American Journal of Agricultural Economics*, **69**, 426-31.

Kloppenburg, J. (1984) The social impacts of biogenetic technology on agriculture: past and future. In Beradi, G. M. and Geisler, C. C. (eds), *The Social Consequences and Challenges of New Agricultural Technologies*, Westview Press, Boulder, Col.

Kloppenburg, J. and Kenney, M. (1983) Biotechnology, seeds and the restructuring of agriculture, *Insurgent Sociologist*, **12**, 3-17.

Knutson, R. D. *et al.* (1983), *Agriculture and Food Policy*, Prentice-Hall, New Jersey.

Koester, V. (1977) The redistributional effects of the common agricultural financial system, *European Review of Agricultural Economics*, **4**, 321–45.

Lewontin, R. C. and Berlan, Jean-Pierre (1986) Technology, research and the penetration of capital: the case of U.S. agriculture, *Monthly Review*, July–Aug., 21–34.

McInerney, J. (1987) Agricultural policy at the crossroads, *Agricultural Progress*, **62**, 11–25.

Marion, B. W. (1985) *The Organisation and Performance of the US Food System*, Lexington Books, Boston, Mass.

Mazur, A. (1983) Public protests against technological innovations. In Summers, G. F. (ed.), *Technology and Social Change in Rural Areas*, Westview Press, Boulder, Col., pp. 29–50.

Nature Conservancy Council (1982) *Conservation of Species of Wild Flora and Vertebrate Fauna Threatened in the Community*, Nature Conservancy Council, London.

Neville-Rolfe, E. (1984) *The Politics of Agriculture in the European Community*, European Centre for Political Studies, London.

Newby, H. (1989) Economic restructuring and rural labour markets in Europe: current policy options. In Summers, G. F. *et al.* (eds) *Agriculture and Beyond*, University of Wisconsin.

O'Connor, R. *et al.* (1983) *A Review of the Common Agricultural Policy and the Implications of the Modified Systems for Ireland*, Economic and Social Research Institute, Dublin.

OECD (1987) *Structural Adjustment and Economic Performance*, OECD, Paris.

OECD (1988) Agricultural reform: a long row to hoe, *OECD Observer*, June–July, 16–19.

O'Hara, P. (1986) CAP structural policy – a new approach to an old problem?. In *The Changing CAP and Its Implications*, An Foras Taluntais, Dublin, pp. 34–69.

OTA (Office of Technology Assessment) (1986) *Technology, Public Policy and the Changing Structure of American Agriculture*, US Government Printing Office, Washington.

Petit, M. (1985) *Determinants of Agricultural Policies in the Unted States and the European Community*, International Food Policy Research Institute, Washington.

Petit, M. *et al.* (1987) *Agricultural Policy Formation in the European Community: the Birth of Milk Quotas and CAP Reform*, Elsevier, Amsterdam.

Power, R. *et al.* (1989), *National Farm Survey 1987*, Teagasc, Dublin.

Rogers, E. M. (1983) *Diffusion of Innovations*, The Free Press, New York.

Roy, E. P. (1972) *Contract Farming and Economic Integration*, Interstate Printers and Publishers, Danville, Ill.

Runge, C. F. and Von Witzke, H. (1987) Institutional Change in the Common Agricultural Policy of the European Community, *American Journal of Agricultural Economics*, **69**, 213–22.

76

Senior-Nello, S. M. (1984) An application of public choice theory to the question of CAP reform, *European Review of Agricultural Economics*, **11**, 261–83.

Tracy, M. (1989) *Government and Agriculture in Western Europe, 1880–1988*, 3rd edn. Harvester Wheatsheaf, Hampstead.

USDA (United States Department of Agriculture) (1988) Public investment in agricultural research, *Agricultural Outlook*, **12**, 31–2.

von Meyer, H. (1988) Environment and rural development in Europe, *E.E.R.*, **2**, 15–20.

Weinschenck, G. and Kemper, J. (1981), Agricultural policies and their regional impact in Western Europe, *European Review of Agricultural Economics*, **8**, 251–81.

Wilkening, E. and Gilbert, J. (1987) Family farming in the United States. In Galeski, B. and Wilkening, E. (eds), *Family Farming in Europe and America*, Westview Press, Boulder, Col., pp. 271–301.

Wimberley, R. C. (1986) Agricultural and rural transition. In Joint Economics Committee, Congress of the US, *New Dimensions in Rural Policy: Building Upon Our Heritage*, US Government Printing Office, Washington, DC, 39–45.

Winters, L. A. (1987) The political economy of the agricultural policy of industrial countries, *Economics*, **14**, 285–304.

CHAPTER 3

Paradigmatic Shift in Agriculture: Global Effects and the Swedish Response

Martin Peterson

Introduction

Whenever specialized knowledge is required paradigmatic shifts will occur at regular intervals. This is valid for most productive sectors including agriculture. In agrarian shifts it is possible to distinguish reasonably sharp contours when most elements involved are changing character. This can take place since, in spite of being constituted by such varied components, the agrarian system presents a notable coherence. It contains an indivisible mix of rational/objective solutions and cultural/subjective considerations. Factors such as a stationary life and particularistic habits and values have not necessarily contradicted the introduction of technology and business thinking into agriculture. They have tended to adjust themselves to these universal logics.

How are agrarian shifts initiated and generated? In most cases exogenous factors have prevailed. The main instigators have been world trade, science push, market pull, social, institutional changes and political upsets. To this list two more general phenomena have recently become relevant: the physical limits with which the environment can cope, i.e. our scientific perceptions of those limits; and secondly, the values connected with a growing consciousness of the effects produced by mechanization (animal factories) and chemicalization of agriculture on choice of food.

Implicit in the treatment of agriculture is a recognition of special and separate interests inherent in the profession of farming. Whereas there is no technology that would entirely replace farming, it has turned out to be virtually impossible to rationalize agriculture along the lines of industry. This induced a special interest in the politics and sociology, even phenomenology of farming, from the 1960s. This had the effect of promoting a changed self-perception of the farmer and of the farming profession. It made farmers even more resistant to mass rationalization as they detected a faltering interest on the part of the State for the family farm during the course of the 1980s. In addition an entrepreneurial self-confidence emerged among farmers as it became increasingly accepted that operating a farm was tantamount to running a small enterprise. To run a farm enterprise implies the command of a number of components and unforeseen factors, which can only be gained by practice. In this position the farmer is unique among unique colleagues.

Out of this new entrepreneurial position two effects have arisen: a self-reinforcing realization with positive effects on professional autonomy and creativity, but also a disinclination to cooperate with others. However, new conditions are prodding farmers to reinterpret the individualism in their entrepreneurship. Whereas earlier the whims of the climate and other cyclical factors of a biological nature added to farmers' calls for an institutionalized safety-net, the post-war combination of science push and new market mechanisms has removed those institutions and cultural filters of protection, which farmers were previously taking for granted. Since the earlier half of the 1980s farmers, collectively, are faced with a new situation with respect to biotechnology and its potential. This implies both a threat and unforeseen opportunities. On the one hand industry, in particular the transnational companies, have reached a level where they will not only appropriate farm products but also be able to substitute new biotechnically derived products for agrarian ones. A greater awareness of nutritional criteria is not reducible to a return to natural wholefoods (Goodman *et al.* 1987). It can equally be met by a balanced diet of bioindustrial food or the products of organic agriculture suitably improved through genetic engineering. A growing volatile demand, which answers to the increasingly complex set of needs and consumption patterns in industrially advanced societies, will more appropriately be met by *flexible production systems*. In this context biotechnology offers advantages to smaller specialized farm units, which can either become subcontractors or try to stay on as independent suppliers. The impact of flexible production systems will, however, ultimately depend on the shape of social institutions and general cultural values. This chapter first considers the nature of paradigmatic shifts in agriculture from an historical perspective. It then, with reference to the Swedish experience, examines the nature of the State regulation during the post-war period. Swedish policy is placed in an international context. In the final sections, discussion focuses on the gradual breakdown of this system and its partial replacement by deregulatory processes and alternative production systems.

Paradigmatic shifts in agriculture

As an introduction to the modern project, in importance on par with the Enlightenment and the Industrial Revolution, agriculture experienced two paradigmatic shifts with somewhat irregular occurrence in time and space. One was of an organizational kind – enclosures and new elements in capital formation – and another was technical in terms of new methods in fertilizing and crop improvement. As technology enabled a regular flow of world trade in agrarian products feasible paradigmatic shifts have occurred with greater regularity. A notable shift took place in the 1870s with European agriculture for the first time exposed to overseas competition. National governments were forced to look for a strategy – a protectionist one or one of stepping up the competitive capacity for an open-market situation. Mechanized inputs and the farm-implements industry then entered the lives of farmers. Such links between agriculture and industry also encouraged a flow in the other direction, i.e. towards an appropriation of agrarian goods for an increasingly more sophisticated market. The basis of the rise of the food industry had its roots in production technology. However, the institutional factor of a smoothly running distribution system preventing bottlenecks in the supply of agrarian products constituted, at the time, an even more decisive factor.

The entry of industry into agriculture became irrevocable as elements of the rural production process appeared amenable to industrial reproduction. In contrast to the industrial transformation of craft products, which often enough took place in the countryside, the capitalist development of agriculture was marked by industrial appropriation such as the processing of agrarian raw materials that was preferrably located in urban areas (Goodman *et al.* 1987). Hence the signals between production units and the market were far more difficult to interpret. Consequently in the wake of one major market upset–such as World War I – disastrous levels of oversupply in agrarian products hit the world market.

The result was the Great Depression of the 1930s that threatened to eliminate the vast majority of small family farmers. During the preceding decades, however, in most of continental Europe both the countryside and the family farm as a social institution had proved their value to state governments as a politically neutralized zone and profession. The countryside represented neutral territory in the sense that it was an uncontested area with a low propensity for social conflict during periods of concentration and rapid industrialization. The family farm, in particular the smaller family farm, bridged in a Kautskian sense the gap and the emerging contradiction between the urban working class and the peasant class. During economic recessions the rural world, where family farm norms were increasingly prevailing, had been able to absorb redundant people thus defusing socially dangerous situations.

The countryside of the 1930s was no longer safe and nor was it neutral. The State had to intervene in order to regulate where there was an imbalance in the agrarian sector to redress. However, every imbalance was seen as temporary and isolated. There was little thought of any coordinated measures nor did there exist any long-term philosophy by the State on the future shape and role of agriculture. The irony of the situation, though, was that similar to the case of the US family farms in the 1880s. European family farms turned out to be relatively more resistant to an economic crisis of the 1930s dimension than the more cycle sensitive larger estates (cf. Friedmann, 1982; Koning, 1983; Peterson, 1987). Big capital had pulled out of farming in the crises of the 1880s and the 1930s when investment returns on land decreased below a minimum point. The possession of larger estates became more of a burden than an asset. Incomes within the farm sector evened out, hired labour became uneconomical, and family farmers stepped into the vacuum left by estate holders. The large farm entrepreneurs turned themselves often enough into family farmers and, not least, tenant farming tended to benefit during this transformation process. Significantly the market for development of large-scale technology was also reduced as the reduction in the number of large enterprises persisted up to World War II (Koning, 1983; Peterson, 1987).

Smaller farm enterprises tended to have a cost advantage by valuing independence relatively more than remuneration according to going market prices. This did not make the family farm more efficient than the larger estate but vastly more economical. Moreover, because family farmers were more self-supporting and without obligation to pay wages, they had more scope to accommodate to the diminished proceeds by even more thrift and parsimony. In addition, the family farm was favoured by the regionalization of economies during the 1930s. A revival of regional networks often based on the skilled crafts of redundant or would-be redundant workers provided a backbone for family farms, which were hard pressed to introduce cost-cutting and productivity-raising innovations.

The dilemma of family farms in this context was that the food industry had created sectors of accumulation by restructuring the inherited 'pre-industrial' agrarian production process. In the industrial sectors constituted by these appropriations, barriers to accumulation were removed as traditional agrarian production processes were subordinated to capital. This made it possible for the food industry to apply pressures on farmers to reduce costs by draining off a part of the potential demand for agrarian products. It is at this point that the process of driving up supply automatically set in. The farmers, who lack the market power to cover any resulting rise in costs, are trapped by a hastened rate of cost-price reducing innovations. Thus over-supply has mainly been generated due to the exclusion of farmer influence over price-setting. Spiralling over-supply conditions have since largely been caused by the lack of influence among agricultural producers over price-setting rather than by any inherently uncontrollable factor associated with a presumed surplus in the number of farmers.

From the outset State intervention was too uncoordinated ever to command the elements leading to this vicious spiral. However substantial this intervention was and however much it affected the foundation of the agrarian sector it tended to assist the food industry in the long run. The industry got a raw material supply at stable and comparatively low prices enabling it to expand its profit margins at the cost of the vast number of smaller farmers. As a result the food industry has had little incentive to reinvest in new buildings and machinery. State intervention provided a safe situation for those farmers associated with production in the short term. In the longer term their overall autonomy has been eroded. Intervention schemes have intermittently been renewed, creating a patchwork of regulations many of which seem contradictory in nature.

Quest for a global solution: the late 1940s

In the wake of World War II agriculture was, for a brief span of time, subject to innovative and exciting visions of a global scope. A new logic of a transnational order was about to take shape in the World Food Board (WFB) proposal initiated by John Boyd Orr, the first Director General of the FAO. The WFB proposal was greeted with enthusiasm by the FAO General Meeting in Copenhagen in September 1946. Only two governments showed doubts. The Americans voiced a certain ambiguity and the British feared that this global system would become more expensive than its own regulatory system, which had enhanced the purchasing power of the labouring classes. As Britain and the US at that time dictated most of the international rules the WFB proposal was doomed. Orr never recovered from this setback, neither did several national governments and a number of prominent scientists.

The WFB proposal embraced both a transnational structure able to handle the global concern of food supply and ample scope for the farmer to develop his capacity. In 1946 the severe food situation had been exacerbated in most of Europe due to a succession of severe winters and droughts. Stocks of agrarian products were depleted. In the US, on the other hand, war-time experiments had enabled an increase in agrarian productivity by 100 per cent, which created a surplus scare. The emerging figures on the food situation in the Third World were much worse than expected. A global regulatory body was indeed a timely proposal. The intention of the WFB was to stabilize prices of agrarian commodities on the world market; to establish an adequate world food reserve to meet emergencies; to provide funds for financing the disposal of surplus agrarian products on special terms to nations most in need; and to cooperate with organizations concerned with international credit for industrial and agricultural development, and with trade and commodity policy (Peterson, 1979; 178).

In stabilizing prices, the WFB would operate through its commodity committees, which would be given power to hold stocks of each of the most important commodities. The Board would decide which world prices would determine the quantities that could currently be marketed. Then it would announce a maximum and minimum price and undertake to buy into its stocks when the world price fell below the declared minimum and sell from its stock when the world price exceeded the maximum. Orr actually had these schemes prepared in the 1930s. Riding on the crest of interest in state interventionism in agriculture, Orr was then convinced that a functioning global food policy would have been operating as soon as the early 1940s. The war interrupted his plans. The Copenhagen meeting of the FAO appointed a Preparatory Committee to work out the detail of the WFB proposal. This Committee was at the time known as 'the world's most qualified seminar'. It did not help the WFB proposal, which was quenched by a thorough dilution process engineered by a then junior Minister of the British Labour government, Harold Wilson.

As a substitute the agrarian sector became subject to national solutions and was drawn into the combined orbits of welfare state politics and market liberalizations for growth. The growing strength of farmers' organizations helped to secure a firm position for the family farm in this process. A neo-corporatist context reinforced the political role of farming on a more centralized national arena. The regional networks of the 1930s, where farming and local industry functioned together on a level of parsimony for a spatially restricted market, were only to be found as residues in German Ackerbürgerstädte and in the revived Italian context of local, small enterprise cultures.

Quest for a global solution: the late 1980s

During the 1950s rationalizations and a heavy input of technology provided predictable structural development and standardized thinking in the agrarian sector. These standards became locked due to the corporatist agreement by organized agriculture and the State, which saw fit to combine such contradictory elements as productivity raising measures with a complex set of regulations. This standardized system was not broken up until the new logic of flexibility began to permeate the advanced economies during the 1980s. In this situation farming made itself accessible to unending knowledge of an unorthodox and alternative sort.

The paradigmatic shift taking place in the 1980s and 1990s has many causes. One is the impact of the global events on local policies and to some extent vice-versa. In fact the Swedish national strategy of agrarian regulation stood as a prototypical model for the CAP of the EC. Towards the end of the 1980s, as Sweden pursues an advanced stage of deregulation, it is once again an open question as to whether or to what extent the EC will follow suit.

Much of how events will unfold is dependent upon the treatment of the various proposals submitted by the Cairns group, the US government, the EC and Japan to GATT in Geneva and the mixed bag that will be the outcome of the tug-of-war between agricultural politics, agricultural ideology and science push. The Uruguay GATT Round in 1987 started a global war of hegemony over agrarian trade. The 1990s will, however, see a mutual adjustment manoeuvring between international institutions on one hand and the special interests of the EC and nation states be they the US, Japan or Sweden.

In the mid-1980s budget costs for agriculture rose dramatically in the US and Western Europe. Declining foreign demand cut farm income while price support systems continued unchanged. Costs to support agriculture soared at the same time as a record number of bankruptcies among farmers occurred. The idea grew that deficiencies in the global agrarian system could only be remedied with corresponding corrective measures on the global level. GATT was the obvious instrument to carry out this change.

In December 1988 trade ministers met in Montreal to follow up the Uruguay GATT round, where it had been established that deregulation and free trade in farm products would be central to world-trade liberalization. The meeting was preceded by the advocates of specific trade ideologies mobilizing their followers. The Cairns Group consisted of 14 nations, among them major exporters such as New Zealand, Australia, Canada, Argentina, Brazil and Hungary. This reflected a resolve to move radically toward greater market orientation in agriculture (cf. Runge, 1988; Lawrence, chapter 4 in this volume). Like the US government this group called for eventual elimination of all domestic subsidies and border protections with distorting effects on trade. Both called for a new liberal framework only allowing decoupled direct income support to farmers and consumers, measures for infrastructure improvement and disaster relief. The only differences lay in implementation schedules.

On the other side were the EC and Japan. In Montreal the EC only envisaged one-year emergency commitments to reduce cereals' prices and over-production in other branches, whereas protectionism for some products might be enhanced in the longer term. For the EC the decision taken in February 1988 on income insurance had created an exhaustion in political inventiveness. This decision implying a Green Book discussing four different models of support – early retirement, temporary subsidies, social income support and support to those who transfer land from farming to an alternative usage – only came about when the Council of Ministers considered the exorbitant costs of a non-decision. The relative absence of unity among member nations had usually meant an inclination to stick to the status quo on agriculture in the EC. It took until early 1989 before a decision was taken on direct income support. Important background material had been constituted by a Delfi-study of 1987. This concluded that the basic features of the CAP should be maintained although in a rationalized form, including a more restricted application of the intervention system, a reduction (10 per cent) of prices on agrarian products, and a payment of a co-responsibility fee by producers. The common guideline stipulates that the support shall be accorded farmers with incomes below 70 per cent of GNP per capita, financed by the EC up to 70 per cent in less-developed regions and up to 25 per cent in other regions. Such payments will, however, be limited to 5 years. Thus the CAP of the EC was to remain essentially intact. The Japanese approach on the other hand was to emphasize the non-economic objectives of farm policies, including rural employment, environmental quality and 'food security' (cf. Runge, 1988). Japan was prepared to fight for these principles in order to protect their rice farmers, from imports from the US. The need for this was demonstrated quite radically during a crisis in the autumn of 1988.

Judging from the firm stand of the opposed camps at Montreal the meeting was bound to yield little. In fact it produced nothing. So in April 1989 the negotiators of the GATT round met again this time in Geneva, well aware that another non-decision would mean disaster. A decision did come forth calling for a freeze of farm product prices as a first step while the more principled issues were still deferred. However, those implying that anything short of a clean sweep would lead to failure had reason to be surprised when the Council of Ministers on 21 April decided to follow suit and freeze prices on farm products. This measure rocked the foundations of the CAP. The symbolism of this act carried more weight than its practical consequences.

In July 1989 there emerged an increasingly clear consensus on the advantages of tariffication over non-tariff barriers. Tariffs are a more visible and measurable form of trade protection. Once tariffs are set GATT negotiations will progress more smoothly. The greatest obstacles will be the powerful domestic farm lobbies such as the US dairy farmers, the rice growers of Japan and the Western European cereal barons. Once export subsidies on farm products have been abolished a paradigmatic shift in agriculture will be further facilitated in terms of production methods and a closer contact between producer and consumer.

The regulation paradigm: the case of Swedish agriculture after World War II

The roots of the Swedish system are to be found in a contradictory political deal, which occurred during the 1930s between the Social Democratic Party and the Farmers' Party. These two parties made up a coalition, which in order to work had to contain certain awkward quid pro quos. The Swedish labour movement supported a liberalization of trade in food products with the working class being highly dependent on low food prices. The farmers, whose trade union organization had just been formed into a militant interest group, were on the other hand struggling to keep prices on agrarian products up. The famous 'red–green deal' implied farmer support to the Social Democrats for a new social policy at the same time as the farmers gained a first regulation of food prices. The shadow of this deal accompanied the ensuing agrarian acts of 1947, 1967, 1977 and the food policy Act of 1985. An enduring tension between goals of Labour Party and Farmers' Party was inherent in every Act.

The 1947 Act set the pattern and pace. The post-war Keynesian consensus strategy could not allow the farmers to lag behind in terms of income and productivity. The Act made explicit that state price support should guarantee farmers incomes equal to other social groups. The primary means should be through customs duties. The State should furthermore contribute to a comprehensive rationalization of the farm sector. The prime target should be to reduce production costs. Production was to be adjusted to domestic needs and the issues of over-supply and export subsidies would never arise.

However, instability in supply between 1945 and the end of the Korean War in 1945 caused rampant surplus production of several agrarian products. This put a downward pressure on world-market prices. Hence the authorities were forced to introduce a substantial export subsidy, which in most nations was financed through import duties and regulation fees. In Sweden the burden of financing export subsidies was eventually laid entirely on the producers themselves. Under such conditions surplus exerts a downward pressure on producer prices whereas consumer prices remain unaffected. By contrast, the CAP of the EC later came to guarantee a full price to the producer wherever the product was sold. Thus the endemic overproduction problem arose at an early stage as a very unintended consequence. Once the over-supply spiral was established whether due to price guarantees or quite simply due to a technology-and-productivity driver – which under any circumstances would generate over production – it appeared impossible to get rid of it under the prevailing regulation paradigm. It had been an illusion to believe that a policy that decided and regulated at the State level could maintain a balance between production and demand levels. It seems that this illusory State model was based on the assumption that change in agriculture was due to endogenous factors that could be regulated from outside. Certainly up to 1950 it had often appeared as if the logic of internal agrarian needs entirely dictated the implementation of technology and the ability of farmers to pick and choose among the results of science and technical progress.

In fact, exogenous factors such as capital and technology/science push have exerted much more influence on agriculture than either farmers or the State have been prepared to admit. After all, developments in genetics and chemistry as well as in mechanization and high energy use were imparted to agriculture. In a similar way the rise of factor prices in agricultural production could, in the main, only have been exogenously determined (cf. Peterson, 1987). In addition the regulation policies in agriculture have promoted quantity over quality, which has generated an unequal treatment of different categories of farmers by the market.

During the 1950s and 1960s the general view among farmers was that technology/science push occupied a more central role than economic factors. It was only through rising factor prices in the 1970s that enterprise economics gained in importance in relation to techniques of cultivation. Capital intensity and size economies then came to rival and sometimes outdistance technology as determining factors for agrarian development. In either case, and with capital and technology mutually reinforcing each other, State regulation was moving further away from being able to balance domestic production and demand.

The workings of the regulation system

The regulation system and the growth economy paved the way for neocorporatist relations between producers, consumers and the state. The producer interest was primarily represented by the national farmers' organizations. This was the case in Sweden to a large degree as well as in most Western European nations with similar conditions. The lack of any *direct* influence by farmers on price movements or price-setting was pervasive up to the 1980s. This circumstance contributed to the imbalance between production and demand. During the 1980s an increasing number of producers have strived to establish direct relations with their customers and thus redress direct farmer influence over prices. It is, however, not expected to have any significant effects within the frame of a new paradigm until well into the 1990s when coinciding with the new GATT rules.

During the 1980s the surplus production debate has had the effect within the EC of slowing down rises in the negotiated farm prices. Swedish farm prices have, on the other hand, continued to rise even faster than inflation. Taking into consideration the prototypical role played by the Swedish agrarian policy on CAP it is of relevance to explore the reasons for this difference. The goals of the CAP and Sweden in terms of productivity, income and stable markets, etc. have been identical. So have the more important policy means such as price policy and structural policy. In both cases price policy measures have been overwhelmingly dominant whereas structural policies have been integrated with other policy programmes such as regional and social funds. Prices have been determined by an administrative process rather than by market forces. Price decisions have been based on cost compensation and income parity motives with deduction for the appreciated productivity growth. At the same time the construction of price regulation varies from product to product and between product groups.

The Swedish regulatory system is based on a protection of the farmer in two ways. There are duties on all imports competing with Swedish production. The import duty is mobile and raises the price of imports from world market levels to ones suitable to the regulated Swedish market. This mobility separates the duty from ordinary customs fees, which, according to GATT rules, cannot be raised above the level it has been tied to. In this way the regulation can completely shut out movements on the world market, whether these have short- or long-term causes such as bad harvests or technological developments.

The guarantee to producers for their quantities of any product delivered to the producer cooperatives is of a similar level of importance in the regulatory system. Product regulations have differed. Sugar beet, oliferous plants and potatoes have been cultivated in contract form. Crops have been paid for at a certain price regardless of quantity and quality; and dairies have been obliged to receive milk at a unitary price followed in the 1980s by a two-price system.

Together the mobile import duties and the guaranteed sales at a safe price have made it possible for farmers to calculate their incomes quite accurately. Simultaneously, these incomes have for the same reason become totally insensitive to world-market prices. In addition farmers have had every encouragement from politicians and the overall economic system to advance technical development. Hence under the regulation paradigm there has existed a built in mechanism directed towards constant overproduction no matter what measures are taken by authorities to discourage surplus capacity. Compensation for rising production costs and a subsidy system directed to the end product of the food chain on the consumer market have driven costs in Sweden up and above those in the EC during the latter half of the 1980s. The Swedish farmer has seen little of these compensations and subsidies, which have mostly fallen on other sectors in the food production system. These favoured sectors have, on the other hand, also been controlled by organized agriculture through the industrial producer cooperatives constituting branches of the National Farmers' Union (LRF). The frustration of farmers and their own limited influence over their incomes and rising capital costs have provided the Swedish agrarian corporatist model with undue cost generating pressures in comparison with the CAP. Swedish farmers have felt themselves less favourably treated than their colleagues within the EC. Accordingly, they have seen themselves compelled to rationalize at a higher rate.

Negotiation proceedings in Sweden

Price negotiations are an annual affair. They take into account how farmer expenses and incomes compare with those of urban occupations. Negotiations have so far been carried out between a delegation from the LRF and a special delegation from a state agency with a mandate from the Ministry of agriculture. A final agreement is put to the government and to Parliament. These two bodies have rarely made any amendments. On the basis of the initial negotiations the State decides price levels twice a year – on 1 January and 1 July.

Cost compensations have generally been calculated before negotiations take place. Figures have been derived from a certain norm calculation, which has been based on the weighing of revenues and expenses of the entire agrarian sector. Included in this calculation have been items such as changed social security fees and the unintended effects of rationalization. Industrial food production has been eligible to similar reimbursement schemes.

As this description indicates the Swedish regulation system has implied a certain automatism. This has been unduly cost-generating and one that legislators tried unsuccessfully to break away from through an amendment presented to Parliament in 1984. At the time the force of the prevailing system seemed overwhelming. Change could obviously only come about through a shift of the entire system. From 1984 a number of coinciding factors initiated a process in this direction. A major factor was the torrent of critique of the regulation system that poured forth from a number of sources outside agriculture such as economists and technocrats, other interest organizations and politicians. This critique would, however, hardly have been possible if *deregulation* had not developed into a legitimate phenomenon more generally during the course of the 1980s. Without this, it would have been extremely difficult to modify the agrarian regulation system.

In Sweden the preconditions for deregulation were more favourable than in the EC where neither consumers nor farmers had been affected so badly by the effects of the regulation system during the 1980s. Swedish households spent almost $7 bn more on food than they would have had to do within the

EC price level. Of the several billion dollars extra paid by Swedish consumers only a very small share has reached the farmers. One reason has been that the consumers have shouldered the burden of covering the costs above the world market price. In some nations, notably the US and the UK before her entry into the EC in 1973, this burden was met by the taxpayer instead. In the EC the consumers have been charged but to a lesser degree than in Sweden. However, the explanation why the Swedish system has fared worse than the EC must be sought elsewhere.

Swedish food prices rose by 116 per cent during the 1980s as opposed to 81 per cent in Western Europe as a whole. On goods other than food the price rise was 5.5 per cent slower in Sweden than in Western Europe. Hence, general inflation could not have had any direct hand in the abnormal rise in Swedish food prices. Farmers receive only 5 per cent of the value of the entire food-consumption in Sweden when interest rates and capital expenditures have been accounted for. Land prices have declined somewhat during the 1980s so there have been no capital gains to drive prices up. However, food prices are high in relation to the standard of food. Consumers cannot spend their income on the same amount of quality food as in other comparable nations. The current drive to improve food quality, which is increasingly demanded by the consumers, is driving up both costs and prices. Flaws have existed concerning the indirect effects of the regulation system encouraging inefficiency in the food industry. These are the result of a number of factors such as slow productivity growth and ill-directed investments of both public and private capital. They have caused high production costs throughout the economy and lowered wage-earner incomes and buying power in relation to those in comparable nations. It has been comparably much easier to restrain labour costs in the industrial sector than in the agrarian one. This is one of the explanations for the disparity in price developments between food products and other consumer goods.

In 1989 the share of state support of the agrarian production value was 60 per cent in Sweden, 49 per cent in the EC and almost 70 per cent in Japan. Protectionist stands have been consistently much stronger in Japan than elsewhere in the advanced economies, constituting a persistent problem in the context of GATT. The only deregulated agriculture so far is that of New Zealand, the success of which is dependent upon other nations following suit. Sweden could clearly not deregulate her own food sector unless it was done in harmony with the EC.

Deregulation and new critical perspectives

Deregulation has often been associated with the extremes of the market economy and with threats to the welfare state. In the early 1980s it became elevated above suspicion even by defenders of the welfare state. For the first time since 1945 an all-encompassing shift away from Keynesianism occurred. Derived from the conditions of the troubled 1970s, deregulation played a major part in this process as a contribution to the solving of stagflation, which Keynesinism had proved incapable of handling.

Capital accumulation had peaked around 1970 in Western Europe and somewhat earlier in the US. As a result giant companies, in particular transnational ones, saw that their market shares were in danger at a global level. They had to restructure or deregulate a too rigid organization. The most spectacular example came with the dismantling of the ATT (American Telephone & Telegraph), which was reorganized into several units with greater strike capacity on the international market. As a rule both regulation and the later deregulation tended first to hit the communication sector, i.e. the means of public transport such as railway, air-traffic, bus-transport, etc. and other means of communication such as telephone, radio and banking. The most conspicuous deregulation drama took place in Britain with the advent of the Thatcher government even though the same process occurred in many nations.

The drive for deregulation coincided with a new direction in industry. This meant moving away from Keynesian standardized and mass-production models, associated with capital intensity, large collectives and the post-war welfare consensus that bore the imprint of social democracy. The new orientation in industry was more labour-and-knowledge intensive. It promoted the ties between production–technology–science, which earlier standardized production models had discouraged. The link between deregul-ation –knowledge/flexibility–science gave this transformation a special legitimacy. At the same time public bodies and collective structures lost their earlier authority and legitimacy (Eckstein, 1982; Lapalombara, 1987). Phenomena such as political overload – too many interests demanding too many favours from the State – and corporatism – an interest mediating form between interest organizations and the State – were increasingly blamed for economic stagnation.

One target for this critique was corporatist linkage that was described as 'iron triangles' by a committee of social scientists appointed by the Norwegian government in the early 1970s to investigate new power constellations in modern welfare society. Supporters of deregulation and the market economy now preferred to see the iron triangles as an effect of public choice theory, which was one way of throwing suspicion over the entire political system.

The agrarian sector became a special scapegoat. Little did it matter under these circumstances that the basis of public choice theory had been undercut by political scientists who maintained that economic concerns do not translate into voting behaviour. Voters do not simply vote for their own pockets. Rather, their preferences follow a more collective reckoning responding to changes in general economic conditions and general symbolic issues (Kinder and Kiewit, 1981).

Nevertheless, the detractors of agrarian regulation took the opportunity to exploit the concept 'iron triangle' to the full in order to attack state subsidy programmes in agriculture for being economically senseless. With the absence of any obvious public interest in these programmes and with optional programmes easily available and conceivably satisfying public goals, the subsidy policy has often appeared inexplicable. These critics have made a distinction between alleged and real motives and in this light they have used public choice theories to provide an understandable explanation to the subsidy programmes. In agriculture, the same critics maintained that the trick has been to concentrate the advantages on a small and well organized group with a substantial political influence and to spread the disadvantages among larger and less well organized groups such as taxpayers and consumers at large. In that way special interests have triumphed over public interests. It has been only too easy to convince urban–industrial groups about the outrageousness in agrarian 'iron triangles'.

By the mid-1980s both the LRF and the State took this critique seriously. This is signified by the faltering attempts both initiated by advocating radically new policies from 1985 onwards. Both have accepted deregulation as a necessary process for the 1990s. Symptomatically they have tried to keep all options open until they were encouraged by the GATT rule in April 1989. Both appear prepared to not only accept but to work for such a paradigmatic shift. Nevertheless, it has been more difficult than they anticipated to shake loose the strictures of the old paradigm.

One case in point concerns the agrarian policy mechanisms. These were more rigid than originally anticipated. For instance, at the time of the foundation of the CAP the EC was still a net importer of agrarian products. When import restrictions are applied by such a large trade block world market prices are inevitably exposed to a downward pressure. This 'terms-of-trade' effect was advantageous so long as the EC remained a net importer, but it was turned against the EC once it had changed position to net exporter. The use of import duties rather than custom duties within both the EC and Sweden reflects, under these circumstances, a will to let the use of resources be guided rather by cost relations within the sector than by national production potentials in relation to those of other nations.

Another matter complicating a transition for both the interest groups in agriculture and the State is the structural differences *between* nations. The price regulation system in Sweden has been much more uniform than the EC in both design and application. Variation of product goals have been more specified in the EC than in Sweden. The favoured treatment of dairy and grains is reflected in the surplus production of them. Grain producers constitute a powerful group in the farmer lobby. It has mainly been the large farms that have cultivated grains due to investment costs and profitability. This has turned meadows into fields for cultivation for the sake of quantitative expansion. The Commission has ostensibly favoured dairy production because of its traditional association with the small family farm.

Whereas Swedish grain production was earlier afflicted with a similar surplus generating problem due to the same price guarantees as in the EC, it has since become subject to a direct link between surplus and costs. The principle of the common financing in the EC has cut the connection between the utility and the costs of member nations for the CAP. In this way advantages could be concentrated and disadvantages spread. In this respect Swedish producers will be more favoured by deregulation than those in the EC.

As shown in Table 3.1 it is only in the UK that the combination of grain and dairy is dominant to the extent that the relative production value of both is above the EC average. The family farm (dairy) profile is abundantly evident in the cases of West Germany and Sweden. The power of their respective farmers' organizations has rested upon a strong alliance between organization leadership, producer cooperatives and the family farm norm as a uniting ideology. Among producer cooperatives (see Table 3.2), which constitute an economically decisive part of organized agriculture, the dairy branch is by far the largest in Sweden. The family farm norm and the relatively favoured position of dairy production gather the majority of persistent small-holders making up 60 per cent of the farmer population and defying the trends of recent decades. As a result of such circumstances this group has been a strong supporter of the LRF, in spite of the fact that the organization has done little to concretely promote their position. Being less than barely subsistent and hanging on to farming because of the life-style they are defensive enough to be grateful for being a fully recognized part of organized agriculture. Most of those who have family households to cater for have other sources of income besides farming. In all about three-quarters of farmer income in Sweden is derived from sources outside of agriculture. Only 30–40 per cent of farmers could realistically survive on farming alone. Many of these also have outside incomes as they belong to a new generation of business-oriented rural entrepreneurs.

Table 3.1 The importance of different agrarian branches in Sweden and the EC in 1986 (share in % of total production value in agriculture)

	Grain	Dairy	Beef	Pork	Fruit/Vegetables
Belgium	6.2	17.2	20.2	20.5	13.6
Denmark	11.7	24.1	9.2	28.0	4.2
West Germany	9.5	27.1	16.6	17.4	6.4
Greece	10.5	9.3	3.6	4.4	22.4
Spain	13.4	9.5	6.7	9.1	22.9
France	17.0	17.6	15.2	5.9	10.6
Ireland	4.6	35.4	38.1	5.3	2.4
Italy	10.4	11.6	10.0	6.3	24.8
Luxembourg	4.9	46.5	26.0	8.1	3.0
Netherlands	1.4	26.7	10.4	18.1	10.8
UK	19.4	22.0	12.5	8.2	9.9
EC	12.0	19.5	13.6	10.6	13.1
Sweden	12.1	40.9	12.5	15.9	–

Source: OECD Statistics 1987, Affärsvärlden, Mar. 1989.

As is evident in Table 3.2 the dairy producers dominate the cooperatives. Symptomatic for the present Swedish context is the fact that producer cooperatives are about to be changed into stock companies in order to be able to cope with deregulation and increased market orientation. This will go hand in hand with an intensified process of internationalization. Under such circumstances decision-making will have to become much faster and there will be an increased demand for capital and multivariate forms of cooperation. This seems to provide new opportunities for external capital to enter farm industrial enterprises. In 1988, for instance, a Swedish law preventing non-farming interests from acquiring farm land was abolished. This has opened up interests outside agriculture to buy up land for other business purposes such as golf courses, deer hunting enclosures and other leisure activities.

Table 3.2 Swedish agrarian producer cooperatives and their recent relative growth in relation to turnover and number of employees in 1987

Ten largest cooperatives	Branch	Turnover 1987 in Skr. (bn)	Change % 1987	Number of employees
Arla	Dairy	9.7	+ 0.9	6,100
S: a Skogsägarna	Forestry	5.4	+ 20.0	4,600
Farmek	Slaughter	2.9	+ 1.0	1,900
Skånska Lantmän	Grain	2.9	− 5.0	1,300
Scan Väst	Slaughter	2.8	− 0.0	1,800
Skanek	Slaughter	2.6	− 14.0	800
Odal	Grain	2.2	+ 4.0	900
Västsv. Lantmän	Grain	1.9	− 4.0	900
NNP	Dairy, etc.	1.8	+ 7.0	1,000
Skanemejerier	Dairy	1.3	+ 1.5	500

The other face of a paradigmatic shift: alternative strategies

When agrarian regulation policies were originally formulated for the new economic–political conditions of the 1950s, they were mainly intended for the benefit of those 25 per cent of the working population who were 'rural' in Western Europe. In 1989 it was less than 8 per cent. If the impact of international market conditions increases and the present tendency of global convergence prevails in agriculture, the farming population of Western Europe will be reduced by another 50 per cent or to a share of less than 4 per cent. Any revival of protectionist measures to expand the inner European market is out of the question since the GATT rule of April 1989. Strategies will need to concentrate on those commodities for which there exists a special aptitude in the respective nations. This could be furthered through the judicious use of price-support policy as a preparation for a deregulated market (Fennel, 1985). The promotion of productivity without additional capital investments would be a possible part of such a strategy. One of the unintended effects of the regulation paradigm was the technology-for-higher-quantity approach induced by an agrarian market that was increasingly managed by corporatist structures. As a result there arose a mistaken belief in an automatic link between new capital investment – new machinery, buildings and equipment – and the achievement of greater productivity (Fennel, 1985). Structural policies have been largely absent in the process. New and imaginative structural measures could substantially improve preconditions for raised productivity. In Sweden a higher productivity level has been gained through unduly costly inputs. Hence neither profitability nor efficiency have been impressive on Swedish farming. The level of production costs would not be automatically reduced by deregulation. Therefore, there is every reason to agree with the LRF and the State that the adjustment of Swedish agriculture to world-market conditions will be a protracted and demanding process. During this process protectionist schemes will have to facilitate the transition. The same is true of the EC where the price guarantee system has helped to raise the value of farm land making alternative rural uses less attractive. Nevertheless, the race to find new alternative products in agriculture with market viability and a capacity for offsetting surplus production has only just begun.

Alternative projects such as farm tourism and the breeding of unconventional animals have gained prominence in most of Western Europe. In Sweden the LRF only started actively to promote farm tourism in conjunction with a new policy line agreed upon at their congress in June 1989. The central issues for a future strategy were announced to be: (i) the environment, alternative products and ecological farming; (ii) a substantially increased role for women in farming and in the farmers' organization; and (iii) gradual deregulation, acceptance of the new GATT rules and membership in the EC (significantly in stark contrast to the anti-EC stand of the Farmers' Party and the Greens in parliament).

The energy and environmental crisis have compelled Swedish farmers to develop new methods and rid themselves of their dependence on oil and its derivatives as base products for their activities. Since the mid-1970s farmers have reduced their use of oil to one-fifth. The use of pesticides and chemical fertilizers has dropped markedly during the latter half of the 1980s. Not only do they want to avoid being a target in the environmental debate, but they also realise that these crises have in fact provided them with arguments for asserting themselves and seeking ways out of their earlier passive dependence on the corporatist-cum-regulation paradigm. This has become manifest in three ways: through the development of alternative products and the move towards integrating ecological methods with 'conventional' ones; attempts at approaching consumers more directly; and thirdly a new collaboration with local industry where farmers will provide raw materials for the development of new products, thus strengthening regional economies.

The drive towards ecological cultivation is attracting new attention and new recruits. The particular challenge is not only one of quality but also one of reviving the accumulated knowledge in farming of one or two generations ago. At the same time it is not certain that retrieved knowledge or even new biological techniques could be automatically applied on a soil that has got so used to chemicals. However intense the exploration of ecological farming – which is really orthodox farming – the process of 'reconquest' may take longer than ecologists envisage. Like the old saying 'while the grass is growing the cow is dying', the biotechnical industry may well encroach upon the entire food-processing industry during the interval. Already the food industry is applying biotechnical processes to 'improve' the standard of mass produced food through additives with 'natural flavours'. This actually means using cheap refuse from sugar refineries, canneries, slaughteries and bakeries. According to this increasingly powerful multibillion and transnational industry, the food of tomorrow is based on cheap raw materials biotechnically processed into 'valuable food' for overpopulated mass markets. According to the same source the quality food of yesterday was only conceivable for a limited market.

However, in Sweden, the new 'professionalism' among farmers seems intent on challenging the effects of biotechnology in this respect. They have received an unexpectedly strong support from the University of Agriculture. This is an institution financed directly by the Ministry of Agriculture but attempts to preserve an academic independence. The positivist spirit that has so far been dominant has been modified moving towards something much more ready to adopt alternative social and cultural factors into consideration. Prominent faculty members now are advocating the support of traditional Swedish institutions (such as cooperatives of the popular movements) as protection and counterforce to an anticipated onslaught by the transnational biotechnical industry. At the same time the research institute of the LRF has contracted high ranking Swedish biochemists to work out harmless substitutes to antibiotics for pigs. The result, which will have positive consequences on an international scale, is encouraging further research concerning poultry and livestock.

In terms of alternative production, two products are particularly in focus. One is *flax seed*, the production of which ceased in the early 1960s because of its lack of competitiveness. Linseed oil was considered superfluous in a world dominated by oil derivatives. Since the mid-1980s production has been resumed in south-western and south-central Sweden on the initiative of private farmers. These have discovered that there is a much wider domain of application than earlier believed. Not only does linseed oil constitute an outstanding, non-toxic element in painting but it is also superior to other animal and vegetable fats in livestock feeding for preventing defects or curing deficiencies. The same cure has been successfully applied to mal-nourished people in the Third World.

A further usage, which has recently been tested with success, is the rubbing of linseed oil on the backs of pigs in order to reduce the presence of malignant elements in the air, which normally promote ill-health in both pig-farmers and the pigs themselves. The linseed oil binds toxic germs and reduces their effectiveness by 80 per cent. Similarly linseed oil could be applied to prevent the circulation of toxic germs in modern houses with air-recycling systems. Moreover a new implement applied to a harvester can reap off the oil kernels leaving the straw intact. This flax-seed straw has found use in the manufacturing industry. This example demonstrates the potential for versatility in many traditional crops, which obviously could be strongly competitive.

The second alternative crop is *salix* or *willow* for energy forest cultivation. The initial energy forest project on a large scale started in 1986 at the instigation of one state agency and a semi-private consultancy agency. The ultimate goal mentioned was 200,000 ha of energy forest. The LRF was initially ambivalent but came out more and more strongly for this project after some years. Strong forest industry interests and several rural economists acted openly against it. The latter advocated that grains for biomass would be commercially more viable as a source of energy. Calculations showed that energy forest would find it hard to break even, whereas grains for biomass demanded little investment and production costs and could show a profit much earlier.

Such calculations however, did, not take into account the much wider use of Salix. Salix works like a vacuum cleaner of polluted air, especially metals. Moreover, certain substances could be derived for the pharmaceutical industry. In all likelihood this is not the end to the applications of Salix.

Salix production is still at an experimental stage, where a number of processes at various stages such as both planting and weeding could be rationalized much further. The ultimate planting machine has not yet been placed on the market although the provisional ones built by farmers have shown much better results than the more expensive models constructed and developed by the State. However, there is little definitive knowledge as to which soil is most suitable and what weeding methods should be preferred.

Both of these alternative crop productions have avidly demonstrated what local initiatives by farmers can achieve, when they are assisted by adequate expertise (as in the case of energy forest). In the case of linseed oil, experts and politicians such as the local governor in a south-central province have come rallying to the farmers. Most interesting of all is the collaboration established with local industry, which has created a re-emergence of regional economic approaches without the aid of allocated State money. In the case of energy forest its economy during the initial stages is to a large extent dependent on subsidies from the State and negotiated deals with the local energy producing industry. Energy forest will be located to the more suitable regions with respect to soil and climate. Grains for biomass are produced in southern and the vast northern regions. Japanese elephant grass is projected for biomass production. It is thought that if fully applied, these programmes for alternative energy production could go a significant way to not only eliminating grain surpluses – which are bound to be growing with new productivity raising methods – but also to preserve farming populations. With a pending abolition of nuclear power production the Social Democratic government is allowing natural gas to take much of the market for biomass fuels. The LRF has, however, mounted a vigorous campaign to make the government switch from its present line in favour of biomass fuels, and in particular, energy forest.

The government has not yet made up its mind conclusively on alternative energy production. A seemingly promising start for ethanol production derived from grains was suddenly given negative signals from the government because it was not considered competitive on the fuel market as long as the price of gasoline kept comparatively low. This policy has not surprisingly met with harsh criticism from farmers and green opinion, which comprises much more than the green parties proper. It is, however, also an indication of the government's intention to give priority to market economy signals on energy matters when a deregulation of farming is about to be introduced.

Transitional policies

The quest for control of alternative energy sources such as energy forest cultivation is an expression of a two-edged farmer approach. This involves preservation of farmer control over rural economies and a safeguard against the prospect of environmental catastrophes or protectionist developments in world trade. It is essential not to become the victims of such distortions but to have access to indigenous resource capacities it is argued.

The concrete task for the government will be, on one hand, to find a modified protective system for the transition from regulation to deregulation, and on the other, to formulate a new agrarian long-term policy. The latter would involve questions of the shape of agriculture in terms of products, methods and farming population.

A transitional protective system could not imply a modified version of the elements in the regulation system including mobile import duties. This would only give farmers the continued illusion of being immune to changes around the world. Two other methods have been proposed. One is quantitative restrictions, which is a fairly recent topic. Such measures would expose at least parts of the Swedish market and yet guarantee the sale of the Swedish farm products. However, the protectionist element involved would be obstructive to the free trade endeavours of the GATT and the OECD.

The other is customs duties, which GATT would favour. When customs levels have been settled in accordance with GATT rules they can in principle only be lowered. In this perspective the movements of world market prices are transmitted into the national economies giving producers a clear signal of what products would be more profitable to concentrate on. It would also be easier to handle administratively. The disadvantages, however, would be that nation-states would lose control over price levels, the relative profitability of certain products, and locally generated agrarian strategies would be secondary to overall provision capacities. National health and the environment may also be adversely affected, which could only be remedied at the cost of legislation and a new regulatory maze.

The problem of income support during the transition to complete deregulation is considered to be difficult enough if the relative profitability of branches is to remain in tact. In the Swedish context, closely followed by the EC, four methods of income support have been considered: a one-time inclusive restitution, acreage related support, income insurance and cultivation support.

The inclusive restitution would be a one time lump sum payment, which could conceivably be issued in the form of state bonds securing the owner an annual allowance. The lump sum would compensate farmers for their losses during the transition from one system to another. The advantage would be that the future orientation of farming would not be distorted. One risk would be the calling for complementary support measures by more exposed groups, which if complied with would encourage further similar demands and undercut the entire idea of lump-sum restitution. A successful application on the other hand would be rewarding in the neoliberal sense in that the constant pressure for political and administrative intervention in agriculture would cease. It has also been advocated by liberal economists.

The most common alternative presented concerns acreage related support, which is in line with a social–liberal mode of thought. It implies an annual flat rate remuneration of say Skr.1000 per hectare for cultivable farm land and a corresponding sum per cow for dairy farmers. In order to encourage the cultivation of certain land there could be differentials in support. This might favour backward regions and farmer groups. One problem arises when the tiller is a tenant and the owner, who gets the support, lives elsewhere. On the other hand the price of land between affluent and depressed could become more equalized. As prices on farm products are exposed to a downward pressure the price of land in affluent areas will follow suit.

The income insurance scheme enacted by the EC in February 1988 has also been considered in the Swedish debate. The individual farmer would get a safe income even though the norm income, on which the support would be based, would be sliding downwards since the historical average of that income would sink step by step as farmers adjusted themselves to this form of support. It would lead to a reduced intensity in production, which, as a result, would eliminate surpluses. The difficulties concern technical applications such as determination of norm income, the income of the individual farmer, the treatment of income from outside sources and the prevention of farms being divided up into several farm enterprises for a widening of the circle of insurance receivers. These aspects have not been dealt with sufficiently on the EC level. New models can be expected to be tested in both the EC and Sweden during the transition towards deregulation.

Finally there is a proposal for a direct farmer support. This model is the one most closely identified with a socialist approach to agriculture. In Sweden it is advocated by one wing of the Social Democratic Party and has support among government experts. It is however rejected by the LRF and its counterparts in the EC (members of COPA) as too blatant a case of social welfare politics. This form of support would be accessible to every kind of farm enterprise irrespective of acreage, yields or orientation of production. This makes it neutral. It could, however, also be differentiated. It would be higher where most needed and concentrated on those farmers who devote most of their time to farming. Being a percentage addition on the net income of the enterprise it would be a stimulant to secure as favourable a net income as possible. Further it would be linked to the farmer's own activities, which would mean an encouragement to a more effective use of resources and a lower intensity. This would in turn result in a possibility to reduce product prices, which would favour the consumers. As prices are lowered chemical fertilizers and pesticides will become relatively more expensive for the benefit of incentives to more new thinking and entrepreneurship not only in relation to ecological methods but with regard to how the farmer would produce his net income. Evidently this form of farmer support would actually be a far cry from social welfare policies. The resistance from the farming community, including rural economists, to this form of support appears to have its origin in culturally determined interpretations of what any dependency on the State will entail. Rural socialism would rather express itself in the transcending of the individual private enterprise form. This would then imply genuine collaboration in production methods around common projects. In fact such tendencies are now visible in local initiatives although conventional divisions into capitalist or socialist agriculture are no longer meaningful nor applicable.

The first transitional policy line was a compromise. The Swedish government opted for acreage (and cow) related support. At the same time the gradual removal of protectionist barriers will proceed. On 1 July 1990 the Swedish government is expected to introduce yet another new agricultural policy on the road towards deregulation. This will be influenced on the one hand by the growing control of the market wielded by transnational bio-technical corporations against which national farmer interests have little to counter but for attempts at mobilizing national counter strategies. At the same time, however, there will be an encouragement to revive regional and local cooperatives far removed from the LRF controlled cooperatives combining the interests of farm inputs – chemical fertilizers, pesticides – agricultural producers and the food industry.

Conclusion

The paradigmatic shift of the 1990s will be marked by the effects of deregulation. This will involve a spread of alternative and ecological production making steady inroads as a growing potential counter strategy to mass redundancies among farmers. Secondly, the calling by the authorities for a scientific combination of biological and chemical methods in order to arrive at a synthesis providing both the highest quality and the environmentally safest method. This will downgrade priorities surrounding productivity rates. Non-farming interests will be investing in farm land for speculative purposes at an increasing rate, which may again raise land prices for the benefit of those farmers surviving the transition to deregulation. Thirdly, there will be a movement away from dependencies on large collective organizations, state protection, national hot-house conditions and large-scale units in general. In that context biotechnology may offer a constructive contribution in the favourable options it provides for small-scale farm enterprises. Fourthly, lessons from neighbouring Finland where the distribution of family farms of modest size is much larger and farming in due course is highly valued both as a profession and as a supplier of quality products, have influenced Swedish politicians attitudes about the closing down of agriculture. Oddly coinciding with deregulation, public interest in farming is also on the rise because of a deep concern with the quality of food and the environment. The negative aspects of farming such as the strains of isolation, absurdly long working hours and the high capital costs involved in individualized private enterprise farming have become strongly associated with the regulation and quantitative growth paradigm. This alienated farmers from the rest of society. To overcome this, new collaborative arrangements have now been initiated firstly in exposed regions involving ownership and use of barns and other diversified means of production. In the 1990s we may very well witness a shift from a paradigm of regulation-cum-capitalism to a deregulation with advanced elements of genuine socialism, even if this word does remain taboo.

Bibliography

Bjärsdal, IJ. (1986) *Lantbrukskooperation och bondefack. Ett unikt samgående: förutsättningar, resultat och möjligheter,* Förlag, Stockholm LTs.

Bolin, O. *et al.* (1984) *Makten över maten,* Stockholm SNS.

Bolin, O. *et al.* (1988) *Åkerfällan,* Stockholm SNS.

Eckstein, H. (1982) The idea of political development: from dignity to efficiency, *World Politics,* **34,** No. 4, 451–86.

Ekman, L. & Nitsch, U. (1988) Datorkraft och bondeförnuft, Swedish University of Agricultural Sciences, Uppsala.

Fennel, R. (1985) A reconsideration of the objectives of the CAP, *Journal of Common Market Studies,* **23,** No. 3.

Finansdepartementet (1987) *Vägar ut ur jordbruksregleringen* Ds Fi 1987: 4, Stockholm Ministry of Finance.

Finansdepartementet (1988) *Alternativ i jordbrukspolitiken, av Wetterberg,* G. Ds 1988: 54, Stockholm Ministry of Finance.

Friedmann, H. (1982) *The Family Farm in Advanced Capitalism: Outline of a Theory of Simple Commodity Production,* Working Paper series No. 33, University of Toronto.

Goodman, D. *et al.* (1987) *From Farming to Biotechnology,* Basil Blackwell, Oxford.

Hayami, Y. and Ruttan V. (1985) *Agricultural Development,* Johns Hopkins University Press, Baltimore.

Kinder, D. and Kiewit, R. (1981) Sociotropic politics, *British Journal of Political Science,* No. 2.

Koning, N. (1983) Family farms and industrial capitalism, *The Netherlands Journal of Sociology,* **19,** No. 1, 29–46.

Johnson, G. (1988) Crisis in international agricultural trade: How it arises and what if nothing is done. Unpublished paper, Conference on world agriculture: Prospects for the reform of farm support policies.

Lapalombara, J. (1987) *Democracy Italian Style,* Yale University Press, New Haven, Conn.

Micheletti, M. (1987) Organization and representation of farmers interests in Sweden, *Sociologia Ruralis,* **XXVII,** No. 2/3, 166–80.

Munk Jensen, A. and Strandskov, J. (1986) *EF's landbrugspolitik*, Kobenhavn.

Nitsch, U. (1988) *Bönderna och deras uppgifter i framtiden*, Swedish University of Agricultural Sciences, Uppsala.

Peterson, M. (1979) *International Interest Organizations and the Transmutation of Postwar Society*, Almquist & Wicksell International, Stockholm.

Peterson, M. (1987) What kind of agriculture? Sources of imbalances in West European agrarian structures. In Thorniley, D. (ed.) *The Economics and Sociology of Rural Communities; East-West Perspectives*, Avebury, London.

Rabinowicz, E. (1989) Jordbrukspolitik i EG och Sverige. In Hamilton, C. B. (ed.) *Europa och Sverige*, UI och SNSs förlag, Stockholm.

Rabinowicz, E. *et al.* (1986) The evolution of a regulation system in agriculture: the swedish case, *Food Policy*, Nov. pp. 323–33.

Runge, C. F. (1988) Agricultural protectionism, *Foreign Affairs*, No. 3, pp. 471–93.

SOU 1984: 86 (1984) *Jordbruks – och livsmedelspolitik*, Stockholm.

Sylwan, P. and Petersson, O. (1985) *Livskraftigt*, LO-Tiden, Stockholm.

Söderström H. T. (1989) *Konjunkturrådets rapport 1989*, Den svenska modellen inför 90-talet, SNS Förlag, Stockholm.

CHAPTER 4

Agricultural Restructuring and Rural Social Change in Australia

Geoffrey Lawrence

Deregulation and rural restructuring

Rural social change in Australia has not been considered a priority area for investigation by researchers or policy analysts. Unlike the US with its tradition of rural sociology or Great Britain with its history of community studies, Australia has tended to rely upon its agricultural economists to provide insights about structural change. The result has been a focus upon the more obvious and readily quantifiable features of rural production. Consequently, research and analysis of the structural forces leading to the growth and decline of farming enterprises, the relationship between agriculture and rural town development, the role of the state in agriculture and social differences between regions has been scanty and theoretically arid.

As a result of the paucity of sociological material on earlier periods of development in Australian agriculture, it is difficult to identify the features that may be specific to the present period of restructuring. What can be asserted with reasonable accuracy, however, is that Australian agriculture and the rural society it supports are undergoing quite rapid change associated with the deregulation of agriculture, the application of new technologies and the integration of the Australian economy into the Pacific Basin region.

Deregulation – the progressive removal by the state of the protective mantle under which much of Australia's private enterprises have operated – began in the mid-1980s and has been pursued with vigour.

All Australia's major political parties (Labour, currently in government and a coalition Liberal and rural-based National Party, in opposition) appear convinced deregulation is necessary for national economic development. The dismantling of tariffs and other import restrictions together with the removal of legislation, which has bound family-farm agriculture to State marketing monopolies, is viewed as a catalyst that will boost production and enhance overseas market penetration. Tariff removal is supported by the farmers because of its cost-reducing effects. It has been estimated that tariffs (originally established to assist local industry compete with overseas manufacturers) have been costing the farm sector up to A$1.5 bn per year – at a time gross value of rural production has been at a level of around A$15 bn (National Farmer, 2–22 January 1986; ABARE, December 1988). The National Farmers' Federation (NFF), the main organization of Australian commodity councils, has argued not only for the total removal of tariffs but also for the deregulation of the labour market. It has argued that if the wages' share of Gross Domestic Product (GDP) were to fall, so farm costs would be lowered via a direct reduction in the farm wage bill and an indirect reduction in the cost of farm inputs (NFF, 1981).

A major initiative of the Federal Labour Government after its election in 1983 was the deregulation of the banking sector, a move that farmers supported because of its supposed benefits by way of enhanced competition and cheaper credit. The dollar was floated as a further possible boost to rural producers and there was a questioning of the role of State-formed statutory marketing authorities in an era of 'free' market agriculture. In 1989 the Wheat Board, which was established at the request of growers who wanted to reduce price fluctuations, was partially deregulated by Labour. Various State governments have followed suit by removing local barriers to free trade in agricultural commodities. The rationale is that not only will the public save money in terms of reduced government expenditure but also consumers will gain through lower prices. Competition will force from agriculture the least efficient producers, and agribusiness will begin to coordinate in a more enterprising manner than has previously been the province of the State (see Department of Trade, 1987).

There is evidence that agribusiness has begun to strengthen its position in Australian agriculture in line with the reduction of state support for farmers (Lawrence, 1989a). With guidelines of the Foreign Investment Review Board having been relaxed, Japanese capital has begun to penetrate agriculture, specifically for the purchase of beef properties and for the construction of beef feedlots and abattoirs. And in the Murrumbidgee Irrigation Area (MIA) – Australia's most important region for the production of irrigated horticulture and rice – the State government has decided to abolish land tenure and water entitlement rights (a system that has favoured the perpetuation of family-farm agriculture) (NSW Department of Agriculture and Fisheries, 1988). MIA farmers remain divided over the possible effects but there is a general belief that deregulation will herald the full-scale corporatization of the region and result in a significant contraction of the rural population (Horticultural Industry and Government Committee, 1987).

Australia is not the only former British antipodean colony undergoing such economic restructuring. Across the Tasman Sea, in New Zealand, more thorough-going deregulation initiatives than those that have been adopted in Australia are considered to have resulted in declining income, increased interest payments and greater debt by farmers as well as on-farm adjustments such as the reduction in employed labour and greater levels of off-farm employment by family-farm members (Cloke, 1989). Similar changes were reported in a major study of rural social relations on Australian farms and in rural towns in the 1980s (see Lawrence, 1987).

What appears to be happening in rural Australia (and New Zealand) is that the progressive development of capitalist agriculture is leading to the removal of farmers. Without any mechanisms in place to create alternative economic opportunities in rural areas, the removal of the farm population is creating a weakening of rural community structures thereby undermining the basis of many country towns. Known in the US as the 'Goldschmidt thesis' (Buttel, 1981) the tendency for the economic development of agriculture to be associated with the economic and social underdevelopment of rural communities has become a feature of inland Australia. Fuelled by government policies of deregulation, industry trends towards rationalization, and with the continued reliance of agriculture upon new and more productive (labour-saving) technologies, the underdevelopment of rural Australia is one of the most obvious outcomes of economic restructuring. This chapter seeks to identify the structural changes occurring in Australia, including the ways technological change and deregulation have combined to force a reduction in the number of rural producers, and more indirectly, to cause the erosion of the economies of many smaller country towns. It attempts to link theoretically the technological dynamic of Australian agriculture, the activities of international corporate capital, the changing role of the state, and the social impact of economic changes occurring in rural Australia.

Australia in the global economy

In the two centuries of European occupation of the continent, the Australian economy has been highly reliant upon the income generated from export agriculture. McMichael (1981) has advanced the argument that up until the 1980s Australia's economic development may be best understood with reference to two major patterns of global capital accumulation; the first corresponding to Britain's pre-eminence in the nineteenth century; the second to a period of US hegemony since the end of World War II. According to McMichael the former period was characterized by capital accumulation within the boundaries of national states, the mediation of international exchange according to interstate demands and by the centralization of finance capital in London. In contrast, the second period has been one of capital accumulation on a global scale organized by transnational corporations, the division of the world system by those corporations, and the internationalization of finance capital.

Whereas in the earlier period of British influence the combined demands of capital and labour led to the growth of a social-democratic state in

Australia (albeit one regulated in a manner that served Britain's interests), in the latter period the redivision of global labour and markets has occurred according to the dictates of corporations that fail to respect any desire for 'relative autonomy' on the part of a small nation-state like Australia (McMichael, 1981). The message from the transnationals has been: restructure or reap the consequences of capital withdrawal.

With hindsight the period immediately after World War II – associated with the imposition of tariff barriers and the use of migrant labour to create an environment for the expansion of domestic manufacturing industry – can now be seen as something of an interlude during which domestic industry could grow. Subsequent growth, however, has been linked intimately to that of transnational firms. In the short period from 1945 to the mid-1960s Australia was decolonized by Britain, only to be recolonized by the US (Crough and Wheelwright, 1982). Australian capitalists, it seems, were quite prepared to adopt compradore status if it meant foreign capital could be harnessed for domestic profit-making. In the 30-year period to the beginning of the 1990s first American, then Japanese (and other South-East Asian countries) capital has entered Australia to take advantage of commercial opportunities in mineral extraction, agriculture and, more recently, tourism. By 1980 Australia was exhibiting one of the highest levels of foreign penetration of any developed nation (Kemeny, 1980). Encouragement for capital inflow has continued such that major control in the oil, pharmaceutical, car, banking, computing, advertising, electrical goods and tobacco industries resides with transnationals (Crough and Wheelwright, 1982). Although, in agriculture, a family-farm (owner–operator) structure prevails in the area of on-farm production, transnationals supply most of the farm inputs and process a small but growing proportion of farm output (Sargent, 1985).

Australia is being progressively marginalized and de-industrialized as it is incorporated into the Pacific Basin as a supplier of raw materials (Crough, Wheelwright and Wilshire, 1980). This has placed the Australian economy in a vulnerable position. Since the 1970s around 80 per cent of Australia's exports have been primary products or minerals (Higgott, 1987). As a consequence the Australian economy has been particularly susceptible to world price fluctuations in traded commodities. With some 70 per cent of the output of Australian farms entering the world market (Longworth, 1988) the impact of severe commodity price falls – as occurred in the mid-1980s – can quickly result in widespread recession. The Australian Bureau of Agricultural and Resource Economics (ABARE) – a federal body established to monitor trends in agriculture – has reported that whereas agriculture's relative contribution to GDP, employment levels and exports has fallen throughout the last 30 years, its relative influence upon growth in the non-farm sector has increased. In fact in the boom times the farm sector displays a quite substantial influence upon the rate of growth in non-farm activities (see Crofts, Harris and O'Mara, 1988).

An important structural feature of the world economy that needs to be recognized as a part explanation for the productivity drive in Australian agriculture is that of the rising cost of manufactured items compared with farm-produced items. The rising cost of manufactured commodities imported into Australia, in conjunction with the general overall decline in commodity prices for agricultural goods, has a major impact upon Australia's terms of trade. The dollar float of 1984 (which lowered the value of the Australian dollar *vis-à-vis* major trading partners) and the growth in private overseas borrowings (associated with corporate takeovers) have exacerbated Australia's debt problem. In one year during the mid-1980s debt servicing jumped from about 16 per cent to approximately 30 per cent of GDP (Higgott, 1987: 12) and, as a proportion of export earnings, presently stands at a level close to that recorded in the Depression of the 1930s. As Higgott (1987) has argued, had Australia been a Spanish-speaking nation located in Central or South America it would certainly have been visited by the International Monetary Fund in the last 3 or 4 years.

In response to structural pressures for economic adjustment, the Federal Government has implemented measures consistent with the desires of foreign corporations. It has removed exchange controls, encouraged the entry of foreign banks, attempted to reduce public sector borrowing as a proportion of GDP, imposed wage restraint on the working class (capital's share of the gross operating surplus increased by 6 per cent in the 5 years to 1988, matched by a corresponding level of decline in the share received by wage and salary workers [Stilwell, 1988:26], and has attempted to stimulate productivity increases via industry restructuring policies.

Despite these initiatives and the stated intention of the Government to build a balanced economy, there has been little sign of a flow of productive capital into areas other than mining and agriculture. The combination of deregulation (and associated currency instability), high interest rate, increasing foreign debt, corporate strategies of take-over and rationalization, together with tighter fiscal and monetary policies on the part of the Government, has led to a fall in total manufacturing production (Toner, 1988). Whereas Government rhetoric is about building a competitive manufacturing sector, manufacturing investment has, in real terms, hardly risen during the 1980s, while the average age of capital stock increased by about 30 per cent between the 1960s and the 1980s (Toner, 1988).

Meanwhile, deregulation of the financial system has transformed the Australian stockmarket into something of a repository for global capital (Wheelwright, 1988). The deficiency in productive investment has been attributed to the disposal of the investible surplus into speculative, rather than productive, ventures (Marzouk, 1987; Stilwell, 1988). This situation is consistent with the view that capitalism is now a global system in which transnational players direct (and redirect) investment to take advantage of the most profitable conditions for capital accumulation. It is the newly industrializing countries in the Pacific Basin that are in receipt of productive capital to be used in industrial expansion. In contrast, capital inflow into Australia is for raw material extraction, for first-stage processing and for speculation.

As a result of its allotted position in the global economy, Australia has increased its dependence upon new technologies supplied from abroad. On the basis of the ratio of a nation's expenditure on technology to that on research and development (a measure, according to the OECD of relative technological dependency) Australia ranks fourth from the bottom among the 15 OECD countries – above Portugal, Spain and Finland (Hill, 1988: 180). In an effort to overcome this dependency the Australian Government has introduced a number of measures to improve economic competitiveness in virtually all sectors of the economy (Australian Government, 1986; Higgott, 1987). Nevertheless, there is little the country can do to break links that have been forged in the past with other, stronger, trading nations. As one economist has noted:

> The message is clear. Australia is part of the Pacific Rim. . . . Consumers in these countries are moving up market . . . [Australia's] major traditional export commodities (wool, wheat, sugar and dairy products) are all likely to be in increasing demand as the consumers living in the Pacific Rim countries became wealthier . . . new export opportunities [are] opening up all the time . . . (Longworth, 1988: 210)

It is traditional agricultural, rather than manufactured, items that are in demand and Longworth (1988: 210) continues:

> If these nations are to purchase more from Australia, there will be increasing pressure on Australia to allow increased exports from these countries. China, in particular, will be looking towards Australia as a market for its cheap manufactures.

Utilizing the orthodox economic theory of comparative advantage policy-makers in the Government have largely decided that for Australia to exploit economic opportunities in the pacific Basin agriculture will need to be transformed. Consequently, a 'high tech'/deregulated/rationalized/verti-cally-integrated farming model – characteristic of corporate agriculture in the US – has been advanced as a possible solution to Australia's economic woes.

A number of assumptions and assertions underlie the endorsement of this proposal. It appears to be taken for granted that the reorganization of agriculture along corporate lines will provide improved benefits for Australians (the current account deficit will be lowered, export markets will be secure, agriculture will be more efficient and so forth). Yet, as will be discussed below, there is little evidence to support this contention and, indeed, much to support the counter view that a corporate model is inappropriate for Australia (see Sargent, 1985). A second assumption is that State controls and regulations are a barrier to progress in agriculture. This view, although based on a belief, now discredited, (Stilwell, 1988) that State investments 'crowd out' private investments, appears to be shared by the Labour Party, Coalition parties and by the NFF.

The evidence suggests that whereas government activity adds to the costs of farming (NFF, 1981), the State's withdrawal leads to increased price instability (Hefford, 1985; Edwards, 1987) and to the demise of certain sections of family-farm agriculture (Lawrence, 1987). That is, whereas the State would appear to have a continuing role to play in smoothing out the fluctuations that lead to inefficient or inappropriate use of the nation's farming resources, such a benefit is rejected by adherents of the free market approach. Yet another assumption is that if Australia dismantles protectionist barriers not only will the farm sector become more internationally competitive, but also the Australian Government will be in a position of strength when it argues, at General Agreement on Tariffs and Trade (GATT) meetings, for the removal of trade barriers and subsidies in the US, Japan and the European Economic Community (EEC). Although it can be demonstrated that Australian agriculture is disadvantaged by protectionist policies and subsidization operating abroad (Edwards, 1987; Miller, 1987; Kirby, *et al.* 1988), any decision to reduce support for agriculture in Australia *in a world environment chracterized by increasing levels of protection* will erode, rather than enhance the position of the Australian primary producer. Those arguing from the morally 'correct' position that protectionism is a major economic cost to capitalist economies have yet to dislodge competing nations from supporting their domestic producers. The mid-term review of multilateral trade in Montreal in December 1988 revealed that virtually no progress had been made in rolling back protectionism. There were, instead, predictions of a widespread trade war between the EEC and the US (*Business Review Weekly*, 1989). Countries with high levels of protection appear quite content to 'export' their farm problem (Lloyd, 1986) by outcompeting (via subsidization and encroachment upon world markets) the minimally-protected exporting countries such as Australia.

Observers have recognized, for example, that the US Export Enhancement Program (EEP) is aimed at winning back world wheat trade that has been lost in previous years to competitions – particularly the EEC. With EEP in place the US share of global market trade in wheat in the 3 years to 1987–8 rose from 31 per cent to 46 per cent whereas the EEC's share dropped from 19 per cent to 16 per cent. Australia – an unfortunate casuality in the so-called trade war – saw its contribution drop from 20 per cent to 10 per cent during the same period (*Australian*, 1988:10).

The Uruguay Round of GATT negotiations has been marked by recalcitrance on the part of the major players to move toward trade liberalization. The rejection by the EEC of the US 'zero 2000' option (under which all subsidies and barriers to trade would be removed by the turn of the century) is evidence that reforms will be slow in coming and that, when they do, they may be superficial. Australian producers are to remain exposed to the so-called 'free market' yet, unlike their counterparts abroad, will receive little assistance from the State. Overseas trade policies, combined with the reluctance to provide support on the part of the Australian Government, is likely to force a large number of Australia's producers from agriculture and many others into contract relations with international agribusiness.

A final assumption of those supporting the corporate model is that it is now the most appropriate vehicle for the delivery of food and fibre to Australia's trading partners. This appears to be implicit in recent policy formulation despite the past importance (and success) of bilateral trade agreements in providing Australian producers with a degree of market security (Campbell, 1980; OECD, 1987). The Department of Trade (1987) has argued that corporate agribusiness is the most rational and cost-efficient means of linking Australia's domestic producers with markets abroad. The view held by the Department is that the worldwide pressures forcing the fusion of farming with agribusiness are so great that Australia cannot afford to resist, and indeed must encourage, corporate integration. In synchronizing production and marketing, agribusiness is seen to be able to develop reliable outlets for Australia's produce: it can do so in a way that adds value, in Australia, to rural-based exports. Contract relations are viewed as an appropriate means of encouraging farmers to produce what the market (that is, the corporation) demands. Contract relations are also seen to encourage producers to use the latest technologies (Department of Trade, 1987). The main barriers to an 'agribusiness future' for Australia are identified as existing state monopoly marketing controls at home and protectionism abroad.

It is asserted that once such impediments are removed Australian agriculture will be leaner and stronger, albeit corporate dominated. The 'obvious' benefits will include greater on-farm productivity, market efficiency and improved sales abroad (Department of Trade, 1987). These assertions are made without any supportive evidence and without discussion of contrary evidence. Yet agribusiness has been implicated in the overcharging of farmers for inputs and of consumers for foods, in transfer pricing activities, in tax avoidance and in environmental destruction (see Sargent, 1986; Lawrence, 1987; Burch, Rickson and Thiel, 1988). The endorsement of the trend away from the ownership and control of farming activities by family-farm operators is nothing less than approval for the further subsumption of Australian farming (see Marsden, Whatmore and Munton, 1987) in the interest of transnational agribusiness. This accords with Australia's role as a key exporter of primary produce for the industrializing Pacific Basin region.

It is in this context that the importance of technology in the restructuring of Australian agriculture needs to be understood.

Farming technology in Australia

Innovation has been a feature of Australian agriculture since the establishment of the first British penal settlement in 1788. When, in the early years of colonization, European farming practices proved to be a failure, new production methods and new plant and animal types were introduced in rapid succession as a means of achieving agricultural self-sufficiency. Later, during the time the industrial revolution in Britain, opportunities for the export of fine wool stimulate pastoral expansion and innovation within the sheep industry. Urbanization in the emerging industrial nations created a demand for fibres, meats and grains that could not be met by domestic producers in those countries. Australian farmers exploited these opportunities, extending crop production into the continent's interior and employing new technologies such as mechanical harvesting equipment, stump-jump ploughs and refrigerated transportation. By the mid-19th century State governments had come to recognize the desirability of creating an infrastructure for the support and stimulation of export agriculture: and by the beginning of the 20th century State and Federal governments began to play a key role in rural research and education.

As new lands opened up and new farming problems were encountered, so the partnership between the commercial farmer and the State developed. Some spectacular successes were to follow. The introduction of the *Cactoblastis* species of caterpillar led to the eradication of the prickly pear infestation of Australian grazing lands; the myxomatosis virus destroyed a rabbit population of plague proportions; and new drought and rust resistant wheat varieties allowed for the extension of farming into drier parts of the continent. Later still, state-supported ventures such as sown pastures, the introduction of new dryland and irrigated crop varieties and tick-resistant cattle breeds, as well as the trial and development after World War II of productivity-boosting chemical fertilizers and pesticides, were to become the mainstays of Australian export agriculture.

Perhaps the most important development, however, was the mechanization of farming. As the Committee of Inquiry into Technological Change in Australia (1980:48) reported:

> developments flowing from the introduction to agriculture of the internal combustion engine wrought unprecedented changes, not only in the structure of rural industry and the rural community, but in the community as a whole. The effect on rural employment has been large: at the turn of the century, a third of the nation's work force was engaged in rural industry – by 1979, the figure was down to 7%.

The figure today stands at 5.4 per cent (ABARE, December 1988), testimony to the seemingly inexorable change wrought by the continued application of technology to agriculture. It is through the adoption of improved technologies (and in particular the substitution of capital for labour) that farmers have sought to increase their levels of productivity and to become more competitive on international markets.

Although there are problems associated with defining and estimating productivity (Powell, 1977; Jarrett and Lindner, 1982) most economists consider it to be a measure of the increase in the level of output per unit of factor input (Committee of Inquiry, 1980). The growth in productivity on Australian farms has been 2.8 per cent per annum over the 20-year period to 1986. This rate compares more than favourably with a 2.0 per cent per annum productivity increase in manufacturing and a 1.1 per cent per annum productivity increase for the economy as a whole during the same period (ABARE, March 1988). Improvements in productivity, and major increases in the volume of rural output have acted to counterbalance the overall decline in output prices relative to input prices. Consequently, since the 1950s, the net real value of production for agriculture as a whole, whereas often fluctuating widely from year to year, has remained reasonably steady.

The way farmers have attempted to prosper in such circumstances is through the acquisition of more land, and through the purchase of more technology. As farm size has increased, the number of farms has dropped. From an estimated 203,350 properties in 1951–2, the number of commercial farms had steadily eroded to a level of 167,200 in 1986–7 (ABARE, December 1988: 428).

A number of reasons have been advanced to explain the long-term decline in the terms of trade for agriculture. The competitive nature of the export market in rural products, protectionist measures in competing nations, reductions in the growth in demand in developing nations, and favourable seasons abroad would seem to be part of the explanation (Curran, Minnis and Barkalor, 1986; Fisher, 1986; Friemann, 1987). But the main force appears to be technology itself. As Frieman (1987: 176) has explained:

> Technological change has allowed sustained growth in production, while also providing consumers of agricultural products with substitutes for some of these products (for example, synthetic fibres). These effects of technological change usually outweigh any increases in demand resulting from population and income growth, thereby causing real agricultural prices to fall.

Somewhat ironically, therefore, the adoption of new technology increases output and so serves to place downward pressure on commodity prices. This forces farmers, in turn, to adopt new technology to offset price falls. If markets could be found for the increased output or if producers in other exporting nations lagged in the adoption of new technologies (or had higher costs of production) Australian producers who had adopted new technologies may be advantaged, at least in the short term. However, the structure of world agricultural production does not usually confer such advantage. Competitors overseas are quick to seize upon the latest innovations and to employ them to reduce costs and boost output, adding further to the problem of oversupply. Governments abroad are placed under pressure by their domestic farm lobbies not only to underwrite the costs of production but also to negotiate bilaterally for the disposal of output under conditions favourable to producers. Such 'distortions' in world trade greatly disadvantage Australian producers.

Since subsidization has become politically unpopular in Australia policy dictates that the rate of structural change in agriculture should be accelerated so that the efficient producer can survive and prosper in the face of increased competition from abroad (NFF, 1981: 53;) (Australian Government, 1986). Farmers reluctant to make the necessary on-farm changes, or those unable to borrow to purchase new lands and technologies are seen to be doomed unless, of course, they can work harder, take off-farm employment to supplement farm income, or can develop novel products or service activities (Lawrence, 1987).

It has been claimed that economic competition in agriculture imposes upon commercial farmers a form of technological dependency. They become increasingly reliant both upon 'upstream' agribusiness firms (supplying the inputs to agriculture) and 'downstream' agribusiness firms (responsible for transporting, processing, packaging and distributing farm produce)

(Sargent, 1985). Farmers, as a group of unlike producers who are geographically spread and who operate with relatively small amounts of capital and labour, are economically weak in relation to the corporations with which they deal. They are placed in a position of asymmetric interdependency (Martinson and Campbell, 1980) with the larger agribusiness firms. The agribusiness firms, usually vertically and horizontally integrated and based upon overseas capital and management, are large conglomerates that can exploit their position of advantage, directing the course of agricultural development while extracting higher levels of economic surplus from farming (Wessel, 1983; Sargent, 1985; Lawrence, 1987). Farmers appear to have little choice but to purchase inputs provided by upstream agribusiness firms. Yet new technology is costly. The only way the individual farmer can compete is to borrow money for the purchase of productivity-boosting inputs. To repay loans farmers seek to achieve maximum production and to lower costs – which usually implies increased specialization and application of the new technology over as greater area (or for a longer period). The purchase of more farm land is a logical outcome because this may allow the farm to capture economies of scale. Consequently, the larger, more capital intensive producers become relatively more dominant, further marginalizing the smaller producer (Kingma, 1985:2). Wessell (1983) believes that all farmers who wish to remain in farming are being forced onto a 'technological treadmill'. They are required 'to run faster just to stay in the same place financially' (1983:25). Whereas the 'technological treadmill' model has come under recent criticism for its theoretical inadequacies (see Godden, 1987), what cannot be denied is that the *formal* subsumption of agriculture by finance and industrial capital is premised upon the continual adoption by farmers, of new technologies. Structural transformation is of a sort that will increase the likelihood of industrial and finance capitals subsuming the farm labour process by helping to alter internal management regimes and indirectly controlling farm production relations via technological dependency, credit provision and market linkages (Goodman and Redclift, 1985:239; Whatmore *et al.*, 1987:31).

Rather than viewing agribusiness as some sort of 'enemy' of farmers (which is a neopopulist response by farmers to the recognition of subservience to big business) the approach of Goodman and Redclift (1985) and Whatmore *et al.* (1987) provides a theoretical understanding of the economic outcomes of the interaction of pre-capitalist forms of production with those operating within the capitalist mode of production.

Concrete examples of the changes taking place in Australia can be found in the area of rural research. During most of the post-war years state-funded agricultural research has been under the indirect control of the farm lobby. It was the farmers who defined their production problems and it was the State that sought to solve those problems. Recent changes in State policy, especially those relating to 'high-tech' agriculture, have began, no matter how slowly, to favour the corporations. The Federal Government has actively sought to encourage collaboration between public research bodies and private corporations (thereby subsidizing corporate research in

Australia); has provided taxation concessions and other incentives for private investment in biotechnology; has strengthened legislation – allowing monopoly rights over the production and marketing of 'new life'; and has initiated an investment promotion programme to facilitate integration of Australian and overseas biotechnology firms (Lawrence, 1987).

The Government has also decided to ignore calls for the introduction of tighter controls over biotechnological research in Australia (Australian Government, 1989: 12). This approach is broadly consistent with the Federal Department of Trade's (1987) view that since transnational corporations have now become the motor force of worldwide agricultural development, all efforts should be made to encourage these firms to apply their new technologies in Australia. Indeed, the Department of Trade has specifically endorsed biotechnology as the means by which family-farm agriculture can be better controlled by agribusiness (Department of Trade, 1987).

The overall point to be made here is that the *formal* subsumption of farm labour allows for the appropriation by large urban capital of absolute surplus value and for the incorporation of family farming into circuits of capital controlled and dominated by transnational agribusiness. The so-called 'independent' commercial farmers, increasingly reliant upon external credit and other inputs, are incapable of altering the 'rules' of capital accumulation. They conform to the needs of agribusiness firms in order to remain in farming.

The more dramatic change from *formal* to *real* subsumption occurs when, through incorporation of the entire farming process, corporate entities can extract surplus value as relative surplus value (Goodman and Redclift, 1985). The fully integrated agribusiness operations, once thought to be purely American phenomenon, are beginning to play a significant role in Australian agriculture (*Business Review Weekly*, 1988). The structural changes resulting at the local level from the growth of agribusiness and the subsumption of the family farm have, in general, terms, been considered beneficial for the nation as a whole.

Yet in most rural areas the decisions of rural producers to expand their holdings to take advantage of economies of scale and to harness new technologies in an effort to boost productivity have had a marked effect on the structure of farming and, indirectly, upon the wider rural community. These developments are usually taken as evidence that agriculture is responding well to change. After all, the most efficient farmers are expanding (displacing those deemed inefficient) and resources are being employed in a manner that is in accord with principles of economic efficiency (reduction in the costs per unit of farm output).

Technology is not only viewed as a positive force that will enrich the world as a result of its ability to stimulate food and fibre production (Campbell, 1980). It is also seen to be the mechanism by which farmers can improve their position *vis-à-vis* competitors and so maintain viability in the face of cost of production increases and deteriorating world prices (Friedmann, 1987; ABARE, 1988). Technology is viewed as an harbinger of progress in the agricultural sector and, by extension, as a positive force in the wider society

(Hill, 1988). It has only been in recent times that the long-term benefits of agricultural technologies have been questioned by social theorists. Technology in the US is thought to have encouraged

> the cannibalistic centralization of farm operations while simultaneously ensuring a secure and expanding market for the purveyors of new agricultural technologies. The benefits of technological improvement in American agriculture since 1930 have accrued principally to agribusiness and to the small groups of farm operators in the technological vanguard. For the vast majority of farmers, however... technological advance has been a nightmare . . . (Kloppenburg, 1984:296).

In Australia, Kingma (1985) has argued that productivity increases in agriculture have not had the beneficial social welfare outcomes posited by neoclassical economic theory. He considers that the present trajectory of Australian agriculture – towards larger-scale farming systems and dependency of farmers upon agribusiness input and supply firms – may actually lead to a decline in the productive capacity of Australian agriculture, result in unacceptable patterns of ownership and control in farming and lead to the erosion of the economic and social base of rural communities. Kingma endorses the need for reconsideration by economists of a 'modified market' analysis that would allow for other criteria (such as impacts upon rural communities, impacts upon the environment and changes in work practices) to be given priority in future productivity studies. However, much of the 'objective' research undertaken by agricultural economists is unashamedly oriented toward fusing the interests of big business with those of farming (Lawrence, 1989b).

Capital intensity in agriculture has the effect of increasing the dependency of farmers upon the industrially-manufactured inputs of agribusiness, upon off-farm credit sources, and (as a result of increased output) upon an unstable world market. The effects, as will be suggested below, are hardly 'neutral'.

The impact of agricultural restructuring

Since the direction of technological change has been capital biased (Powell, 1982: 229) productivity gains have been achieved by a reduced labour input in on-farm production. Employing a model that assumed constant price levels, Lewis *et al.* (1988) concluded that new technological applications in Australia appear to be responsible for the reduction in the demand for farm labour by approximately 2 per cent per annum. The agricultural workforce dropped from 476,000 in 1951–2 to 393,900 in 1987–8, the time during which total employment in Australia grew from 4.2 m to 7.2 m workers (ABARE, 1988). Between 1969 and 1979 the number of rural establishments fell at a rate of about 4 per cent per annum, with a much faster decline in industries such as dairying. At the same time farm size grew at an annual average rate of about 4 per cent, with average farm size increasing from 1996 hectares to

2670 hectares during the decade. There was an unexpected growth in rural employment in 1982-3 and again in 1985-6 thought to be attributable to an increase in part-time and hobby farming, a reduction in off-farm employment opportunities for commercial operators and a redefinition of the role of women in farm activities (Johnston and Girdlestone, 1983: 23; BAE, 1987). One trend has been for increasing levels of family labour to be used in periods of economic decline and for women to assume increased responsibility in farm activities (reflected in the change from sole ownership to partnerships in Australian farming [BAE, 1983: 341]). Another trend has been toward the displacement of hired labour on family-farm (owner-operated) properties and for the growth of contract services. There has been an accompanying increase in multiple job holding amongst farm family members (BAE, 1983).

Whereas such developments may be taken as evidence that 'appropriate' structural adjustment is occurring on the farm it is important to recognize the social impact of such change. Onko Kingma (1985: 3) has asserted that:

> labour-saving technology will impact on the way in which time is used in paid work and non-paid 'work' pursuits. As productivity increases in paid work relative to non-work time, the opportunity cost of non-work time increases, causing intensification of effort in non-work time, a change in the nature of activities undertaken in non-paid work time and an additional emphasis on money earnings.
> ... Changing patterns of time use brought about by (labour minimising) productivity increases may thus... produce rapid and possibly undesired social change.

Kingma also suggests, somewhat speculatively, that as technology becomes more sophisticated and more expensive, and as farmers become more closely linked with those who 'engineer' the agricultural environment for the ultimate service of urban industry, so farmers experience individual and collective impotency. Such powerlessness, he postulates, may lead to passivity and feelings of inadequacy that are in turn manifested in *lower* levels of output (1985: 3).

What *is* clear is that stress-related health disorders are increasing amongst farmers and farm workers and that in terms of general illness, psychiatric disorder, and heart disease rural Australians appear to be amongst the worst affected in the workforce (Kellehear, 1988).

Problems such as back injury, breathing disorders, chemical poisoning and hearing impairment are directly attributable to the on-farm use of sophisticated agribusiness technologies (*Australian Farmer*, 1985; Roberts, 1986). Rural workers also have a shorter life expectancy, and, in terms of ill-health and accidents, farming is considered to be one of the most dangerous occupations. The number of farmers and farmworkers injured in any 2-year period in Australia is purported to exceed the total number of Australian soldiers wounded in action throughout World War II (*National Farmer*, 7 August 1980: 5; *National Farmer*, 16 October 1985: 25; Lawrence, 1987; *National Farmer*, 24 July 1987: 5).

The shedding of farm labour has important effects on rural social interaction and community viability. In 1947 approximately 31 per cent of Australians lived in non-metropolitan regions. This figure currently stands at about 12 per cent (Lawrence, 1987). Despite evidence of general interest in rural living among urban populations and a desire by those currently residing in rural areas to remain in the country (see Department of Decentralization, 1979) the forces of concentration and centralization in agriculture have reduced the economic viability of rural service centres. Whereas there is growth in most of the larger provincial cities, about one-third of Australian country towns are experiencing irreversible population decline associated with the reduction of service functions as farm size has increased (Rural Development Centre, 1985: 14).

There was evidence, in the 1976–81 intercensal period, of a 'population turnaround' in smaller rural settlements (Smailes and Hugo, 1985) but figures from the most recent period (1981–6) have revealed a return to the longer-term trend toward rural population decline (Balanced Development Association, 1989; Planning Research Centre, 1989).

In line with existing tendencies the smaller inland rural settlements, especially those with population levels below 10,000, are most affected (Henshall Hansen Associates, 1988; Planning Research Centre, 1989). It appears that decentralization initiatives have failed to contain the population losses associated with the application of new technologies in agriculture (O'Connor, 1986). Moreover, inequalities between rural and urban centres have begun to appear as a consequence of population loss and the reluctance, under the new regime of deregulation, for governments to provide infrastructural expenditure to maintain services in the smaller centres. Of the 37 poorest electorates in Australia some 33 are located in rural areas. Family income levels in those electorates were found to be less than half those recorded in the more affluent city suburbs (Commonwealth Electoral Division, 1988). Not surprisingly, poverty and unemployment levels have been shown to be higher in rural than in urban regions and the range of work opportunities is much narrower (Monk, 1980; Powell, 1986). Research has revealed that the level of domestic violence is higher in the country than in the city (Wallace, 1986; Coorey, 1987b), whereas many health problems, exacerbated by government service withdrawal in line with funding rationalizations (Kellehear, 1988; Williams, 1989), appear also to have a greater incidence in non-metropolitan Australia. Rural populations experience well above national average levels of premature mortality and of death through ischaemic heart disease, cancer, suicide, tuberculosis and malnutrition. In rural areas of the State of New South Wales the mortality rate among Aborigines is four times that of the white population (Department of Community Services and Health, 1986). The life expectancy of Aborigines in Australia is some 15 to 20 years less than non-Aborigines and this is seen to be directly attributable to the lack of appropriate health services to Aboriginal communities in inland Australia (Sanders, 1982; Lincoln et al. 1983).

Governments at State and Federal levels have begun to impose 'critical mass' criteria in the delivery of human services (Lawrence and Williams, 1989). 'Per head of population' calculations, which form the basis of critical mass decision-making in service delivery, tend to ignore spatial isolation, and this is an important characteristic of life in rural Australia. Accordingly, the chronically ill, the mentally ill and disabled persons in rural regions have neither access to the same services nor to the same level of services currently available to those residing in metropolitan areas (Kellehear, 1988). In New South Wales half the State's rural hospitals lack basic diagnostic equipment and the staff to treat general respiratory problems and heart disease (Lawrence and Williams, 1989). The metropolitan ratio of general practitioners per head of population is 1:300 whereas in Western NSW it is as low as 1:1500. The physical and mental exhaustion and isolation associated with medical practice in many rural regions of the State is considered responsible for doctor out-migration and the inability of smaller towns to attract new doctors (*Land*, 3 August 1989: 12). The lack of suitably qualified medical staff remains despite the over-representation of illness, and of the elderly, in rural regions of the State (Planning Research Centre, 1989).

According to the Government's own records people living in communities of fewer than 100,000 face 'considerable' disadvantage, whereas those living in towns of less than 5,000 face 'extreme' disadvantage in relation to service availability. Gross inequalities and inequities in care provision remain throughout rural Australia (Auditor-General, 1988). The reductions in the level of health-care and welfare services – justified in terms of newly-imposed 'user pays' and public accountability criteria – are not being taken up by the voluntary health and welfare sector. Married women, who have traditionally been responsible for volunteer work in rural Australia, have been conspicuously absent during the present period of restructuring. Many who might otherwise have made their time available have been preoccupied with both on-farm work activities and off-farm employment as a means of maintaining the farm (Baxter *et al*, 1988; James, 1989). There has been no time left for involvement in community service activities (Coorey, 1987a; Dunn, 1987).

It is the structural characteristics of the smaller inland communities that militate against economic growth. With the general lack of private and public investment in secondary and tertiary industries in country towns – and with many of the value-added activities associated with primary industries located in metropolitan areas – there has been little opportunity for country towns either to keep or to attract workers. Displaced farm workers tend not to remain in smaller rural settlements and there is a problem of 'depth' in the professional and skilled occupations even in larger country towns (Powell, 1986). As the agricultural economy and the demand for services declines there is a consequent loss of the (relatively more mobile) people possessing specialized skills. Sociologists have established that it is the privately employed professionals and state-employed officers who are most likely to be the community influentials and motivators, taking on responsibilities in voluntary social organizations and giving a town vitality and a spirit of community (Oxley, 1981; Wild, 1981). As Martinez-Brawley (1987: 23–6) has written:

In our increasingly bureaucratic and impersonal world, not all human needs can be satisfied in large, anomic structures . . . [yet in many towns industry closure] can have profound effects on the community ranging from increased demands for benefits to mental health services. The survival of small farms and small entrepreneurs is essential to maintain viable rural communities and to provide opportunities for rural youth. Rurality is neither all good nor all bad, but there is much about it that is attractive and should be valued and preserved.

Kingma (1985) and Lawrence (1987) have argued that when, in the context of the concentration and centralization of capital in farming, rural communities are reduced to 'nodes' in the wider production network, power is lost from those communities, social services contract and a loss of community self-determination is often experienced.

In terms of the so-called 'Goldschmidt thesis' rural restructuring means, at one and the same time, the improvement in the productive capacity of agriculture and the decline in the life chances of rural dwellers. As rural to urban migration proceeds governments, anxious to rationalize services, withdraw funding from rural regions, leaving the older, poorer and generally more vulnerable citizens in a deteriorating socioeconomic environment. People remain trapped as money and services are removed from the community. Unable to sell their homes for prices that might allow them to settle elsewhere, the most disadvantaged rural dwellers – those in need of social services – find that they must travel increasing distances for basic health, welfare and education. The progressive closure of schools, courthouses, railway stations, hospitals and welfare offices throughout rural Australia is having major social consequences (Lawrence, 1987; Williams 1989). Yet Local Government appears constitutionally, financially and politically unable to alter this downward trajectory (Sorenson, 1989). The direction of social change is not, however, inevitable. It is based upon the dynamics of capital accumulation in a class-based society and legitimized by neoclassical economic theory and free-market ideology.

Capital accumulation, technology and the state

If, despite the purchase and application of new technologies, farmers find they are facing continuing economic problems, if rural communities continue to contract and if existing agronomic practices result in environmental deterioration why is it that the State does not intervene to alter the course of agriculture in Australia? It is argued in this section that the State is structurally bound to the present pattern of accumulation in agriculture and is, therefore, incapable of altering the 'high tech' trajectory.

As was stated earlier, the conditions of the global market to which Australia supplies a high proportion of its agricultural output, the activities of agribusiness in manipulating input prices and controlling the sale of farm output, and the long-term decline in importance of farming in the Australian economy, are all factors that must be considered, along with that of technology, in any discussion of the path of agricultural development in

118

Australia. In this section, however, the discussion will be limited to an analysis of the 'inner logic' of the capital accumulation cycle for Australian agriculture.

The model of capital accumulation was first outlined by Marsden (1984) and was later developed (Lawrence, 1987) to account for the effects of increased output on the activities of the State and upon overseas markets. The model highlights the forces responsible for the concentration and centralization of capital in agriculture. In the following discussion, the italicized concepts refer to those employed in the model (Figure 4.1).

Figure 4.1 The capital accumulation cycle for Australian agriculture

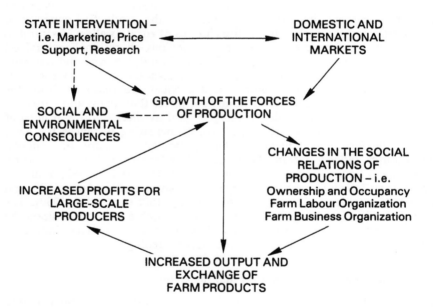

Source: adapted from Marsden (1984).

Farmers producing commodities for exchange act upon signals from *domestic and international markets* in determining what is to be produced, in what quantities, at what times, and with what combination of inputs. Agricultural markets have been characterized by commodity saturation and price volatility, making it particularly difficult for farmers to ensure that the costs of input outlays will be covered by the sale of agricultural commodities. The farmer is compelled to find ways of lowering costs, increasing factor efficiency and raising productivity. The usual method has been to adopt new technologies. In sociological terms there has been a *growth in the forces of production*. The farmer will seek to employ the new (and usually costly) technology in a manner that ensures that maximum individual benefit can be obtained. In the case of mechanical technologies this may mean using the latest machinery over a larger area or for a longer period. The first requires the farmer to purchaser adjacent farm land in order to improve further output levels. In the second case the farmer may contract out machinery, (and more often, the labour of family members) to earn supplementary income. As the most usual trend has been toward the purchase of more land (the 'cannibalization' of existing farms), larger farm size is an outcome. This, in turn, *increases output* and usually alters the *social relations of production* in farming. In general terms the social organization of production undergoes change. The farmer may begin to rely upon computer information for decision-making. If the farm is large enough a manager or other full- or part-time employees may be hired. New management strategies such as the use of more productive plant or animal types, the use of fertilizers and agrichemicals and irrigation will lead to the intensification of production that hastens on-farm adjustment or reorganization. As Kingma (1985: 12–14) has asserted:

> it is mainly through farm enlargement [and the substitution of capital for labour] that incomes in agriculture have been maintained ... Characteristics of resulting production systems have [included]
> - the dominant use of material inputs purchased off the farm;
> - increased capital intensity, associated with the use of large machinery and reduced labour input;
> - a reliance on off-farm corporate business and bureaucracies in the supply of inputs and the processing and sale of outputs;
> - an increasing division of labour. ... Farmers are now keyed into a program of forced and continued productivity increase and an expansion of output per person.

It appears that the State's research effort – one based upon a 'bigger is better' philosophy – benefits the larger producer at the expense of the smaller producer. This is reflected in the decline of the individual owner–operators responsible for overall control of the farm, and the rise of 'larger-than-family-farms' that require labour input from off-farm sources (Buttel, 1981). The family-based operation gives way to employer/employee relations altering, in the process, the class composition of agriculture (Marsden *et al.*, 1987; Gross, Rodefeld and Buttel, 1980).

Farms that utilize the new technologies and alter their management regimes have the capacity to *increase output* that can be *exchanged* in the market-place. The arrival of the products of Australian farmers on *domestic and international markets* has two consequences. Under conditions of oversupply a signal is given to producers that their returns are likely to fall unless they can become even more efficient in the next round of production (that is, it places pressure on farmers to utilize new technologies, leading to the *growth of the forces of production*). It also leads to pressures on the state to seek ways of disposing of unwanted surplus, of propping up flagging prices for farm goods, of subsidizing input costs and of investing in productivity-related research on behalf of farmers. (Just which policies are selected will be determined at the political level.) This completes the right-hand side of the circuit in Figure 4.1.

The *increased output and exchange of farm products* holds other effects. Large-scale farmers whose increased output enables them to capture the benefits of early adoption of new technologies are able to reinvest that economic surplus in newer technologies in the next production round. As Fliegel and van Es (1983:23) have discovered innovations are not scale neutral. As the scale of farming increases so too does the opportunity for the bigger farms to purchase the increasingly large capital investments represented by the new technologies. These technologies are supplied, almost exclusively, by the agribusiness input sector. In this way the larger farmers become inexorably linked to the decisions of transnational corporations that aim not only to generate increasingly higher profits from agriculture but which also control the sorts of technological developments upon which farmers are reliant. Farmers become dependent on these firms for the supply of new technologies yet, in reality, have little role in determining the direction in which future research will proceed. In Australia today, the research activities of the State, so important in the past in assisting family-farm agriculture (Jarrett and Lindner, 1982) are influenced to a significant degree by the 'efficiency' and 'productivity' drives that are the preoccupations of the larger farmers and the agribusiness firms upon which they depend. As Kingma (1985:33) notes

> the current bias towards large scale . . . technology . . . may not be in the best interests of the agricultural community . . . because . . . the majority of farms are smaller farms for which this technology may be inappropriate.

When efficiency criteria are given absolute priority in determining structural change in agriculture, the *increased profits for large-scale producers* results in further rounds of innovation represented as *the growth of the forces of production*.

The second effect of the increased output is to encourage the State to become involved in agriculture (completing the left-hand side of the circuit in Figure 4.1). Where the efficiency drive precludes measures such as underwriting and subsidization the State's role is redefined as one of aiding capital accumulation. It can do this by undertaking productivity-related research (as, in the case of biotechnology, in collaboration with corporate agribusiness) or by attempting to dispose of the increased volume of goods through bilateral and multilateral trade negotiations. The state can seek to develop new markets abroad through direct negotiation and can argue, at GATT meetings and other fora, for the dismantling of protection abroad. In seeking to find new markets for farmers' produce and by engaging in research and the provision (via extension agencies) of pro-agribusiness advice to farmers, the State not only encourages expanded production (increased farm *output*) but also assists in the *growth in the forces of production*.

As was discussed earlier in the chapter, the growth in the forces of production has certain outcomes. The social impact is that farm labour is displaced, rural communities decline and there are problems of rural unemployment and poverty associated with the changes. The environmental impacts of new technologies (alluded to only briefly in this chapter) include soil erosion, desertification, salination, eutrophication, the reduction in ecological diversity, the development of resistant strains, and the application of ever more toxic chemicals in the ecosystem (Lawrence, 1987; Watson, 1989).

It is possible for the State to address these negative consquences (see vertical broken arrow in Figure 4.1). It can, for example, provide social security benefits for unemployed members of farm families; it can promote decentralization schemes; it can enact laws to ban the use of undesirable chemicals; and it can give farmers taxation concessions for initiating soil conservation measures. But the State can do very little to address the *causes* of the problems affecting rural Australia.

To assist the smaller producers the State would need to increase levels of regulation, price support and market control. Not only is this unlikely in a period of fiscal austerity, but it would also appear to run counter to the interests of the larger operators and agribusiness firms who can capture greater benefits through *less* government involvement in the agricultural economy.

The State remains reliant upon agriculture to generate export income. It is unlikely to interrupt or 'distort' the existing pattern of capital accumulation for fear that it might retard the growth of the economy (leading to reduced profits, reduce investments and hence, to the onset of a recession or depression). As was highlighted earlier in the chapter the State is acting to increase dramatically the productive potential of agriculture by fostering the development of high-tech farming. Biotechnological innovations, in particular, promise to ensure the strengthening of the links between large-scale farming and corporate agribusiness in Australia, thereby fuelling the cycle described in Figure 4.1.

Conclusions

The argument of this chapter is that Australia is reliant upon a heavily-mechanized, chemically-dependent and energy-consuming agriculture whose development is geared to the productivity-boosting technologies of transnational agribusiness. Much of the new research and much of the advice provided to farmers by State agencies and agribusiness is framed within a narrow set of economic and technological assumptions. Very little choice is provided to the farming community. Technology is reified and its economic and social effects rarely questioned. The current trajectory of modern farming is consonant with the concentration and centralization of capital in agriculture. Such a trajectory runs counter to the development of a sustainable and socially beneficial agriculture in Australia (see Fritz and Wynen, 1987).

As a number of writers (Stent, 1976; Hodge, 1983; Kingma, 1985; Lawrence, 1987) have argued, the predominant concern of agricultural economics with prices and markets means that current economic models systematically ignore what are construed to be 'subjective' judgements about rural community life and the environment. But the issue here is one of whether the sophisticated technologies available to farmers will provide the widespread benefits that their proponents forecast.

Furthermore, economists utilizing neoclassical economic theory proceed from the assumption that free markets are inherently preferable to State regulated markets. Once this is accepted it becomes possible to argue, from the point of view of comparative advantage, that Australia should seek to encourage the development of an efficient and 'outward looking' agricultural sector (Australian Government, 1986; Longworth, 1988) and progressively to deregulate the economy. Blind faith in market forces, in the absence of appreciation of class issues relating to the ownership and control of resources in Australia, has led to recommendations for the 'streamlining' of export agriculture and mining industries and the removal of support from the previously protected sectors.

There is no guarantee that biotechnological or other high-tech advances will provide the economic boost needed to reassert Australia's previously strong position in world agricultural trade. Not only are traditional food and fibre importing nations looking to biotechnology to provide self sufficiency, but also the protectionist policies of Australia's trading competitors (like the US and EEC) have become major barriers to the increased sale of Australian products on world markets. The present course of Australian agriculture provides no guarantee that farmers will have control over economic developments in agriculture or that the benefits from productivity-related innovations will be generalized throughout the community. Indeed, like many Third World countries, Australia has become reliant upon the export of agricultural commodities whose prices are declining in relation to the costs of manufactured imports.

Australia's economic reliance upon an export agriculture that is geared to agribusiness and that requires continued technological innovation as the main means of sustaining farm ownership is likely to have serious implications for rural society. The main consequences include the increasing incidence of social pathology (poverty, unemployment, domestic violence and general illness), which, together with the loss of population through immigration and the subsequent removal by the State of appropriate health, welfare and educational services, will result in major inequalities between rural and urban localities. When a country town is in decline, public and private investment often falls to a level that further promotes the demise of that town. 'Self help' projects may be undertaken with success in some communities – particularly those that can become tourist destinations for overseas visitors. These are almost exclusively towns in coastal locations that would have grown, in any case, as a result of investments by those retiring or wanting recreation. Just as there is an economic cost associated with 'propping up' a town in decline so there is an economic cost associated with letting that decline continue. It is a cost in terms of underdeveloped human resources and the underutilization of fixed physical assets (Planning Research Centre, 1989: 10). It is also a cost relating to the establishment elsewhere of new infrastructures to support those who have migrated. The population pressure on Australia's large urban areas is quite significant and is reflected in a different sort of social pathology (homelessness, crime, drug taking and the existence of an underground economy). Yet governments have not been convinced that more spatially balanced economic development will advantage Australians. Governments have been prepared to allow 'free market' forces to determine industrial location: and metropolitan centres have been the favoured locations.

To-date Australia has not seen the growth of any discernible movement seeking to redress the negative consequences of rural community decline. The most likely force for change in rural Australia is the urban-based 'green' movement. Although influential in Australian politics, environmental groups are noted for their preoccupation with forest and wilderness destruction. They have rarely addressed the issue of the incremental damage that results from unsound agricultural practices and they have stopped short of endorsing the development of sustainable communities alongside their models for sustainable agriculture. There has, in fact, been little challenge to the hegemony of commercial export agriculture and modern technology.

If, however, the economic crisis of agriculture comes to be seen less as a problem to be solved via corporate agribusiness and biotechnology, and more as one of the economic and social *irrationality* of existing production systems, there may be a basis for the rejection of inappropriate technologies. A challenge to the corporate powers of control and domination in late capitalism may be an outcome of the realization that technical rationality is a narrow ideology that justifies a course of economic polarization and environmental destruction. Such a challenge cannot be expected from Australia's farming community. Although being progressively exposed to the forces that have led to the demise of their own numbers and to the destruction of rural communities, farmers seem reluctant to oppose the trajectory of modern farming. Instead, they support a political party and a farmers' organization that are strong proponents of 'new right' philosophy and policies. They have become willing victims of an economic strategy that strengthens agribusiness at the same time as it reduces their own independence. They have become champions of free enterprise in spite of the erosion of their own freedoms by the very processes they support. Few, it seems, understand the nature or implications of the global restructuring of agriculture.

124

References

Auditor-General (1988) *Efficiency Audit Report: Department of Community Services and Health, Home and Community Care Program*, Australian Government Publishing Service, Canberra.

Australian (1988) 14–15 May.

Australian Bureau of Agricultural and Resource Economics (ABARE) (1988) *Quarterly Review of the Rural Economy*, 10, No. 4, Dec.

ABARE (1988) *Quarterly Review of the Rural Economy*, 10, No. 1, Mar.

Australian Farmer, (1985) June.

Australian Government (1986) *Economic and Rural Policy*, Australian Government Publishing Service, Canberra.

Australian Government (1989) Biotechnology in Australia, Media release from the Minister for Industry, Technology and Commerce.

Balanced Development Association (1989) *Policy Statement on Balanced Development*, Balanced Development Association of Victoria.

Baxter, J. Gibson, J. Kingston, C. and Western J. (1988) *The Lives of Rural Women: Problems and Prospects of Employment*, University of Queensland, St. Lucia.

Bulletin (1988) 26 July.

Burch, D. Rickson, E. and Thiel, I. (1988) Contract farming and social change. In Hindmarsh, R. Hundloe, T. McDonald, G. and Rickson, R. (eds) *Papers on Assessing the Social Impacts of Development*, Institute of Applied Environmental Research, Brisbane.

Bureau of Agricultural Economics (1986) *Farm Surveys Report*, Australian Government Publishing Service, Canberra.

Bureau of Agricultural Economics (1987) *Quarterly Review of the Rural Economy*, 19, No. 3, Sept.

Business Review Weekly, (1989) 13 Jan.; (1988) 22 Dec.

Buttel, F. (1981) W(h)ither the family farm?: toward a sociological perspective on independent commodity production in US agriculture, *Cornell Journal of Social Relations*, 4, Cornell University, New York.

Buttel, F. and Newby, H. (eds) (1980) *The Rural Sociology of the Advanced Societies*, Allenheld, New Jersey.

Campbell, K. (1980) *Australian Agriculture*, Longman Cheshire, Melbourne.

Cloke, P. (1989) State deregulation and New Zealand's agricultural sector, *Sociologia Ruralis*, 29, No. 1.

Committee of Inquiry into Technological Change in Australia (1980) *Technological Change in Australia*. Vol. 2, Australian Government Publishing Service, Canberra.

Commonwealth Electoral Division (1988) *Comparison of 1986 Census Characteristics*, Current Issues Paper no. 11, Legislation Research Service, Commonwealth Electoral Division, Canberra.

Coorey, L. (1987a) Rural women access to services. In Dunn, P. (ed) *Community Welfare Services: a Rural Focus*, Riverina and Murray Neightbourhood Centres Group, Wagga Wagga.

Coorey, L. (1987b) The nature of continued domestic violence in country areas, *Regional Journal of Social Issues*, 21, Dec.

Crofts, B. Harris, M. and O'Mara, P. (1988) Variations in farm output and its effects on the non-farm sector, *Quarterly Review of the Rural Economy*, 10, No. 3, Sept.

Crough, G. and Wheelwright, T. (1982) *Australia: a Client State*, Penguin, Victoria.

Crough, G. Wheelwright, T. and Wilshire, T. (eds) (1980) *Australian and World Capitalism*, Penguin, Victoria.

Curran, B. Minnis, P. and Barkalor, J. (1987) Australian agriculture in the international community', *Quarterly Review of the Rural Economy*, 9, No. 1, Feb.

Department of Community Services and Health (1986) *The Home and Community Care Program*, Australian Government Publishing Service, Canberra.

Department of Decentralization (1979) *Regional Developer*, 1, Mar./Apr.

Department of Trade (1987) *Agribusiness: Structural Developments in Agriculture and the Implications for Australian Trade*, Department of Trade, Canberra.

Dunn, P. (ed) (1987) *Community Welfare Services: a Rural Focus*, Riverina and Murray Neighbour Centres Groups, Wagga Wagga.

Edwards, G. (1987) Agricultural policy debate: a survey, *Economic Record*, 63, 8, Jan.

Edwards, K. (1988) 'How Much Soil Loss Is Acceptable', *Search*, 19, No. 3, May/June.

Fisher, B. (1986) Policy options for Australia's rural recession, *Australian Quarterly*, Winter.

Fliegel, F. and van Es (1983) The diffusion – adoption process in agriculture: changes in technology and changing paradigms. In Summers, G. (ed) *Technology and Social Change in Rural Areas*, Westview, Boulder, Col.

Friemann, J. (1987) Australian agriculture: its future structure and role, *Search*, 18, No. 4, July/Aug.

Fritz, S. and Wynen, E. (1987) *Sustainable agriculture: a viable alternative*, National Association for Sustainable Agriculture, Australia.

Godden, D. (1987) Cochrane's technology treadmill revisited: modelling technological change in agriculture. Paper presented to 31st Annual Conference of the Australian Agricultural Economics Society, Adelaide, 9–12 Feb.

Goodman, D. and Redclift, M. (1985) Capitalism, petty commodity production and the farm enterprise, *Sociologia Ruralis*, 25, No. 3/4.

Goss, K. Rodefeld, R. and Buttel, F. (1980) The political economy of class structure in US agriculture: a theoretical outline. In Buttel F. and Newby, H. (eds) *The Rural Sociology of the Advanced Societies*, Allenheld, New Jersey.

Hefford, R. (1985) *Farm Policy in Australia*, University of Queensland Press, St Lucia.

Henshall Hansen Associates (1988) *Study of Small Towns in Victoria*, Henshall Hansen Associates, Melbourne.

Higgott, R. (1987) *The World Economic Order*, Australian Institute of International Affairs, Canberra.

Hill, S. (1988) *The Tragedy of Technology*, Pluto, London.

Hodge, I. (1983) Rural employment and the quality of life, *Review of Marketing and Agricultural Economics*, **51**, No. 3.

Horticultural Industry and Government Committee (1987) *Review of Horticultural Production Controls in New South Wales*, Department of Agriculture, Sydney, NSW.

James, K. (ed) (1989) *Women in Rural Australia*, University of Queensland Press, St Lucia.

Jarrett, F. and Lindner, R. (1982) Rural research in Australia. In Williams, D. (ed). *Agriculture in the Australian Economy*, 2nd ed, Sydney University Press.

Johnston, B. and Girdlestone, J. (eds) (1983) *Implications for Future Research of Recent Developments and Trends in Agriculture*, Bureau of Agricultural Economics/CSIRO, Canberra.

Kellehear, A. (1988) Country health: another side of the rural crisis, *Regional Journal of Social Issues*, **21**.

Kemeny, J. (1980) Dependent economy, dependent ruling class. In Crough, G. Wheelwright, T. and Wilshire, T. (eds) *Australian and World Caplitalism*, Penguin, Victoria.

Kenney, M. and Buttel, F. (1985) Biotechnology: prospects and dilemmas for Third World development, *Development and Change*, **16**, No. 1.

Kingma, O. (1985) Agribusiness, productivity, growth and economic development in Australian agriculture, *Research Monograph No. 22*, Transnational Corporations Research Project, Sydney University Press.

Kirby, M. Haszler, H. Parsons, D. and Adams, M. (1988) Early action on agricultural trade reform, *Australian Bureau of Agricultural and Resource Economics Discussion paper No. 88, 3*, Australian Government Publishing Service, Canberra.

Kloppenburg, J. (1984) The social impacts of biogenetic technology in agriculture: past and future. In Berardi, G. and Geisler, C. (eds) *The Social Consequences and Challenges of New Agricultural Technlogies*, Westview Press, Boulder, Col.

Land (1989) 3 Aug.

Lawrence, G. (1987) *Capitalism and the Countryside*, Pluto, Sydney.

Lawrence, G. (1989a) Agribusiness and inequality. In Social Justice Collective, *Growing Inequality*, Left Book Club (forthcoming), Sydney.

Lawrence, G. (1989b) Genetic engineering and Australian agriculture: the agenda for corporate control, *Journal of Australian Politicial Economy*, **25**.

Lawrence, G. and Williams, C. (1989) The dynamics of decline: implications for social welfare delivery in rural Australia. Paper presented at the Tenth National Conference of Student Initiatives in Community Health, Charles Sturt University–Riverina, 26–28 Sept.

Lloyd, A. (1986) *Rural Economic Study*, A Report to the Minister for Agriculture and Rural Affairs, Victorian Government, Melbourne.

Lewis, P. Martin, W. and Savage, C. (1988) Capital and investment in the agricultural economy, *Quarterly Review of the Rural Economy*, **10**, No. 1, Mar.

Lincoln, R.Najman, J. Wilson, P. and Matis, C. (1983) Mortality rates in 14 Queensland reserve communities, *Medical Journal of Australia*, Apr.

Longworth, J. (1988) Export markets: the real challenge, *The Australian Quarterly*, Winter.

McMichael, P. (1981) Redivisions of world labour and Australian state-formation, Paper presented at Organisation Economy Society Conference, Brisbane, July.

Marsden, T. (1984) Land ownership and farm organisation in capitalist agriculture. In Bradley, T. and Lowe, P. (eds) *Locality and Rurality*, Geobooks, Norwich.

Marsden, T. Whatmore, S. and Munton, R. (1987) Uneven development and the restructuring process in British agriculture: a preliminary exploration, *Journal of Rural Studies*, 3, No. 4.

Martinez-Brawley, E. (1987) Young people in country towns, *Australian Social Work*, **40**, No. 1, Mar.

Martinson, O. and Campbell, G. (1980) Betwixt and between: farmers and the marketing of agricultural inputs and outputs. In Buttel, F. and Newby, H. (ed) *The Rural Sociology of the Advanced Societies*, Allenheld, New Jersey.

Marzouk, G. (1987) *The Flow of Funds and Monetary Policy in Australia*, Australian Professional Publications, Mosman.

Miller, G. (1987) *The Political Economy of International Agricultural Policy Reform*, Australian Government Publishing Service, Canberra.

Monk, J. (1980) Social change through education: problems of planning in rural Australia. In Avery, W. Lonsdale, R. and Volgyes, I. (eds) *Rural Change and Public Policy*, Pergamon, New York.

National Farmer, (1987) 24 July; (1986) 2 Jan.; (1985) 16 Oct.; (1980) 7 Aug.

Natinal Farmers' Federation (1981) *Farm Focus: the 80's*, National Farmers' Federation, Canberra.

New South Wales Department of Agriculture and Fisheries (1988) *Report of Committee to Examine Charges to Land and Water Controls in Southern NSW*, NSW Department of Agriculture and Fisheries, Sydney.

O'Connor, K. (1986) Why towns change, *Inside Australia* 2, No. 1.

Organisation for Economic Cooperation and Development (OECD) (1987) *National Policies and Agricultural Trade*, OECD, Paris.

Oxley, H. (1981) The Two Towns . . . . In Bowman, M. (ed) *Beyond the City*, Longman, Melbourne.

Planning Research Centre (1989) *Rural Settlements Project. Volume 1 Overviewed Summary*, Planning Research Centre, January, Sydney.

Powell, R. (1977) Productivity growth in the Australian farm sector. In Kellogg Rural Adjustment Unit (ed) *Productivity in Agriculture and Farm Incomes*, University of New England, Armidale.

Powell, R. (1982) Farm investment. In Williams, D. (ed) *Agriculture in the Australian Economy*, 2nd ed., Sydney University Press.

Powell, R. (1986) Forgotten workers, *Inside Australia*, 2, No. 1.

Roberts, P. (1986) The impact of structural change in agriculture on the agricultural workforce, Symposium on Changing Patterns of Work in Australia, Centre for the Study of Work and Labour Market Studies, University of Wollongong.

Rural Development Centre (1985) The new rush for the land, *Inside Australia*, **1**, No. 3.

Sanders, W. (1982) Delivering services to the remote aborigines. In Loveday, P. (eds) *Service Delivery to Remote Communities*, ANU North Australia Research Unit, Darwin.

Sargent, S. (1985) *The Foodmakers*, Penguin, Victoria.

Smailes, P. and Hugo, G. (1985) A process view of the population turnaround, *Journal of Rural Studies*, **1**, No. 1.

Sorenson, T. (1989) Forum, *Urban Policy and Research*, (forthcoming).

Stent, B. (1976) Critique of the methodology of Australian agricultural economics, *Australian Journal of Agricultural Economics*, **20**, No. 1, Apr.

Stilwell, F. (1986), *The Accord . . . and Beyond*, Pluto, Sydney.

Stilwell, F. (1988) Speculation or productive investment?, *Journal of Australian Political Economy*, **23**, Aug.

Toner, P. (1988) The crisis of equipment investment in Australia, *Journal of Australian Political Economy*, **22**, Feb.

Wallace, A. (1986) *Homicide: the Social Reality*, NSW Bureau of Crime Statistics and Research, Sydney.

Watson, C. (1989) A countryside reeling, *Bulletin*, 31 Jan.–7 Feb.

Wessel, J. (1983) *Trading the Future*, Institute for Food and Development Policy, San Francisco.

Whatmore, S. Munton, R. Little, J. and Marsden, T. (1987) Towards a typology of farm businesses in contemporary British agriculture, *Sociologia Ruralis*, **27**, No. 1.

Wheelwright, T. (1988) The stock market crash and the world economy, *Journal of Australian Political Economy*, **23**, Aug.

Wild, R. (1981) Social status and political power in a small town. In Bowman, M. (ed) *Beyond the City*, Longman, Melbourne.

Williams, C. (1989) Growing old in rural New South Wales, *Regional Journal of Social Issues*, (forthcoming).

CHAPTER 5

Rural Labour-Market Changes in the United States

Gene F. Summers, Francine Horton and Christina Gringeri

Introduction

During the 1970s growth and revitalization of rural communities and economies led to a general optimism about the future of rural America. Communities experienced population growth where decline had been the trend. Manufacturing employment and service sector growth more than offset the continued decline in agricultural employment. There was talk of a 'rural renaissance'.

The experiences of the 1980s have brought a return of more pessimistic views. Downturns in many of the industries important to rural economies (agriculture, mining, energy, forestry, manufacturing) have resulted in near double-digit unemployment, a rise in business failures, fiscal crises in local government, declining public services and a renewal of the long-term trend of net outmigration and population declines. To many observers, the turnaround appears to have turned around again (Fuguitt, 1985; Richter, 1985).

In a nation as geographically vast and economically diverse as the United States, description of these trends is complex and theoretical interpretations are at least as diverse as the trends themselves. Nevertheless, in the next section we will attempt to summarize the trends as they pertain to the conditions and performance indicators of labour-markets situated in rural areas. In the second section we will review theoretical interpretations of trends in labour-markets in the US; especially those that have addressed changes in rural labour-market areas. In the final section we argue that it is increasingly necessary to link directly the mainstream theoretical arguments with rural labour-market changes.

Throughout the review we distinguish *labour-markets* from *market-areas*. In doing so the term 'labour-market' will refer to the social relations between buyers and sellers of labour and 'labour-market areas' will refer to localities in which market relationships occur. Within any geographic area, or administrative unit, there may be numerous labour-markets operating. Some may involve only local buyers and sellers (e.g. the farm labour-market or the local retail sales labour-market), others may involve buyers and sellers who participate in a regional or national market (e.g. physicians, corporate management or university professors), and others may involve mixtures of local, regional and national markets. However, for any locality the labour-markets operating within its boundaries combine to create the characteristics of employment in the local labour-market area. We hope this distinction will minimize the confusion found in the literature deriving from the frequent failure of authors to distinguish markets from the geographic areas in which markets operate. One major drawback in analyses that attempt to link market areas and labour-markets has been the lack of satisfactory data for spatial areas. Recent work in the Economic Research Service of the US Department of Agriculture has attempted to address this problem by compiling labour-market data for market areas (Tolbert and Killian, 1987).

It is especially important to separate markets from market areas when determining the most appropriate public policy strategy to deal with employment issues. If locality is of no consequence, the employment issues may be reasonably addressed by macroeconomic policies. However, if there is great diversity among labour-market areas, regional policies may be required and additionally may need to be more targeted along the lines of industrial sectors, occupational groupings, social divisions or population sectors (Deavers and Brown, 1984; Brown and Deavers, 1988; Deavers, 1988, esp. pp. 116–23; Osterman, 1988).

Trends

Since the mid-1950s the rural economy of the US has shifted from a very heavy dependence on agriculture and other natural resource-based industries to a greater diversity of economic activities. Rural labour-markets in the US are no longer primarily agricultural or natural resource-based; a point that has been made repeatedly in recent publications by American economists and sociologists who study rural labour issues, among them Brown and Deavers (1988); Castle (1988); Summers *et al.* (1988); Weber, Castle and Shriver (1988); Duncan (1989); Drabenstott and Henry (1988); Falk and Lyson (1988).

Indeed, primary industries provided only 5.0 per cent of rural employment in 1984. The whole food and fibre system – from the farmer to the retail merchant – is in decline as a source of employment. In 1975 this system employed 21.0 per cent of the civilian labour force in the United States. Ten years later it employed 18.5 per cent. Moreover, the farm sector's contribution to GNP is declining; from 2.7 per cent in 1975 to 1.8 per cent in 1985 (Duncan, 1989). Against this employment downturn in agriculture and natural resources, the growth in manufacturing and service industries in rural economies has been particularly noticeable and important to public policy.

Employment by industry sector

The service sector clearly dominated the growth in labour demand over the period 1960 to 1980. In 1980 there were 33.8 m more persons employed than in 1960 and 29.4 m of them worked in the service sector. Manufacturing provided employment for about 4.0 m additional workers. These trends were especially pronounced in the rural (non-metropolitan) labour-market. Service sector employment growth doubled from 2 m during the 1960s to 4 m during the 1970s, acounting for nearly 75 per cent of the non-metropolitan employment growth during the 1970s. Manufacturing added about 1.0 m new jobs each decade to the non-metropolitan labour-market, which amounted to 16.9 per cent of the employment growth during the 1970s (McGranahan *et al.*, 1986: 21–2).

Trends in the relative contribution of industrial sectors to total employment also is instructive. In 1960 the service sector accounted for 50 per cent of employment in non-metropolitan areas. By 1984 that proportion had risen to 69 per cent. Manufacturing followed a pattern of 22.6 per cent in 1960, 25.5 per cent in 1970, 23.5 per cent in 1980 and 20 per cent in 1984. In sharp contrast, the relative contribution of primary industries in 1960 (20.7 per cent) had declined to only 5.0 per cent in 1984. (Primary industries include agriculture, mining, forestry and fishery [McGranahan *et al.*, 1986: 24; Brown and Deavers, 1988: 7].)

From 1969 to 1976 the rate of service employment growth in non-metropolitan areas exceeded that of metropolitan areas. According to Miller and Bluestone (1988) this growth was closely linked to the manufacturing growth because this was also a period of rural industrialization. After 1976, the rate of service sector employment growth fell in rural areas and increase in the metropolitan labour-markets, again following the metropolitan–non-metropolitan differences in pattern of goods-producing employment. They also report that most service industries were under-represented in non-metropolitan areas in 1984; consumer- or household-oriented services being the exception.

As the service sector so dominates labour-markets situated in rural areas and because it covers such a wide range of economic activities it is instructive to re-examine these trends for subsectors. McGranahan *et al.* (1986) grouped service activities into three broad subsectors: household-oriented (health care, education, retail trade, personal services, entertainment and recreation), business-oriented (business and repair services, finance, insurance, real estate, wholesale trade and professional services), and other services (communication and utilities, transportation and public administration).

They report that 35.8 per cent of the total 1980 employment in rural areas is in household-oriented services with retail trade accounting for 15.6 per cent. The comparable metropolitan proportions are 36.4 and 16.3 per cent respectively. This distribution gains in importance when one notes that employment in household-oriented services accounted for more than 40 per cent of the growth in both metropolitan and non-metropolitan areas during the 1970s. Much of the growth can be linked to the expansion of health-care services. With the continued 'ageing' of the population this promises to be a significant growth sector for several decades to come (Hirschl and Summers, 1982).

Business services as a subsector accounted for 13.2 per cent of the non-metropolitan total employment and 20.8 per cent of metropolitan employment. Overall the subsector had a better than 40 per cent rate of growth in both metropolitan and non-metropolitan areas but its impact is somewhat diminished when one notes the relatively smaller contribution the subsector makes to total employment. Other services contributed 11.0 per cent to rural employment and 13.0 per cent to metropolitan employment.

Broad trends in the restructuring of the US economy can be seen in these statistics, but they provide only a crude measure of the changes taking place. The richness of the diversity and the complexity is made more apparent by examining changes among regional and local labour-market areas. Comparative analyses reveal the details of the spatial division of labour among industries and occupations. They also provide descriptions of several dimensions of the social division of labour and lead to further consideration of social and cultural institutions in the operation of labour-markets.

In a recent study of rural labour-market areas, Killian and Hady (1988) found that agriculture remained the predominant industry in only 32 of the 182 areas. Twelve were led by mining and 8 were heavily dependent upon wood products. By contrast, textile and apparel manufacturing was dominant in 12 market areas and durable manufacturing in 6. Public education and administration led the employment roster in 26 of the rural labour-market areas, and 86 were classified as 'diversified'. When these figures are considered in conjunction with the national labour-market data, it is very evident that the nationally calculated 5.0 per cent who are employed in primary industries are concentrated in a relatively small number of rural labour-market areas. Moreover, only 28.6 per cent of the rural labour-market areas are dominated by employment in the primary industry sector.

Turning to the overall economic performance of these 182 rural labour-market areas, Killian and Hady (1988) found that those specializing in durable manufacturing had the worst record, far worse than those specializing in primary sector industries. (Their summary index was based on six measures of income and employment.) On the other hand, labour-market areas specializing in public education and administration, and those with a diversified industrial base, consistently had the better economic performance records.

Bloomquist's analysis of rural manufacturing performance partially clarifies the Killian and Hady findings (Bloomquist, 1988). By grouping rural manufacturing according to the product cycle model of industrial organization (cf. Thompson, 1965; Norton and Rees, 1979), he found that 'bottom of the cycle' firms dominate manufacturing employment in non-metropolitan areas. These industries are distinguished by their demand for labour with relatively low technical skills and their low wage rates.

Employment by occupation

The growing importance of service and manufacturing industries in rural labour-markets is also revealed in the distribution of employment by occupation if one accepts the argument that white-collar occupations are predominantly in the service producing industries and that manufacturing industries are dominated by blue-collar occupations. Using data from the 1980 Census of Population, McGranahan *et al.* (1986) report that nearly half of the rural work force was employed in white-collar jobs; 18.2 per cent were employed as managers or professionals and 24.2 per cent were working in low-skill white-collar occupations (technical, sales or administrative support).

Blue-collar occupations provided jobs for another 37.2 per cent of the rural workers; 22.7 per cent in low-skill blue-collar jobs (operators, fabricators and labourers) and 14.5 per cent in high-skill blue-collar occupations (precision production, craft and repair).

Using statistical reports from both the Bureau of Economic Analysis and the Bureau of the Census covering the period 1969 to 1984, Bloomquist (1988) concludes that 'While the rural manufacturing sector has had substantial growth in recent years, most of the growth has been in manufacturing industries that provide low-skill and low-wage jobs' (Bloomquist, 1988: 49).

In a related analysis McGranahan (1988) divided manufacturing into 'complex and routine' industries based on the proportion of the industry employment in managerial and professional–technical jobs as a percentage of total industry employment. He found that the routine industries are more commonly located in rural areas. Consequently, only 10 per cent of the professional and technical jobs are located in rural labour-markets. On the other hand, occupations such as 'machine operator' and other less-skilled blue-collar jobs have a disproportionately high presence in the manufacturing sector of rural labour-markets.

It appears that rural manufacturing tends to be composed of small firms with routine operations and larger multiple-location firms that locate their routine production in rural branch plants. There is considerable evidence that even the 'high-tech' industries follow the same pattern of buying labour for routine production in rural labour-markets and entering urban labour-markets to secure technical and professional labour requirements (Glasmeier, 1986; Falk and Lyson, 1988, esp. pp. 44–9; Barkley, 1988; Malecki, 1989).

The human resource base

In theory, labour-market outcomes are determined as much by the attributes of the available supply of labour as by the industrial and occupational characteristics of the demand for labour. In this context, it is an historical fact that the human-resource base of rural areas have been at a disadvantage when compared with urban areas (McGranahan, 1988). Although the gap in years of formal education has been closing, it still remains; especially for males. The apparent movement toward equality of education between rural and urban adults almost certainly is due, in part, to the urban to rural migration of older adults and, therefore, only partially indicates an improvement in the retention of pupils in the educational system in rural areas. An important point to note is that the traditional measure of human capital – years of schooling completed – has become less adequate as a measure of levels of human capital in an area and of an individual's ability to function in modern labour-markets.

With the turnaround in population movement to a net out-migration pattern for many rural areas, non-metropolitan America has seen a net loss of people, particularly of young adults, to metropolitan areas in each year since 1983. Non-metropolitan areas had a significantly lower proportion of adults in 1980 between the ages of 20 and 44 and a higher proportion of people over age 55 than did metropolitan areas. Net migration rates by age in 1985–6 show that this older age distribution is becoming even older as the 1980s progress (Swanson and Butler, 1988: 177).

Dislocated workers who made their living in declining occupations or in declining industries in rural areas often are unable to adjust to new high-growth occupations and industries without considerable retraining and re-education. Many find that once-valued highly specialized manual skills, which had been learned on the job, are not easily transferable to the jobs now available in the local labour-market. Some do not have the basic literacy skills to be retrained at all, creating a pool of hard-to-employ workers (Ross and Rosenfeld, 1988: 338).

Labour-market outcomes

Growth in the aggregate demand for labour over the past 15 years has been quite impressive in view of the fact the US economy weathered two major economic recessions during that period. However, trends in the aggregate demand for labour reveal nothing about the outcomes for participants in the labour-market, i.e. the proportion who found employment and whether that was partial or full-time employment, the level of earnings provided by employment or how the employment was distributed among the many persons seeking work.

Unemployment has increased in rural labour-markets from 1973 to 1988 despite the good record of job creation in the national economy. Moreover, the gap in unemployment rates between metropolitan and non-metropolitan areas has been steadily widening. Whereas in 1973 rural labour-markets had a lower rate of unemployment than the metropolitan labour-market (4.4 per cent compared to 5.1 per cent), in 1988 their respective rates were 6.2 and 5.3 per cent. If these unemployment rates are adjusted to include discouraged workers and one-half of the workers employed only part-time for economic reasons, the plight of rural labour-markets is considerably worse. In 1973 the non-metropolitan and metropolitan adjusted rates were both 7.1 per cent; by 1988 the metropolitan areas had recovered to an annual average of 7.9 per cent while the non-metropolitan areas remained at 10.1 per cent (Parker, 1989). The increasing disparity is attributable to two trends. First, each of the two recessions hit rural labour-markets harder. Second, recovery has been slower and less complete in the rural labour-markets. Since 1985 there have been distinct signs of recovery in both metropolitan and non-metropolitan labour-markets, but relief from unemployment has been noticeably slower in coming to rural labour-markets. Conditions that could produce these results include structural and institutional elements, but only recently have they attracted the attention of researchers.

Part-time employment has also been increasing as a proportion of those employed in rural labour-markets. This is a national trend because it also has been increasing in metropolitan labour-markets. It appears to be partially a function of the performance of the national economy because the yearly averages of part-time employment rates follow the same pattern of unemployment across the recessionary and recovery periods of the 1970s and 1980s. But also as with unemployment, part-time employment has been pushed up more rapidly in the rural labour-markets during recessions and the recovery has been less complete than in the metropolitan labour-markets. Thus, in 1988, the annual average of part-time employment for economic reasons in rural labour-markets stood at 5.9 per cent while in the metropolitan markets it was 4.2 per cent (Bureau of the Census, *Current Population Surveys, 1973–1988*; Parker, 1989). In 1973 the comparable percentages were 3.6 and 2.7 respectively for non-metropolitan and metropolitan labour-markets.

Interpretation of these two trends is quite contentious. As both trend lines follow the pattern of recession and recovery it can be argued that the rise in unemployment and part-time employment rates over the past 15 years is due to the failure of the economy to function at a level nearer full capacity. This is a result of increased international competition, capital flight to foreign investments and deliberate efforts to control inflation through the use of macro-level fiscal and monetary policies. The cost of greater competition and inflation control is higher levels of partial employment and unemployment. The association of trends with these factors notwithstanding, it can be argued also that structural and institutional changes are contributing to the shrinking levels of employment (Duncan, 1989).

Earnings of rural workers are below those of urban workers and the situation is getting worse. Even when other income sources are added to earnings, non-metropolitan families and households are worse off than metropolitan residents. In 1980 the median income of non-metropolitan families was $16,592 compared to $21,128 for metropolitan families, i.e. the incomes of non-metropolitan families was only 78.5 per cent of their metropolitan 'cousins' (Census of Population, 1980). If households are considered rather than families, the same ratio obtains. But according to the 1987 Current Population Survey, the ratio had declined to 73.1 per cent.

Racial and ethnic minorities in non-metropolitan areas are particularly disadvantaged (Fuguitt, Brown and Beale, 1989; Snipp, 1989). In 1987 the median total money income per household member of black persons living in non-metropolitan areas was $4758 and Hispanics did only slightly better – $5424. By contrast, whites living in metropolitan households had incomes of $13,786. Those are the extremes, but even among non-metropolitan households the whites have incomes that are about double those of blacks ($9985 and $4578 respectively) and Hispanics do only slightly better (Bureau of the Census, 1989). No figures are available for native Americans although it is well documented that their incomes are lower even than blacks' (Snipp, 1989). These conditions have prompted some to refer to the plight of minorities in rural America as the 'Third World in America'.

Poverty persists in rural households and is spreading to regions outside the South (Brown and Warner, 1989). In 1973, 14.0 per cent of all non-metropolitan residents had incomes below the official poverty level. In 1985 the percentage had risen to 18.3 per cent, at least partly due to the rising rates of unemployment and underemployment. Even when 'in-kind' transfer payments are added to other income, 13.2 per cent of the non-metropolitan people failed to have enough income to meet minimal basic needs. In metropolitan America the figure was 9.3 per cent. In 1987 the non-metropolitan poverty rate had dropped to 16.9 per cent showing some slight improvement. Rural poverty is still concentrated in the southern region, but it is increasing in the Midwest and in the Northwest regions due to the economic downturn of industries disproportionately located there (agriculture and manufacturing in the Midwest and fishing, mining and forestry in the Northwest) (Deavers, Hoppe and Ross, 1988).

The 'working poor' is a more common phenomenon in rural areas than in cities. Labour-market participation is higher among poor families in non-metropolitan than in metropolitan areas. Over two-thirds of the non-metropolitan poor families had at least one member active in the labour-market. One in four had at least two income earners and still they were poor (Brown and Deavers, 1988). There is little doubt that this is partially due to the lower wages and salaries of rural workers, but it also reflects the higher rates of unemployment and underemployment (Osterman, 1988).

Social and economic changes have caused a dramatic rise in women's participation in the work force (Bokemeier and Tickamyer, 1985; Rosenfeld, 1985; Haney and Knowles, 1988). In 1980, 45 per cent of the non-metropolitan women aged 16 and over were active in the labour-market (Ross and Rosenfeld, 1988).

Recent rural labour-market studies reveal the existence of a clear and deep social division of labour that is manifest in various labour-market experiences and outcomes (Horan and Tolbert, 1984; Bloomquist, 1988; Falk and Lyson, 1988; Killian and Hady, 1988; Tickamyer and Bokemeier, 1988, 1989; and Snipp, 1989). White women and racial and ethnic workers of both genders are more likely to have jobs with lower earnings, less stability and fewer opportunities for advancement. There is some evidence the situation may be worsening (Goudy et al., 1986).

Labour-market theories

Recent trends in rural labour-markets and labour-market areas are beginning to attract the attention of economists and sociologists all whose approaches to explanation have a clear heritage in more general theories of work and society, i.e. demand-oriented, supply-oriented and institution-oriented theories. The demand-oriented explanations emphasize global, national and regional changes in the structure and volume of product demand and other factors that affect labour demand. The supply-oriented explanations draw heavily on human capital theory with its stress on the importance of education and training of workers in competitive labour-markets. The institution-oriented explanations emphasize organizational and institutional factors in the operation of labour-markets in a manner that is reminiscent of institutional economics.

As neoclassical economic theory figures so prominently in the debate, it may be useful to review its principal propositions. A labour-market is composed of relations among buyers and sellers of labour. Therefore, a labour-market is an institution that governs the exchange of labour services and thereby distributes labour among occupations, industries and labour-markets to yield the maximum efficiency in the use of a society's resources (Kreps, Somers and Perlman, 1974; Shaffer, 1989). According to Mark Henry (1989: 29):

> Economists usually analyze labour markets from the perspective of aspatial behavioral models in which there is a profit maximizing employer who desires to hire labour so that the last unit of labour hired is paid a wage that is equal to the added value of the product obtained from that labour unit. The market also reflects the behavior of households that attempt to maximize utility in a leisure – income tradeoff process and thus offer different quantities of labour services as the prevailing wage rate varies.

Thus, labour-market outcomes are demand- and supply-driven with wage being the key instrument for reaching an equilibrium.

The assumptions underlying neoclassical labour-market theory are extremely restrictive. These include the following: that workers and employers have complete knowledge of all opportunities, that both are rational and will maximize either their satisfaction or their profits, that workers and employers are sufficiently numerous that neither can influence the wage rate through collusion or other means, that labour within a market is homogeneous and therefore workers are interchangeable (there is no discrimination) and that no barriers exist to interfere with mobility of labour among occupations, industries or geographic locations. Therefore, unemployment occurs only when these assumptions are not met or when there are other reasons for market failure.

Within the neoclassical model, unemployment is seen as differentiated according to the sources of the market failure and is often divided into demand-deficient unemployment, structural unemployment and frictional unemployment. The proper choice of public-policy instruments is deter-

determined by the source of the market failure. Demand-deficient unemployment occurs when the product market demand falls below the point where job vacancies are equal to the available workers.

Structural unemployment occurs when there is a mismatch between job requirements and skills available. This is usually taken to mean one or more of the assumptions regarding the supply of labour have been violated. For example, it recognizes that barriers may exist to complete knowledge, that workers may not be interchangeable, that there are barriers to mobility or that rules of hiring and/or promotion may exclude some potential workers. Where unemployment is deemed to be structural in origin, the public policy response usually is to intervene to remove the barriers to mobility or to train (and retrain) workers for the existing job vacancies.

Frictional unemployment recognizes the failure of the simultaneity assumption. Mobility of labour and other factors of production do not move instantaneously or simultaneously from where they are not needed to where there is an effective demand. Time is required for adjustments to occur. Consequently, at any moment in time there are likely to be some unemployed workers. This level of unemployment may be regarded as an irreducible minimum as there does not appear to be a policy instrument for correcting this failure of the market (Shaffer, 1989).

Demand-oriented theories

The demand for labour consists of employment opportunities that are structured according to occupations, industries, skill requirements and location of work; all of which may vary over time. The demand at any time and place is affected by several factors. These include the demand for the output (good or service) that labour produces, the productivity of labour (a combination of capital, technology and worker skill), and the price of factors of production other than labour. Effective demand for the output is governed by the degree of competition in the product-market and consumer preferences. Similarly, prices in the factor-markets are assumed to be competitive (Shaffer, 1989). Some demand-oriented theorists use national labour-markets as their unit of analysis whereas others address spatial differentiation within the nation. In either case, an attempt is made to explain the ups and downs of labour-market conditions by facing outward in search of exogenous factors to account for labour-demand changes in labour-market areas. In its broadest perspective, one must begin with the changing conditions in the global economy that affect the local demand for labour.

Global economic restructuring

Since the mid-20th century, the world has experienced many economic, social and political changes that might reasonably be summarized as the global diffusion of capital, technology and skills (Galston, 1988). As these critical factors of production have diffused throughout the world, a truly global economy with intensive global competition has been generated. This places greater pressure than previously on the economy of the United States. In particular the traditional extractive and goods producing sectors face greater international competition that forces firms in these sectors to seek ways of increasing efficiency in productivity, i.e. increasing the value of output per unit cost of inputs. Obviously, these sectors have been the predominant sources of demand for labour in rural markets. Thus, the global restructuring has hurt rural labour-markets and market areas even more than labour-markets in urban areas.

For at least a century, the trend has been toward lower real prices of natural resource-related commodities (Castle, 1988: 12). Today the real prices of raw materials are at their lowest levels in recorded history relative to manufactured goods and services. This is in sharp contrast to the predictions of widespread shortages and rising prices that were being made a decade ago. Indeed, global agricultural outputs and production of practically all forest products, metals and minerals are at all-time highs, with the greatest percentage increases coming from less-developed nations. There is little reason to expect the total raw-materials output to decrease, despite the depressed prices; most nations are committed to a political strategy of self-sufficiency in food and raw materials and now possess the production technology needed for high output.

Yet, the depressed global state of the primary goods economy has not led to a global industrial depression. This appears to be due largely to the diminished structural importance of primary goods production in the economies of developed nations, a situation which T. W. Schultz anticipated many years ago (Schultz, 1951). In most developed countries, raw materials and food production account for less than 10 per cent of the GNP and an even smaller proportion of the labour force. This major structural change in the world economy has had serious implications for the rural economy of the United States.

In the manufacturing sector, primarily because of technical change, labour input has become an increasingly small part of the value of industrial production (Bluestone and Harrison, 1982; Summers, 1984; Drucker, 1986). In all industrial nations, manufacturing output has steadily increased and maintained its share of the GNP while employing fewer workers. This has been accomplished by substituting capital and technology for labour. With promises of 'high-technology' for even greater production efficiency, there is little reason to expect this structural change to reverse. A recent study by the National Academy of Sciences Panel on Technology and Employment concluded that whereas more jobs are created by technology than are eliminated, the negative impact of technology falls heavily on those persons without basic skills and with poor education (Cyert and Mowery, 1987).

Thus, rural labour-market areas in the US that are heavily dependent on low-skill, low-wage manufacturing for employment and are experiencing a declining labour demand, may expect to find little relief by pursuing a singular strategy of rural industrialization. Similarly, agriculture and raw materials extractive industries have little potential for generating additional employment in rural labour-market areas.

At this point the prescriptive debate separates into macro-level and micro-level issues. At the macro-level the debate centres on selection of the most appropriate national economic policies for revitalizing the competitive position of the US in the global economy and incorporates discussion of international trade, industrial, fiscal and monetary policies. The micro-level debate centres on the spatial and sectoral distribution of economic activities, whatever may be the relative position of the US in the global economy. If people hope to live in small cities and rural areas while still sharing equitably in the fortunes of the US economy, it will be essential to find ways of stimulating the growth of non-traditional labour-markets in rural labour-market areas.

Export base theory

According to export base theory the economy of any spatial system may be divided into two broad sectors; those economic activities that produce goods and services for external markets and those activities that produce goods and services for internal markets. It is assumed the export activities drive the internal economic activities and consequently the export sector is sometimes called 'basic' and the domestic sector regarded as 'secondary'. The critical element in the theory is the generation of a money flow into the local economy that is then spent internally. In this manner, exports are able to create a demand for labour directly in the export activities and in the secondary sector through the spending and respending of the money that is brought into the economy via the export activities (Andrews, 1954; North, 1955; Tiebout, 1956; Thompson, 1973).

Agricultural products, raw materials and manufactured goods have composed the bulk of the expert sector for many rural labour-market areas, but global and national trends in these product markets threaten the labour demand in areas with a strong dependency on them (Killian and Hady, 1988). However, it is not necessary to limit the export sector of rural labour-market areas to these traditional activities. Any activity that generates an in-flow of money may be regarded as an export activity. By redefining the traditional conception of exports to include exportable services, high-tech manufacturing, recreation and tourism and residential development for persons with passive incomes, export base theory provides a possible guide for increasing the demand for labour in rural labour-market areas. The notion receives broad support from Killian and Hady's (1988) study of 182 rural labour-market areas. The best performances were recorded by the areas with 'diversified' economies and those specializing in 'public education administration'. Support for the argument is also provided by several recently published case studies.

Smith and Pulver (1981) and Smith (1984) have shown that non-manufacturing businesses can generate significant amounts of export activities. In a survey of 385 non-manufacturing businesses in rural Wisconsin, they found that 27 per cent of the businesses made over half their sales outside the local area. Smith, Hackbart and van Veen (1981) and

Hirschl and Summers (1982) have shown that passive income (investment returns, pensions, retirement payments) to rural community residents has the ability to generate jobs in the local labour-market area. Both studies reported greater secondary job-generating efficiency for passive income than manufacturing payroll. In many rural communities and labour-market areas, passive income is more than half the total personal income and provides a potentially strong source of increased consumer goods and services demand as well as a source for development capital (Summers and Hirschl, 1985). It should be noted that recipients of passive incomes are not welfare recipients; the incomes of retirees is nearly equal that of persons under age 65 and the proportion of the US population over age 64 will increase well into the next century. Retirees are a growth-market.

The list of non-traditional rural economic activities that have a potential for generating exportable goods and services is quite large and the range of possibilities has not been fully explored. However, advocates argue that it surely includes medical centres that serve a non-local clientele, universities and colleges attracting non-local students, recreation and tourist activities, research and development laboratories, military installations, regional offices and laboratories of the federal and state governments and some business and consumer services. The technological changes in communications favour a spatial dispersion of both production activities and producer services; advances in telecommunications and transportation have overcome the cost of distance for at least some non-metropolitan labour-market areas (Noyelle, 1983; Garnick, 1984; Leven, 1985).

Spatial location theories

There is an enormous general literature on the subject of spatial location of economic activities. For the most part, it is urban-oriented with population density, the value of space and the cost of distance being central. To the extent that rural labour-market areas have been treated at all in these theories, it has been assumed that agriculture and other natural resources predominate in rural economic activities (Castle, 1988). Contemporary evidence clearly contradicts that assumption. Indeed, it is precisely these industries that are responsible for labour demand deficiencies and the consequent unemployment, underemployment and low earnings in many rural labour-market areas. Attention is being directed toward goods and service sectors not traditionally found in rural areas in search of those where demand may be growing, and for which rural labour-market areas may have a competitive advantage. The hopeful speculation of export-base proponents is questioned by location theorists and their several derived models. The more widely studied theories of spatial location are industrial location theory, product cycle theory and central place theory.

Industrial location theory attempts to explain how firms (and households) make economic decisions that involve a spatial dimension. A narrow interpretation of location theory is that it deals only with the relocation of businesses, but that is too restrictive. The theory also deals with questions of where to start a new business, where to purchase inputs, where to expand markets, where to acquire capital, where to sub-contract. Thus, industrial location theory is relevant to the issue of stimulating the growth of non-traditional labour-markets in rural areas because it addresses spatial aspects of new business start-ups, expansion of existing firms and relocation of firms (Greenhut, 1956; Moses, 1958; Smith, 1966; Moriarty, 1980; Shaffer, 1989). Within industrial location theory there are four well-established models to account for the location of economic activities.

The 'least-cost' model of location closely parallels the neoclassical economic development theory with assumptions of pure competition in factor markets, complete information about all relevant factors, absence of barriers to spatial mobility, homogeneity of institutional factors among sites and perfect elasticity of product demand and factor inputs at fixed locations (Greenhut, 1956; Moses, 1958; Smith, 1971; Meyer, 1977; Shaffer, 1989). In these circumstances firms make decisions to start up a new business, expand or relocate by seeking to minimize their total cost of production and transportation. When a firm produces a single product that it sells to a fixed-location market, as it the case for many small-scale manufacturers, the least-cost model may have some utility in explaining location decisions.

The 'demand-maximization' model presumes that a seller of a product (good or service) will select a business site that provides access to the largest possible market area (Greenhut, 1956; Smith, 1971; Shaffer, 1989). It also assumes that consumers will make their purchases in order to minimize the price paid for delivered product. This model is particularly relevant for firms selling to dispersed buyers, such as retailers, wholesalers and service providers, with their focus on minimal market needs for profitable operations. With maximum sales as the firm's primary goal, a site is selected to minimize the cost of making those sales, which may not be the site of least-cost.

The 'profit-maximization' model declares that location decisions are determined by which site will generate the greatest difference between costs and revenues, i.e. the greatest profit (Greenhut, 1956; Shaffer, 1989). This may not be the site with the lowest cost or the largest demand. Many up-scale, high priced specialized market-oriented businesses appear to follow this model of location decision-making, but the model need not be limited to high-cost, high-profit businesses.

The 'behavioural' model allows the relaxation of many of the rational 'economic man' assumptions by permitting personal and non-economic goals, incomplete information, inaccurate use of information and uncertainty to enter the calculus of site selection (Pred, 1967). By relaxing these economic rationality assumptions, the location decision process is made more realistic, but also more complex (North, 1974; Massey, 1975; Tornquist, 1977; Shepard, 1980; Shaffer, 1989). By using game theory and bounded rationality, decision-makers are 'permitted' to set multiple objectives for their firm, including purely non-monetary goals. Sales must at least equal costs, of course. It is assumed that decision-makers do not have complete information and might not be able to process it even if they did.

Some decision-makers are more sensitive to non-economic information than others and all of them filter information through their own experiences and perspectives (Lloyd and Dicken, 1977). Similarly, information about future events and conditions are assumed to be uncertain and therefore decision-makers view them in probabilistic terms.

The product-cycle theory stresses the relationship between the stage of product development and labour requirements. It is argued that in the initial stage of product development labour with a high degree of skill is required. Later, when the product has reached a stage of standardized production, the labour requirement is for low-skill, tedious and repetitive work. When a product has reached an advanced developmental stage, it may be cost minimizing for the manufacturing firm to relocate to an area of lower labour cost. Or in the case of multiple-product, multiple-location firms, it may be cost effective to locate the routine production activities in lower labour cost areas. As rural labour-market areas often have relatively lower wage rates than urban areas, the product-cycle theory would lead to expectations of a 'filtering down' of bottom of the cycle production to rural labour-markets (Alderfer and Michl, 1942; Thompson, 1965; Averitt, 1968; Norton and Rees, 1979). Bloomquist's (1988) assessment of rural manufacturing certainly provides strong support for this theoretical model. The product-cycle theory is also employed to explain the further movement of bottom of the cycle production to 'off-shore' locations; especially to free enterprise zones in Third World nations (Falk and Lyson, 1988).

The central-place theory uses an image of hierarchical spatial organization of economic activities to account for differences in the size and functions of urban places (Losch, 1954; Christaller, 1966). Rural service centres and the surrounding farms, viewed as the 'hinterland' of these smallest urban places, are the basic elements in the hierarchical system. Larger urban places develop to serve the smaller ones with each layer in the hierarchical system providing a distinctive set of economic activities not found in the smaller urban places. In a sense, this is reminiscent of the 'demand-maximization' model, except that the demand is generated by markets in the smaller places. The hierarchical organization of places constitutes a system of areas wherein each higher level has a larger central place with a broader range of economic activities and a larger subordinate area (or hinterland).

As the theory emphasizes economic interdependence among urban places of varying sizes, it promises to offer guidance for those searching for ways of stimulating labour demand in rural labour-market areas by linking the system of cities with export base theory. Unfortunately, the empirical work in the US based on the central place theory has been largely concerned with descriptive comparisons of the economic characteristics of places of different size. However, it has provided a basis for arguing that service industries cannot provide a stimulus for increasing labour demand in rural labour-market areas. Applying a logic reminiscent of the product-cycle theory, Miller and Bluestone (1988) argue that household-oriented services will be distributed in relation to population size, whereas business-oriented services that can market over large geographic areas will continue to locate in metropolitan areas where they can take advantage of the cost and marketing advantages of agglomeration. If this argument holds, rural labour-market areas face a future of 'residual specialization in certain consumer services of the kind provided by government, recreational, and retirement businesses, and some distributive activities' (Miller and Bluestone, 1988: 139).

Supply-oriented theories

The supply of labour consists of the number of workers willing to sell their labour at a specified wage rate and stipulated set of skill requirements. A great many factors may operate to determine the labour supply that include the time required to acquire skills, the proportion of the population with the ability to acquire the requisite skills, competing opportunities for work activities and non-monetary goals of the potential workers. Institutional factors may also operate to shape (or distort) the supply of labour as when hiring rules operate to exclude certain categories of workers (Kerr, 1983).

The neoclassical model as described above serves as the starting point for a number of contemporary labour-market theories that differ largely in their choice of neoclassical model elements requiring refinement. Human capital theory (Becker, 1971, 1985) emphasizes labour supply in explaining the operation of labour-markets. According to this theory, workers are hired and retained because of their productivity, which is a function of their skills and knowledge, acquired through schooling, training or work experiences. Workers are paid a wage-rate based upon their productivity relative to competing workers. Therefore, workers may increase their future earnings by investing in productivity-increasing activities, i.e. schooling and training. By assuming that all individuals follow this rational model of investment, the human capital differences among individuals, therefore, are said to result from variations in their expectations for annual returns on investments, in costs of acquiring human capital, in total returns on investments, in calculations of discount rates and variations in their talent or ability. The theory makes no concession to labour-demand factors or to hiring rules that may limit the access of some individuals or groups to full participation in the labour-market. Moreover, it leads to public policies that place the burden of labour-market adjustments entirely on the workers.

Institution-oriented theories

Critics of the human-capital theory and demand-oriented theories argue that they ignore important aspects of the organization of work, the interplay between work structures and markets, the interrelations among work structures (industries, firms and locations) and their impact on the operation of labour-markets (Kalleberg and Berg, 1987; Farkas and England, 1988; Osterman, 1988; Whitener, 1989). Kalleberg and Berg have proposed an analytic framework in which they argue, 'Work structures describe the ways in which labour is divided, tasks allocated, and authority distributed...' (1988: 3). Moreover, they believe that research has shown 'that many work-related inequalities among individuals are generated by correlates of such work structures as firms, industries, occupations, classes and unions' (Kalleberg and Berg, 1988: 3). Among the labour economists and sociologists who emphasize organizational and institutional factors there are three major discernible approaches: those that focus on internal labour-markets, those concerned with dual and segmented labour-markets, and those calling attention to the informalization of labour-markets.

Internal labour-markets

J. R. Commons (1924) emphasized that economic activity is social, and that the basic unit of analysis is the transaction (employment being one type). He identified two aspects of the organization of production (referred to as the 'going concern'): (1) the *technological process* of production, consumption, etc. of physical things (commodities) and (2) the *business process* of 'buying, selling, borrowing, lending, commanding and obeying according to shop rules, working rules or laws of the land' (1924: 8). Economizing is limited by laws, rules and norms of behaviour, which generally have been neglected in economic theory. Institutional theory claims that there is something more fundamental than supply and demand forces – the context within which a market is permitted to operate. Internal labour-market (ILM) theory is an institutional approach to the political economy of employment transactions. As such, it seeks to understand the context, the rules, the institutions (formal and informal) that structure labour-markets, and within which, more or less, supply and demand forces are permitted or encouraged to operate. Rules at the level of the employment transaction are related to rules at the national level and economic policy more generally, so that institutional labour economics can be thought of as a subfield of institutional economics.

Much has been written over the last 20 years on ILMs, particularly as they relate to dual and segmented theories (next section) of structured markets. There is considerable debate, however, as to what ILMs are, their origins historically, what factors influence their proliferation, decline or transformation, and how to distinguish different types in different settings (e.g. cross-cultural, regional, occupational, industrial or organizational). The rest of this section intends first, to clarify some of the definitional issues and second, to suggest some applications of ILM theory to the recent trends in rural labour-markets.

ILMs were first discussed by a group of 'neoinstitutional' labour economists in the US (among others, Reynolds, 1951; Kerr, 1954; Dunlop, 1957). Labour-markets are conceptualized as structured with internal and external aspects[1]. The internal aspects are defined by institutionalized rules, either formal or informal, and of two types: the *craft* markets, which represent job mobility across firms and the *industrial* markets, which represent mobility within the firm or establishment. According to Kerr (1954), unions are the most important institutions structuring labour-markets and influencing the market context. Seniority is the source of employment security for the industrial type ILM, whereas the accumulation of skills and the regulation of the supply of skilled workers is the source of worker security for the craft ILM. The procedures and substance of rules are historically determined matters, thus, institutional theory maintains an inductive orientation.

In the . recent past, ILMs have been given a more neoclassical interpretation. Based primarily on human capital theory and the distinction between general and specific job training, ILMs are explained as resulting from a maximizing logic that, for the most part, benefits both workers and employers (Doeringer and Piore, 1971; Williamson, Wachter and Harris, 1975). In order for the firm to reduce turnover in those jobs that require specific training (human asset specificity), it is economically rational for the firm to offer job security through job ladders and lifetime employment opportunities. What is emphasized in these analyses is the economic rationality of ILMs from the employer's point of view.

Edwards' (1979) account of the spread of ILMs is fundamentally consistent with this view, however, he emphasizes the need for control of the labour force rather than efficiency concerns. Still, ILMs are thought to be rational and in the employers' best interest because employee cooperation and employer discretion, required for the exploitation of labour, is being exchanged for worker job-security and internal mobility. Craft or occupational type ILMs and unions[2] generally are neglected in these more recent analyses, which partially explains why ILMs have come to be understood simply as labour-market internal to the firm. We wish to maintain a broader conceptual framework. Accordingly, ILMs are loosely defined here as relatively homogeneous groupings of workers, the boundaries of which are determined by barriers protecting insiders and excluding outsiders. These barriers take a variety of institutional forms, such as unions, certification and credentialing, personnel practices and discrimination.

Several typologies, all of which are variations on Kerr's original categories, have been proposed (Doeringer and Piore, 1971; Althauser and Kalleberg, 1981; Osterman, 1984). Kerr's emphasis is on unions, either of the craft or industrial types. Doeringer and Piore outline three variable aspects of the craft and industrial types: first, they can be open or closed with many or few ports of entry; second, they can have broad or narrow job clustering and opportunity for movement; and finally, they can emphasize job advancement by seniority, ability or a combination of the two. Althauser and Kalleberg distinguish ILMs (either occupational or industrial) by ongoing training; and Osterman, in addition to the craft and industrial types, adds a third type of ILM that has relevance for the analysis of rural labour-markets. He calls it the 'Secondary ILM'[3] referring to low-skilled, poorly-paid, short-ladder job groups, which may or may not have long tenure.

None of the typologies has been applied in a comprehensive way to the examination of structured labour-markets. An integrated institutional approach would include such factors as technology and skills (Doeringer and Piore, 1971; Berger and Piore, 1980), the needs and motivations of employers

(Edwards, 1979; Osterman, 1984; Williamson, Wachter and Harris, 1975), the organization of labour (Kerr, 1954; Rubery, 1978), the role of the state in the formation of relevant institutions (Loveridge and Mok, 1979; Loveridge, 1983), and an understanding of the historical context that threads these factors into a coherent institutional complex (Jacoby, 1984).

Doeringer (1984) conducted a study of two rural labour-market areas in Maine in order to assess the nature of ILMs in rural areas. The areas he selected are 99 per cent white, so his results are limited in their generalizability, particularly to Southern regions of the US. His main objective is to explain the trend of the 1970s for higher employment growth in non-metropolitan areas than metropolitan areas, as well as the conditions of rural employment more generally. In the two case studies Doeringer finds a predominance of jobs and outcomes that in some ways are characteristic of the 'unstructured' secondary labour-market. For example, they are low-wage and low-skilled jobs. Yet, in other ways these jobs have characteristics of ILMs in the primary sector in that tenure can be long, not because of job specific training or craft skills, but due to informal agreements between employers and employees.

According to Doeringer, it is not the work ethic of rural employees, and it is not the stick of unemployment and underemployment that explains the loyalty of workers. Rather, it is 'paternalism', informal agreements, quid pro quo exchanges of an assortment of uncodified benefits (relative job security being one of the most important) for loyalty, low wages, and flexibility in deciding employment levels. Referring to these practices as gift exchange, Doeringer makes the point that '[t]he employers' gift, however, is harder for the worker to replace than it is for the employer to find another loyal worker' (1984: 285). The power differential favours the employer so that rural ILMs are less secure, for example, than the craft or industrial types.[4] As a result of the prevalence of informal job arrangements and low-wage, low-skilled jobs in rural compared to urban areas, it has been relatively easy for industry to either relocate (possibly outside the US) when new locations become preferable or to cut back levels of employment. It is the permeability of the barriers that permit easier shifting of employment levels in rural areas. ILM theory does provide some explanatory power for recent changes in rural labour-markets. More extensive research is required, however, to confirm the relevance of the theory across the variety of rural locations in the US.

Dual and segmented labour-markets

Dual and segmented labour-market theories are the conceptual cousins of ILM theory as proposed by Kerr, but differ in at least two ways. First, these theories simplify the fragmentation issue. Dual Labour-Market (DLM) theory groups ILMs into a single primary sector, distinct from the secondary sector, which is the external, unstructured market (Doeringer and Piore, 1971). Segmented Labour-Market (SLM) theory identifies two or more segments in the primary sector, and the external labour-market becomes the 'residual' or secondary sector (Loveridge and Mok, 1979). Second, DLM and SLM theories, seek to understand the fragmentation process by analysis of the barriers to mobility across sectors. These are alternatives to neoclassical theory as explanations of wage differentials and mobility patterns.[5] The focus is on sex and race discrimination and the disproportionate location of women and racial and ethnic groups in the secondary or residual sector. They have made a contribution by their concern for the poor and disenfranchised groups in society and by their attention to the lack of institutional supports and power bases from which these groups can build their own protective structures or institutions (Gordon, 1972; Loveridge and Mok, 1981). Policy concerns have been central to the arguments. However, for the most part (Loveridge and Mok are exceptions), these theories have tended to neglect the importance of the organization of labour into unions or bargaining units and have therefore neglected the motivations and capabilities of labour in the barrier building process, including the perpetuation of discriminatory practices.

There have been many empirical studies attempting to prove the existence of duality or segmentation in the labour-market. Some have built upon the dual-economy dynamic described by Averitt (1968) and applied the core–periphery industry distinction to labour-force participants who work in these industries (Beck, Horan and Tolbert, 1978, 1980a, 1980b; Hodson, 1978; Oster, 1979; Tolbert, Horan and Beck, 1980; Tolbert, 1982). The logic is that core industries are more likely to be structured in their employment practices along lines suggested by the primary sector, with periphery industries more likely to maintain secondary-sector employment patterns. Others have used occupational distinctions comparing those occupations that generally involve either primary or secondary sector-type conditions of employment and then proceed by some method to test the different outcomes (usually wages) for employment in each of the sectors (Osterman, 1975; Rosenberg, 1978). More recently, Dickens and Lang (1985) sought to overcome selection bias and the *ad hoc* method of testing the theories with a method that does not decide *ex ante* which occupations or industries ought to be in which sector, acknowledging that each industry or occupation can contain both sectors. Their results confirm the theory, but have been questioned on the grounds that the model used is sensitive to specification whereas the factors influencing wage outcomes are far more complex than their model suggests. There have been comprehensive critiques of DLM and SLM research methods and their theoretical foundations (Cain, 1976; Zucker and Rosenstein, 1981; Taubman and Wachter, 1986). Without empirical support using quantitative modelling methods, the importance of dual, segmented and internal labour-market theories for the general field of labour economics is probably limited.

Doeringer finds DLM and SLM theories insufficient and inconclusive as explanations of labour-market conditions in rural areas. He states: 'Anecdotes from employment and training officials in rural areas . . . suggest that neither human capital models nor segmentation theories based upon sex, race, or industrial divisions in the labour market are applicable'

(1984: 272). There is ambiguity in characterizing many rural jobs as part of the secondary or residual sector. The dual and segmented distinctions emphasize technology and skills as the most important determinants for the lifetime employment patterns of workers, where there is a positive correlation between low-wage, low-skill and high turnover. Rural labour-markets do not fit this pattern.

The emerging informalization of labour-markets

To the contemporary reader, industrial homework may sound like an artefact of bygone days, an activity left behind in America's early industrial days with the Ford Model T. Even among the research of social scientists and labour statisticians, homework as an informal economic activity is quite invisible. It was assumed to have existed only in an 'earlier, harsher stage of capitalism, when nakedly greedy men exploited unorganized and defenseless workers' (Leidner, 1987). The Fair Labor Standards Act of 1938, which prohibited the most common forms of homework, was thought to have succeeded permanently in eradicating homework in the United States.

That does not seem to be the case. Starting in the 1970s, the popular press once again began exposing the resurgence of 'illegal sweatshops' and cottage industries in the older industry of garment-making, and in the newer clerical and electronics industries (Christiansen, 1985; Boris, 1986; Leidner, 1987). Today, as in earlier periods in the United States, homework is paid by the piece or unit of production, and is characterized by an absence of fringe benefits or job security. Homework is defined as income-generating activity done in the residence for an outside employer or an intermediary. Usually, urban centres are mentioned as the locations where industries employ most homeworkers (Lipsig–Munné, 1983; Sassen–Koob, 1986). More recently, however, some press attention has centred on 'farm-factories', the relocation of industries to depressed rural areas and the employment of rural families in farm-based assembly work.

This resurgence of homeworking is seen by some authors as part of a more inclusive process of increasing use of informalized labour that is not confined to the United States, but is an international development. Whereas Sassen–Koob (1986) has examined informal labour and homework in New York City, and Katz and Kemnitzer (1983) expose homework in the high-technology Silicon Valley, other researchers are investigating homework abroad. For example, Benería and Roldán (1987) document the use of homework in Mexico City, Portes and Benton (1984) in Latin America generally, Truelove (1987) in rural Colombia, and Fernandez–Kelly (1983) examines informal activity relative to the Border Industrialization Program situated on the US–Mexican border. Castells and Portes (1986) further the comparative perspective by focusing on informal activities in developed economies such as Italy and Spain, as well as within the United States. These examples, it is argued, indicate that the resurgence of homeworking and other informal activities are not the result of random cases of profit-seeking or vestiges of our pre-industrial era, but are a response to a more fundamental and global process.

The informal economy is defined as a dynamic process, rather than a concrete or static object, which is characterized by the following: 'it is unregulated by the institutions of society, in a legal and social environment in which similar activities are regulated' (Castells and Portes, 1986: 2). Whereas the product of this relationship is usually an item legitimately sold in the market, the terms of the relationship may not be, and usually involve lack of protection, underpayment, insecurity and dependence for the worker. Homework is one type of informal activity, as are sweatshops.

Protagonists argue that the resurgence of informal economic activity is a response to global restructuring initiated to overcome the structural crisis in capitalism occurring during the 1970s (Fernandez–Kelly, 1983; Portes and Benton, 1984; Castells and Portes, 1986; Sassen–Koob, 1986; Portes, Benton and Castells, 1989). There are several underlying causes for the increase in informalization on the international level, which apply to rural as well as urban informal activity. Most often mentioned is industry's reaction to growing working-class strength during the 1960s. Unions impede capital accumulation by organizing workers' demands for insurance, health and safety standards, and higher wage and benefit packages. Informalization is a way to decentralize and isolate the labour force in order to avoid the costs of unionization. In Italy, the strong and developed informal sector of the 1980s has come on the heels of strong labour organization gains in the 1960s. Fiat slowed down production in the 1970s, increasingly moved toward an informal labour force, and has resurfaced in a strong financial position in the 1980s (Castells and Portes, 1986).

Sassen–Koob (1986) links informalization with the growth of the service sector in the United States, which is an indicator of manufacturing downgrading. She notes that areas experiencing sharp declines in unionization are also experiencing rapid growth in high-technololgy and service industries. Union weakness opens the door to increasing informalization, as seen also in Miami, where use of union labour dropped from 90 per cent in 1960 to 10 per cent in 1980, and where informal contracting abounds.

A second aspect of global restructuring leading to increased informalization concerns employers' reactions against increased state regulation of the economy, especially in areas of labour legislation. Informalization becomes a means to reduce production costs involved in taxes, social insurance, and maintenance of health and safety standards, all of which are passed on to homeworkers: 'The rise of the welfare state promoted subsequent informalization, directly, by stimulating companies' efforts to escape its reach and, indirectly by weakening the resistance of the working class to new forms of labour organization' (Castells and Portes, 1986: 18).

The impact of international competition in all industries has resulted in competition to decrease labour costs, resulting in an increase in informal economic activity. Industrial capital is increasingly integrated internationally and thus the industries in developed countries find themselves searching for ways to compete with low-wage sectors of workers in newly industrializing as well as in re-industrializing countries.

Piore and Sabel (1984) argue that 'flexible specialization' is an important industrial strategy coming into increasing use as a means to reduce labour costs, increase capital productivity and thus sharpen international economic competition. Under this strategy, workers develop a variety of skills that allow them to adapt rapidly to constant innovation. A flexible, multi-skilled workforce enables a given industry to adjust to the frequent changes required by small-batch production without the expenditures of retraining and retooling. Furthermore, workers are seen as benefiting from this revised 'craft-oriented' organization, as the basis of their value to a firm will be the skills they accumulate. Piore and Sabel believe these shifts will result in greater worker autonomy and control over the work process.

Not all authors in this area share their enthusiasm (Greenwood, 1988). The benefits of increased skills and autonomy are seen as the harvest of a small proportion of white-collar workers. The workforce in general, however, will experience greater segmentation as a larger proportion of blue-collar workers will enter downgraded jobs in the secondary labour sector. Just as technology allows for greater skill accumulation for some workers, new technology allows jobs to be 'deskilled' by breaking down the labour process into basic components which are then dispersed among workers. These jobs require less skill than previously, and the production process gains both mobility and dispersion.

A fourth underlying cause of increased informal labour is contained in the process of industrial development in previously underdeveloped areas. These countries respond to international industrial competition by informalizing their labour force in order to attract investment.

Finally, Castells and Portes (1986: 20) cite informal labour as a response to increased harsh living conditions resulting from the economic crisis. People may choose informal types of labour both as a means of survival and because it represents more personalized working conditions: 'The informal economy is both the mirage of individual economic opportunity and the means for personalized survival out of the crisis'.

One other factor suggested by the neoclassical economic literature is the increasing availability of pools of immigrant labour that readily absorb informal labour. However, the available evidence refutes this position by noting that homework is performed for US electronic firms by white, Anglo-women in New York and California (Katz and Kemnitzer, 1983; Sassen-Koob, 1986), for Italian shoe and cycle firms by native non-immigrant women, and for Spanish garment and footwear industries by native Spanish women (Castells and Portes, 1986). In Latin America, most homework is performed by domestic migrants, often moving from rural to urban areas (Benería and Roldán, 1987).

Castells and Portes (1986) and Sassen-Koob (1986) note several economic effects of the trend toward informalization. They are: decentralization of the work force and of production, flexible production, delays in the trend toward full automation, decreased labour productivity, increased capital productivity, decreased labour costs and destabilization of the welfare state. Fernandez-Kelly (1983) also notes that informalization allows industry to diversify its economic and political risks, and that it brings married women in Latin America into the wage labour force. Lipsig–Munné (1983) points out that fragmentation of the labour force stimulates competition among homeworkers and between home and factory workers, weakens potential for unionization, contributes to the growth of contracting and subcontracting and undermines full-time factory jobs.

Two other general aspects of informal labour are important. First, the informal sector is not isolated or marginalized relative to the formal sector, but is an integrated and significant component. Italy's economic recovery has been credited, in large part, to the increasing use of informal labour in the last decade. Second, the informal sector tends to develop and flourish under the knowing tolerance – even active encouragement – of the state. In Latin America, 'governments tolerate or even stimulate informal economic activities as a way to resolve potential social conflicts or to promote political patronage' (Castells and Portes, 1986: 16). Meanwhile in Europe, the governments of developed industrial nations have come to depend on informalization as a means of reducing unemployment and stimulating economies out of recessionary periods. In some rural areas of the US local governments are actively pursuing companies that engage in homeworking and encourage their use of local labour as part of an overall economic development strategy (Gringeri, 1989).

That informal labour relations are 'at home' in rural areas should come as little surprise, given the trends discussed earlier. The greater prevalence of routine manufacturing jobs, and the documented growth in low-wage and low-skill work in rural areas suggest that the line between formal and informal activities in this context may indeed be quite fine. Higher rates of poverty in spite of the presence of an earner in the household, higher rates of unemployment and underemployment, and greater disparity between metropolitan and non-metropolitan household income all point to the potential for growth of informal activities. The depressed agricultural economy means greater numbers of people seeking work may be willing to accept low piece-rates, job insecurity and no benefits in exchange for a somewhat increased household cash flow.

Industrial homeworking is an indicator of industry's efforts to implement restructuring in response to the fiscal crises of the previous decade. Homework in the US is increasing precisely when unionization is diminishing, and, in the case of rural areas, is increasing precisely where unions have never been dominant. Industrial relocation thus avoids urban potential for unionization, and basks in rural areas almost outside of unions' reach. Especially when the final product is destined for the domestic market, industrial homework in local areas makes increasingly 'good sense' to industrial managers.

In this era of deregulation and fiscal conservatism, we can expect to see industrial homework developing under the tolerance of at least local governments, especially in rural areas. Informal work as a normative relation of production is illustrated not only in the Latin American context but also in the context of rural America: family farms have a long history of casual, cash-based economic activities, such as 'egg money', which set the foundation for the acceptance and entrance of informal labour-like homework. Thus, industrial homework in rural America is a relatively and practically unexplored piece of a larger, international mosaic.

The agricultural labour-market and the diversity of rural economies

The unvarnished truth is that neither labour economists nor sociologists have turned their attention to the task of explaining the rural labour-market trends outlined above; especially with reference to these theoretical perspectives. The exception is a relatively small body of literature dealing with the agricultural labour market that has been summarized recently by Leslie Whitener (1989). Historically, there have been studies of farm labour, the transition of workers from agricultural to non-agricultural pursuits and status attainment processes among rural youth. However, these studies were designed primarily to describe conditions apparent in earlier decades; principally those of rural America from the end of World War II until the mid-1970s. When attention was given to rural labour-markets, not just farm labour-markets, the focus of attention was on human resource development, employment and income, and employment and training problems (Marshall, 1971, 1974; Leonardson and Nelson, 1977; Rungeling *et al.*, 1977). Almost without exception this literature was dominated by the logic of neoclassical labour economics; human behaviour is rational and profit maximizing under varying constraints and is the product of interactions of *individual* decision-makers in competitive markets.

As we analyse above, the more recent accounts stress segmented labour-markets and reject the neoclassical assumptions of homogeneity and interchangeability of labour. Moreover, they argue that segmentation extends beyond two or three sectors and generates a multiplicity of smaller and more specialized labour-markets. Horan and Tolbert (1984) appear to have demonstrated that among 51 labour-market areas in the south-eastern US, it is reasonable to argue that market areas dominated by agriculture are measurably different from urban and other rural labour-market areas. Workers in agricultural labour-market areas encounter different market conditions and experience differences in labour-market outcomes, such as earnings, employment and family income, when compared to workers in non-agricultural labour-market areas.

Other researchers have pushed the heterogeneity argument further and suggest that the agricultural labour-market is a heterogeneous mix of work structures, relations and locations (Lancelle, 1981; Lyson, 1982; Friedland, 1984; Whitener, 1985). For example, Lyson argues that the agricultural labour-market can be disaggregated into three meaningful occupational families: production agriculture, agribusiness and agricultural education/research. His empirical analysis led him to conclude that the three differ in terms of socioeconomic composition, economic well-being, and in the earnings determination process itself. Friedland (1984) takes a more class analysis route and distinguishes between family farm labour and four groups of hired farm workers: managers and supervisors, permanent year-round employees, career farmworkers and casual farmworkers. He argues that each group operates under a different set of factors affecting labour supply, equity and costs and benefits and is joined in this belief by several other researchers who have identified segmentation in the hired farm labour-market. Lancelle (1981) concludes that the hired farm labour-market is segmented into primary and secondary jobs, and this parallels the work of Osterman (1988). Others have noted market differentiation by commodity, region, size of the farming enterprise, and type of farm activity (Emerson, Walker and Andrew, 1976; Glover, 1984; Martin *et al.*, 1985).

Although it is clear that contemporary studies of the agricultural labour-market are incorporating the concepts of the segmented labour-market theory, the research is largely descriptive at this point. It is too soon to tell whether studies will move beyond the descriptive stage and achieve an integration with the broader theory. Given the increasing size of farming enterprises and the expanding use of hired labour, it seems reasonable to expect further developments along the lines of segmentation studies. At the same time the recently enacted legislation regarding US immigration policy and the current financial conditions of US farms could have implications for the supply and demand of labour in agricultural labour-markets. In this regard the processes of informalization of labour seem particularly relevant although very little theoretically-related empirical research has been directed to this set of issues.

Such studies, focusing on the agricultural labour-markets, tend to ignore the restructuring of rural economies toward greater diversity. This has several important implications. As manufacturing and service industries become more significant elements in local economies, the conditions and organization of work associated with them come to play a greater role in shaping the conditions and performance of rural labour-markets and market areas. For example, rural areas with a greater reliance on manufacturing linked labour-markets are more open to the consequences of shifts in production technology. Similarly, rural labour-markets are more linked to national and international economies, which makes them more sensitive to macroeconomic policy, business cycles and global competition.

These shifts also signal the increasing relevance of broader labour-market theories of sociology and economics for understanding the conditions of rural labour-markets and rural labour-market areas. Rural areas and markets are no longer isolated from the mainstream processes of the economy, society or politics. Consequently, theories that treat work and labour-markets in rural areas as 'ghetto' phenomena are largely undermined and irrelevant.

Similarly, these shifts have dramatically altered the context for rural policy. Where once rural policy was closely aligned with agricultural policy, the options are now far more diverse and complex. Moreover, the diversity among rural areas of the US means that a single rural policy is unlikely to be equally adept in addressing the problems of all rural areas. Brown and Deavers (1988: 26) have summarized the situation quite cogently.

The diversity of rural economic conditions indicates diverse paths to economic viability. Some areas will consolidate their economic development efforts around current activities; others will seek to transform and diversify their economies from goods-producing to a broader representation of services; others will specialize in residential and consumer service activities. Some areas will be successful in maintaining or expanding their levels of economic activity. Others will experience decline. Recognizing that rural areas are increasingly interrelated with each other and with the Nation as a whole, go-it-alone, community-specific economic development efforts appear to be increasingly inappropriate in tomorrow's rural America.

Acknowledgments

The preparation of this manuscript was supported by the University of Wisconsin–Madison, College of Agricultural and Life Sciences, the Wisconsin Agricultural Experiment Station through Hatch Project No. 3219, Gene Summers, Principal Investigator and by the Graduate School of the University of Wisconsin–Madison. In addition, preparation was supported by a grant from the Woodrow Wilson Foundation Rural Policy Fellowship (Christina Gringeri, researcher). We wish to express our appreciation for the helpful comments on earlier drafts that we received from E. M. Beck, Leonard Bloomquist, Emery Castle, William Falk, Thomas Hirschl, Arne Kelleberg, Molly Killian, Thomas Lyson, Terry Marsden, Svend Otto Remoe, Peggy Ross, William Saupe, Ron E. Shaffer, Eldon Smith, C. Matthew Snipp and Charles Tolbert.

Notes

1. Lloyd Fisher's (1951) detailed analysis of the 'unstructured' agricultural labour market in California could be considered the first explication of the 'secondary sector' in much of the later Dual Labor Market literature. What is interesting to note is that he distinguishes the unstructured market by five conditions: (1) no unions, (2) impersonal relations between employer and employee, (3) unskilled work with no skill hierarchy, (4) pay by piece rates rather than by time, and (5) 'little or no capital machinery'. He identifies two main barriers to mobility into nonagricultural employment, discrimination by employers and restrictive practices (including race prejudice) by unions to limit their labour-market supply. He also relates the barriers to mobility to the wage differentials between the structured and 'unstructured' markets.
2. Edwards discusses unions as having an indirect influence on the development and spread of ILMs. According to this view, ILMs are a device to ward off unionization and labour unrest, and unions are not described as key negotiators of ILM rules.
3. Osterman's terminology is somewhat confusing because in the Dual Labor Market literature, the 'secondary sector' is outside and separate

156

from structured ILMs. The secondary sector in Dual and Segmented LM theories is conceptualized as the external competitive labour market distinct from internal market clusters. Osterman's 'Secondary ILMs' are less secure with less mobility than craft or industrial ILMs, but still they are job clusters with internal patterns of mobility.
4. Rural ILM arrangements, as described by Doeringer, are closer to Osterman's 'Secondary ILMs'.
5. Cain (1976) reviews the Dual, Segmented and Neoclassical approaches.

References

Alderfer, E. B. and Michl, H. E. (1942) *Economics of American Industry*, New York, McGraw-Hill.

Althauser, Robert P. and Kalleberg, Arne L. (1981) Firms, occupations, and the structure of labour markets: a conceptual analysis, in Berg, Ivar (ed) *Sociological Perspectives on Labour Markets*, New York, Academic Press.

Andrews, Richard B. (1954) Mechanics of the urban economic base: general problems of base identification, *Land Economics*, **20**, 164–72.

Averitt, Robert T. (1968) *The Dual Economy: the Dynamics of American Industry Structure*, New York, W. W. Norton.

Barkley, David L. (1988) The decentralization of high-technology manufacturing to nonmetropolitan areas, *Growth and Change*, **19**, No. 1, 13–30.

Beck, E. M., Horan, Patrick M. and Tolbert, Charles M. (1978) Stratification in a dual economy: a sectoral model of earnings determination, *American Sociological Review*, **43**, 704–20.

Beck, E. M., Horan, Patrick M. and Tolbert, Charles M. (1980a) Social stratification in industrial society: further evidence for a structural alternative, *American Sociological Review*, **48**, 712–19.

Beck, E. M., Horan, Patrick M. and Tolbert, Charles M. (1980b) Industrial segmentation and labour market discrimination, *Social Problems*, **28**, 113–30.

Becker, Gary S. (1971) *Human Capital: a Theoretical and Empirical Analysis with Special Reference to Education*, 2nd ed., New York, Columbia University Press.

Becker, Gary S. (1985) *Human Capital*, New York, National Bureau of Economic Research.

Benería, L. and Roldán, Martha (1987) *Crossroads of Gender, Race and Class: Industrial Homeworking in Mexico*.

Berger, S. and Piore, M. (1980) *Dualism and Discontinuity in Industrial Societies*, Cambridge University Press.

Bloomquist, Leonard E. (1988) Performance of the rural manufacturing sector, in Brown, David L. *et al.* (eds) *Rural economic development in the 1980s*, Rural Development Research Report No. 69, Washington, DC: USDA, Economic Research Service, pp. 49–75.

Bluestone, Barry and Harrison, Bennett (1982) *The Deindustrialization of America: Plant Closings, Community Abandonment, and the Dismantling of Basic Industry*, New York, Basic Books.

Bokemeier, Janet L. and Tickamyer, Ann R. (1985) Labour force experiences of nonmetropolitan women, *Rural Sociology*, **50**, No. 1, 51–73.

Boris, Eileen (1986) *'Right to work' as a 'Women's Right': the Debate Over the Vermont Knitters, 1980–1985*, Working Paper, University of Wisconsin, Institute for Legal Studies.

Brown, David L. and Deavers, Kenneth L. (1988) Rural change and the rural economic policy agenda for the 1980s, in Brown, David L. *et al.* (eds) *Rural Economic Development in the 1980s*, Rural Development Research Report No. 69, Washington, DC: USDA, Economic Research Service, pp. 1–28.

Brown, David L. and Warner, Mildred E. (1989) Persistent low income areas in the United States: some conceptual challenges, Paper presented to the National Rural Studies Committee in Stoneville, Mississippi, May, Ithaca, NY: Cornell University, Department of Rural Sociology.

Cain, Glen G. (1975) The challenge of dual and radical theories of the labour market to orthodox theory, *American Economic Review*, **66**, pp. 16–22.

Cain, Glen G. (1976) The challenge of segmented labour market theories to orthodox theory: a survey, *Journal of Economic Literature*, **14**, 1215–57.

Castle, Emery N. (1988) Policy options for rural development in a restructured rural economy: an international perspective, in Summers, Gene F. *et al.* (eds) *Agriculture and Beyond: Rural Development Policy*, University of Wisconsin, College of Agricultural and Life Sciences, pp. 11–27.

Castells, Manuel and Portes, Alejandro (1986) World underneath: the origins, dynamics, and effects of the informal economy, Paper presented at the Conference on Comparative Study of the Informal Sector, Harper's Ferry, West Virginia.

Christaller, Walter (1966) *Central Places in Southern Germany*, translated by Baskin, C. W., New Haven, Conn., Gustav Fischer.

Christiansen, Kathleen E. (1985) Women and home-based work, *Social Policy*, **15**, 54–7.

Commons, J. R. (1924) *Legal Foundations of Capitalism*, New York, Macmillan.

Cyert, R. M. and Mowery, D. C. (1987) *Technology and Employment: Innovation and Growth in the U.S. Economy*, Washington, DC, National Academy of Science Press.

Deavers, Kenneth L. (1988) Rural economic conditions and rural development policy for the 1980s and 1990s, in Summers, Gene F. *et al.* (eds) *Agriculture and Beyond: Rural Economic Development*, University of Wisconsin, College of Agricultural and Life Sciences, pp. 113–23.

Deavers, Kenneth L. and Brown, David L. (1984) A new agenda for rural policy in the 1980s, *Rural Development Perspectives*, **1**, No. 1, 38–41.

Deavers, Kenneth L., Hoppe, Robert A. and Ross, Peggy A. (1988) The rural poor: policy issues for the 1980s, in Nagel, Stuart (ed) *Rural Poverty Policies*, Garden City: Greenwood Press.

Dickens, William T. and Lang, Kevin (1985) A test of dual labour market theory, *American Economic Review*, **75**, 792–805.

Doeringer, Paul B. and Piore, Michael (1971) *Internal Labour Markets and Manpower Analysis*, Lexington, Mass., D. C. Heath.

Drabenstott, Mark and Henry, Mark (1988) Rural America in the 1990s, in Drabenstott, Mark and Gibson, Lynn (eds) *Rural America in Transition*, Federal Reserve Bank of Kansas City, pp. 39–58.

Drucker, Peter (1986) The changed world economy, *Foreign Affairs*, Mar.

Dunlop, John T. (1957) The task of contemporary wage theory, in Taylor, G. and Pierson, F. (eds) *New Concepts in Wage Determination*, New York, McGraw Hill.

Duncan, Marvin R. (1989) U.S. agriculture: hard realities and new opportunities, *Economic Review*, pp. 3–20.

Edwards, Richard (1979) *Contested Terrain*, New York, Basic Books.

Emerson, R. C., Walker, T. S. and Andrew, C. O, (1976) The Market for citrus harvesting labour, *Southern Journal of Agricultural Economics*, **8**, July, 149–54.

Falk, William W. and Lyson, Thomas A. (1988) *High Tech, Low Tech, No Tech: Recent Industrial and Occupational Change in the South*, State University of New York Press.

Farkas, George and England, Paula (eds) (1988) *Industries, Firms, and Jobs: Sociological and Economic Approaches*, New York, Plenum Press.

Fernandez–Kelly, Maria Patricia (1983) *For We Are Sold, I and My People: Women and Industry in Mexico's Frontier*, State University of New York Press.

Fisher, Lloyd (1951) The harvest labour market in California, *The Quarterly Journal of Economics*, **65**, Nov.

Friedland, W. H. (1984) The harvest labour market in California, in Busch, Lawrence and Lacy, William B. (eds) *Food Security in the United States*, Boulder, Co., Westview Press.

Fuguitt, Glenn V. (1985) The nonmetropolitan population turnaround, *Annual Review of Sociology*, **11**, 259–80.

Fuguitt, Glenn V., Brown, David L. and Beale, Calvin L. (1989) *Rural and Small Town America*, New York: Russell Sage Foundation, esp. chs 5 and 11.

Galston, William (1988) U.S. rural economic development in a competitive global economy, in Summers, Gene F. *et al.* (eds) *Agriculture and Beyond: Rural Economic Development*, University of Wisconsin, College of Agricultural and Life Sciences, pp. 1–9.

Garnick, Daniel H. (1984) Shifting balances in U.S. metropolitan and nonmetropolitan area growth, *International Regional Science Review*, **9**, No. 3, 257–73.

Glasmeier, Amy K. (1986) High tech industries and the regional division of labour, *Industrial Relations*, **25**, 197–211.

Glover, R. W. (1984) Unstructured labour markets and alternative labour market forms, in Emerson, Robert D. (ed) *Seasonal Agricultural Labour Markets in the United States*, Iowa State University Press.

Gordon, David M. (1972) *Theories of Poverty and Underemployment*, Lexington, Mass., D. C. Heath.

Goudy, Willis, Saenz, R., Burke, S. and Rogers, David (1986) Occupation segregation in selected Iowa communities: 1960–1980, Paper presented at the Annual Meeting of the Rural Sociological Society, Salt Lake City, Utah, Iowa State University, Department of Sociology.

Greenhut, Melvin L. (1956) *Plant Location in Theory and Practice*, University of North Carolina Press.

Greenwood, Robert (1988) The local state and economic development in peripheral regions, Dissertation Proposal, School of Industrial and Business Studies, University of Warwick.

Gringeri, Christina (1989) Industrial homework as a rural development strategy, Dissertation Proposal, Department of Social Welfare, University of Wisconsin.

Haney, Wava G. and Knowles, Jane B. (eds) (1988) *Women and Farming: Changing Roles, Changing Structures*, Boulder, Col., Westview Press.

Henry, Mark S. (1989) Some economic perspectives on rural labour markets, in Falk, William and Lyson, Thomas (eds) *Research in Rural Sociology and Development*, Vol. 4, Greenwich, Conn., JAI Press, pp. 29–54.

Hirschl, Thomas A. and Summers, Gene F. (1982) Cash transfers and the export base of small communities, *Rural Sociology*, **47**, 295–316, Summer.

Hodson, Randy (1978) Labour in the monopoly, competitive, and state sectors of production, *Politics and Society*, **8**, 429–80.

Horan, Patrick M. and Tolbert II, Charles M. (1984) *The Organization of Work in Rural and Urban Labour Markets*, Boulder, Col., Westview Press.

Jacoby, Sanford (1984) The development of internal labour markets in American manufacturing firms, in Osterman, Paul (ed) *Internal Labour Markets*, MIT Press, pp. 23–69.

Kalleberg, Arne L. and Berg, Ivar (1987) *Work and Industry: Structures, Markets, and Processes*, New York, Plenum Press.

Kelleberg, Arne L. and Berg, Ivar (1988) Work structures and markets: an analytic framework, in Farkas, George and England, Paula (eds) *Industries, Firms, and Jobs: Sociological and Economic Approaches*, New York, Plenum Press, pp. 3–17.

Katz, Naomi and Kemnitzer, David S. (1983) Fast forward: the internationalization of Silicon Valley, in Nash, June and Fernandez–Kelly, Patricia (eds) *Women, Men, and the International Division of Labour*, State University of New York Press.

Kerr, Clark (1954) The Balkanization of labour markets, in Bakke, E. Wright, Hauser, P. M., Palmer, G. L., Myers, C. A., Yoder, D. and Kerr, Clark (eds) *Labour Mobility and Economic Opportunity*, MIT Press, pp. 92–110 (reprinted in Kerr, Clark (1977) *Labour Markets and Wage Determination*, University of California Press.

Kerr, Clark (1983) The intellectual role of the neorealists in labour economics, *Industrial Relations*, **22**, No. 2, 298–318, Spring.

Killian, Molly Sizer and Hady, Thomas F. (1988) The economic performance of rural labour markets, pp. 181–200 in Brown, David L. *et al.* (eds) *Rural Economic Development in the 1980s*, Rural Development Research Report No. 69, Washington, DC, USDA, Economic Research Service.

Kreps, Juanita, Somers, Gerald G. and Perlman, Richard (1974) *Contemporary Labour Economics: Issues, Analysis and Policies*, Belmont, Calif., Wadsworth Publishing.

Lancelle, M. A. (1981) *The Labour Market Experiences of Hired Farm Labourers: Gender, Ethnicity, and the Influence of Human Capital*, Ph.D. Dissertation, Pennsylvania State University.

Leidner, Robin (1987) Home work: a study in the interaction of work and family organization, in Simpson, Ida Harper and Simpson, Richard L. (eds) *Research in the Sociology of Work*, Vol. 4, Greenwich, Conn., JAI Press.

Leonardson, G. and Nelson, D. (1977) *Rural Oriented Research and Development Projects: a Review and Synthesis*, Research and Development Monograph No. 50, Washington, DC, US Department of Labour.

Leven, Charles L. (1985) Regional development analysis and policy, *Journal of Regional Analysis*, **25**, No. 4, 569–92.

Lipsig-Munné, Carla, The renaissance of homeworking in developed economies, *Relationes Industrielles*, **38**, No. 3, 545–66.

Lloyd, Peter E. and Dicken, Peter (1977) *Location in Space: a Theoretical Approach to Economic Geography*, 2nd ed.. New York: Harper and Row.

Losch, August (1954) *The Economics of Location*, translated by Woglom, W. H., New Haven, Conn., Yale University Press.

Loveridge, Ray (1983) Sources of diversity in internal labour markets, *Sociology*, **17**, No. 1, Feb.

Loveridge, Ray and Mok, L. (1979) *Theories of Labour Market Segmentation*, London, Martinus Nijhoff Social Sciences Division.

Lyson, T. A. (1982) Notes on a sectoral model of the agricultural labour market, *Rural Sociology*, **47**(2), 317–32.

Malecki, Edward J. (1989) What about people in high technology?: Some research and policy considerations, *Growth and Change*, **20**, No. 1, 67–79.

Marshall, F. Ray (1971) Human resource development in rural areas, in *Human Resource Development in the Rural South*, University of Texas, Centre for the Study of Human Resources, Ch. 12.

Marshall, F. Ray (1974) *Rural Workers in Rural Labour Markets*, Salt Lake City, Ut., Olympus Publishing.

Martin, P., Vaupel, S., Amaya, W., Fish, C. and Amon, R. (1985) The fragmented California farm labour market, *California Agriculture* (Nov.–Dec.) 14–16.

Massey, Doreen (1975) Approaches to industrial location theory: a possible spatial framework, in Cripp, E. L. (ed) *Regional Science: New Concepts and Old Problems*, London, Pion, pp. 84–108.

McGranahan, David A. (1988) Rural workers in the national economy, in Brown, David L. *et al.* (eds) *Rural Economic Development in the 1980s*, Rural Development Research Report No. 69, Washington, DC, USDA, Economic Research Service, pp. 29–47.

McGranahan, David A., Hession, John C., Hines, Fred K. and Jordan, Max F. (1986) *Social and Economic Characteristics of the Population in Metro and Nonmetro Counties, 1970–80*, Rural Development Research Report No, 58, Washington, DC, USDA, Economic Research Service.

Meyer, D. R. (1977) Agglomeration economics and urban industrial growth: a clarification and review of concepts, *Regional Science Perspectives*, 7(1), 80–92.

Miller, James P. and Bluestone, Herman (1988) Prospects for service sector employment growth in nonmetro America, in Brown, David L. *et al.* (eds) *Rural Economic Development in the 1980s*, Rural Development Research Report No. 69, Washington, DC, USDA, Economic Research Service, pp. 135–57.

Moses, Leon N. (1958) Location and theory of production, *Quarterly Journal of Economics*, 72, 259–72.

Moriarty, Barry M. (1980) *Industrial Location and Community Development*, Chapel Hill, NC, University of North Carolina Press.

North, David J. (1974) The process of location change in different manufacturing organizations, in Hamilton, F. E. I. (ed) *Spatial Perspectives on Industrial Organization and Decision Making*, New York, John Wiley, pp. 213–44.

North, Douglass C. (1955) Location theory and regional economic growth, *Journal of Political Economy*, 63, 243–58.

Norton, R. D. and Rees, J. (1979) The product cycle and the spatial decentralization of American manufacturing, *Regional Studies*, 13, 141–51.

Noyelle, Thierry J. (1983) The rise of advance services: some implications for economic development, *Journal of the American Planning Association*, 49, No. 3, 281–90.

Oster, Gerry (1979) A factor analalytic test of the theory of the dual economy, *Review of Economics and Statistics*, 61, 33–51.

Osterman, Paul (1984) White-collar internal labour markets in American manufacturing firms, in Osterman, Paul (ed) *Internal Labour Markets*, MIT Press, pp. 163–89.

Osterman, Paul (1975) An empirical study of labour market segmentation, *Industrial and Labour Relations Review*, 28, 508–23.

Osterman, Paul (1988) *Employment Futures: Reorganization, Dislocation, and Public Policy*, New York, Oxford University Press.

Parker, Tim (1989) Nonmetro employment: annual averages, 1988, Press Release, 27 Feb. 1989, Washington, DC, USDA, Economic Research Service.

Piore, Michael J. and Sabel, Charles F. (1984) *The Second Industrial Divide*, New York, Basic Books.

Portes, Alejandro and Benton, Lauren (1984) Industrial development and labour absorption: a reinterpretation, *Population and Development Review*, 10, No. 4.

Portes, Alejandro, Benton, Lauren and Castells, Manuel (eds) (1989) *The Informal Economy: Studies in Advanced and Less Developed Countries*, Baltimore, Johns Hopkins University Press.

Portes, Alejandro and Sassen-Koob, Saskia (1987) Making it underground: comparative material on the informal sector in Western market economies, *American Journal of Sociology*, 93, No. 1, 30–61.

162

Pred, Alan R. (1967) *Behavior and Location: Foundations for Geographic and Dynamic Location Theory*, Lund Studies in Geography, Part 1, Uppsala, Sweden, Lund University.

Reynolds, Lloyd (1951) *The Structure of Labour Markets*, New Haven, Conn., Yale University Press.

Richter, Kary (1985) Nonmetropolitan growth in the late 1970s: the end of the turnaround?, *Demography*, **21**, No. 4, 245–63.

Rosenberg, Sam (1978) The determinants of occupational standiang in the contextd of the dual labour markets hypothesis, Research Paper No. 15, Department of Economics, Williams College, Williamsontown, Mass., 01267, RP-15, Aug.

Rosenfeld, Rachel A. (1985) *Farm Women: Work, Farm, and Family in the United States*, Chapel Hill, NC, University of North Carolina Press.

Ross, Peggy J. and Rosenfeld, Stuart A. (1988) Human resource policies and economic development, pp. 333–357 in Brown, David L. *et al.* (eds) *Rural Economic Development in the 1980s*, Rural Development Research Report No. 69, Washington, DC, USDA, Economic Research Service.

Rubery, Jill (1978) Structured labour markets, worker organization and low pay, *Cambridge Journal of Economics*, **2**, Mar.

Rungeling, B., Smith, L. H., Briggs Jr., V. W. and Adams, J. (1977) *Employment, Income and Welfare in the Rural South*, New York, Praeger.

Sassen-Koob, Saskia (1986) The dynamics of growth in post-industrial New York City, Paper presented at the Workshop on the Dual City, New York City.

Schultz, T. W. (1951) The declining importance of agricultural land, *Economic Journal* Dec., 725–40.

Shaffer, Ron (1989) *Community Economics: Economic Structure and Change in Smaller Communities*, Iowa State University Press.

Shepard, Eric S. (1980) The ideology of spatial choice, *Papers of the Regional Science Association*, **45**, 197–213.

Smith, David (1966) *Industrial Location: an Economic Geographical Analysis*, New York, John Wiley.

Smith, David (1971) *Industrial Location*, New York: John Wiley.

Smith, Eldon D., Hackbart, Merlin M. and va Veen, Johannes (1981) A modified regression base multiplier model, *Growth and Change*, **12**, 17–22.

Smith, Stephen M. (1984) Export orientation of nonmanufacturing businesses in nonmetropolitan communities, *American Journal of Agricultural Economics*, **66**, No. 2, 145–55.

Smith, Stephen M. and Pulver, Glen C. (1981) Nonmanufacturing business as a growth alternative in nonmetropolitan areas, *Journal of the Community Development Society*, **12**, No. 1, 33–47.

Snipp, C. Matthew (1989) *American Indians: the First of This Land*, New York, Russell Sage Foundation.

Summers, Gene F. (ed) (1984) Deindustrialization: restructuring the economy, *The Annals of the American Academy of Political and Social Science*, Vol. 475, Beverley Hills, Calif., Sage Publications.

Summers, Gene F., Bryden, John, Deavers, Kenneth, Newby, Howard and Sechler, Susan (eds) (1988) *Agriculture and Beyond: Rural Economic Development*, University of Wisconsin, College of Agricultural and Life Sciences.

Summers, Gene F., Evans, Sharon D., Clemente, Frank, Beck, E. M. and Minkoff, Jon (1976) *Industrial Invasion of Nonmetropolitan America: a Quarter Century of Experience*, New York, Praeger.

Summers, Gene F. and Hirschl, Thomas A. (1985) Retirees as a growth industry, *Rural Development Perspectives*, 1, No. 1, 13–16.

Swanson, Linda L. and Butler, Margaret A. (1988) Human resource base of rural economies, in Brown, David L. *et al.* (eds) *Rural Economic Development in the 1980s*, Rural Development Research Report No. 69, Washington, DC: USDA, Economic Research Service, pp. 159–79.

Taubman, Paul and Wachter, Michael L. (1986) Segmented labour markets, in Ashenfelter, Orley and Layard, Richard (eds) *Handbook of Labour Economics*, Elsevier Science Publishers, BV.

Thompson, Wilbur R. (1965) *A Preface to Urban Economics*, Baltimore, Johns Hopkins University Press.

Thompson, Wilbur R. (1973) The economic base of urban problems, in Chamberlain, N. W. (ed) *Contemporary Economic Issues*, Homewood, Ill., Richard D. Irwin, pp. 1–48.

Tickamyer, Ann R. and Bokemeier, Janet L. (1988) Sex differences in labour-market experiences, *Rural Sociology*, 53, No. 2, 166–89.

Tickamyer, Ann R. and Bokemeier, Janet L. (1989) Individual and structural explanations of nonmetropolitan women and men's labour force experiences, in Falk, William and Lyson, Thomas A. (eds) *Research in Rural Sociology and Development*, Vol. 4, Greenwich, Conn., JAI Press, pp. 153–70.

Tiebout, Charles M. (1956) Exports and regional economic growth, *Journal of Political Economy*, 64, 160–9.

Tolbert, Charles M. (1982) Industrial segmentation of men's career mobility, *American Sociological Review*, 47, 457–77.

Tolbert, Charles M., Horan, Patrick and Beck, E. M. (1980) The structure of economic segmentation: a dual economy approach, *American Journal of Sociology*, 85, 1095–116.

Tolbert, Charles M. and Killian, Molly Sizer (1987) *Labour Market Areas for the United States*, Staff Report No. AGES870721, Washington, DC, US Department of Agriculture, Economic Research Service.

Tornquist, Gunnar (1977) The geography of economic activities: some viewpoints on theory and application, *Economic Geography*, 53, Apr., 153–62.

Truelove, Cynthia (1981) The informal sector revisited: the case of the Talleres Rurales Mini-Maquilas in Colombia, in Tardanico, Richard (ed) *Crises in the Caribbean Basin*, Beverley Hills, Calif., Sage, pp. 95–110.

US Department of Commerce, Bureau of the Census (1989) *Money Income of Households, Families, and Persons in the United States: 1987*, Current Population Reports, Series P-60, No. 162, Washington, DC, US Government Printing Office.

164

US Department of Commerce, Bureau of the Census (1973–88) *Current Population Survey*, Washington, DC, US Government Printing Office.

US Department aof Commerce, Bureau of the Census (1980) *1980 Census of the Population and Housing*, Washington, DC, US Government Printing Office.

Weber, Bruce A., Castle, Emery N. and Shriver, Ann L. (1988) Performance of natural resource industries, in Brown, David L. *et al.* (eds) *Rural Economic Development in the 1980s*, Rural Development Research Report No. 69, Washington, DC, USDA, Economic Research Service, pp. 103–33.

Whitener, Leslie A. (1989) The agricultural labour market: a conceptual perspective, pp. 5–79 in Falk, William and Lyson, Thomas A. (eds) *Research in Rural Sociology and Development*, Vol. 4, Greenwich, Conn., JAI Press, pp. 55–79.

Whitener, Leslie A. (1985) Migrant farmworkers: differences in attachment to farmwork, *Rural Sociology*, **50**(2), 163–80.

Williamson, O. W., Wachter, M. and Harris, J. E. (1975) Understanding the employment relation: the analysis of idiosyncratic exchange, *Bell Journal of Economics*, **6**, 250–80.

Zucker, Lynne G. and Rosenstein, Carolyn (1981) Taxonomies of institutional structure: dual economy reconsidered, *American Sociological Review*, Vol. 46, 869–84.

CHAPTER 6

Class and Change in Rural Britain

Paul Cloke and Nigel Thrift

On rural change and class: the way we were?

An understanding of social stratification in rural communities has been impeded by a neglect of class-based analyses. Work on rural social change has remained largely descriptive, and few attempts have been made to link it to the evolution of property and labour relations or to the wider processes of economic restructuring (Cloke and Little, 1989). This aversion to notions of class reflects rural ideology which traditionally presents the countryside as an essentially classless society even if an unequal and hierarchical one. Although refuting this position we do not advocate instead the concept of a specifically *rural* class structure. Rurality *per se*, we would maintain, possesses no explanatory power (Cloke, 1987). What we seek is a fuller understanding of economic restructuring and social recomposition in all types of localities, including those officially or popularly recognized as rural.

The basis of this critique of the traditional wisdoms of rural social change lies in an over-standardization in previous studies of 'newcomers' and 'locals'. In some of the research of the 1960s and 1970s, and in the repro-duction of that research in the textbooks of the 1980s, there has emerged a rather stylized impression that rural change can be summarized as a class of newcomers being superimposed on a class of indigenous residents, with resulting inter-class conflict. Such a view exerts a draconian holism on those social groups moving in and those locals just waiting there to do battle with them. It suggests that class conflict in rural localities is largely inter-class (presumably middle-class 'newcomers' against working-class 'locals') rather than intra-class, and carries over the expectation that the growing middle-class presence will act as a cohesive unit rather than as a series of fractions (Cloke and Thrift, 1987). It further suggests that the polarization between local 'class' and newcomer 'class' has been dominant in the social and cultural changes occurring in rural communities.

165

The discussion by Phillips and Williams (1984: 94) on social polarization in rural settlements raises a number of important conceptual questions about the muddle that arises from an over-simplified intermixing of class and length of residence criteria:

> Although polarization may include an element of newcomers-versus-locals, it is based essentially on social class, with the division occurring between the working class and the middle class. The former group is largely made up of locals while the latter mainly comprises newcomers, but the class dimension is paramount. These groups have different accessibility levels and are subject to different life-style constraints. . . . Since the working class is most affected by these constraints, it is more likely that a characteristically working class will develop than a distinctly middle class. The latter will be more likely to develop activity patterns typical of the middle class nationally.

The basis of our assertion of the need for new insights into the relationship between class and change can be teased out from this conceptual muddle. We agree that class divisions should be seen as paramount. The notion of 'middle class' in the rural context should not be seen as interchangeable with that of 'newcomer'. Recent work on the middle class suggests that there exists a series of complex intra-class divisions that tend to cut across traditional occupational class divides. It therefore seems extremely unlikely that just one distinctive middle-class group will have evolved in rural areas. Instead we should expect to encounter different fractions of middle-class presence, and if these fractions bring with them characteristic behaviour patterns then they are likely to have a powerful influence on culture, society and community in rural localities.

What has been lacking previously is an understanding of the impact that different middle-class fractions have in all aspects of rural life. *Intra-class* conflict has become a factor of major importance in the study of contemporary rural social change. In the remainder of this chapter, we further explore the current debates over the links between class, consciousness, and economic, political and cultural activity; examine the notions of differential class fractions; offer an example of intra-class conflict in rural areas relating to service classes; and finally offer a short agenda of outstanding research issues to achieve a more mature understanding of class relations and rural social change.

On the importance of class

Reviews of recent sociological literature on class clearly indicate something of a demolition job on traditional class analysis. The links between class structure, attitudes and behaviour, conventionally regarded as reflexive, have proved to be far more complex. The assumption of causal relationships between class, social consciousness and political action now provokes heated debate, suggesting that rural studies would benefit from more sophisticated class analyses. Without in any way wishing to become enmeshed in the detailed complexity of these issues (see Rose, 1988, for a clear synopsis) it is necessary, all the same, to broach a few of the salient questions currently besetting the analysis of class so that rural researchers can benefit from the experience of, what Pahl and Wallace (1988: 129) have called, 'these effective exercises in demolition and constructive criticism'.

Perhaps the first fundamental question to be answered is whether class matters any more. According to Hobsbawm (1981) and Lukes (1984) among others, Britain's society exhibits new divisions that represent a breakdown of class-based stratification. Technological change, state intervention in economic markets, the shift to service industries from manufacturing and increasing participation of women in the labour force have all served to blur the distinction between non-manual and manual labour. Indeed, it is argued by some that such a distinction has become almost irrelevant. Moreover, new sectional divisions have sprung up that seem to cross-cut class boundaries. People formerly from different parts of the class system appear to have accepted the inevitability of a dominant moral code ordered by an acquisitive society. Many have become ensconced in a mood of 'informed fatalism' and are content merely to pursue private satisfaction and, where necessary, involve themselves in conflicting sectional demands. As Michael Mann was suggesting as early as 1970, social cohesion is reliant on pragmatic role acceptance, which in turn is structured through education, the media and other apparatus of socialization employed by the state.

Given these apparent new social alignments and societal trajectories towards self-interest and sectionalism, is class now an irrelevant framework for the study of social change? Our answer would be a firm no, on two principal grounds. First, there has been important new empirical evidence on social class in modern Britain produced by Marshall *et al*. (1988), which clearly suggests that class remains of paramount value. Naturally any large-scale survey based on highly structured interviews (as this was) is open to the cynical suggestion the researchers find what they set out to find. It is apparent, however, that the Essex research team were aware of this potential criticism, and did all that was possible to ensure the integrity of their findings. The conclusions of this empirical study are clear:

> ... our data suggest that, in so far as the identities, beliefs and values investigated in this study are socially structured, then the source of this structuring lies in social class differences rather than more fashionable sectoral cleavages. (p. 184)

> The 'demise of social class' is a thesis not well supported by the evidence from the British survey of class structure and class consciousness. Sectionalism associated with possible sectoral cleavages is relatively unimportant when set alongside class phenomena, in particular the persistence of class identities, and the unequal class mobility chances associated with unchanging 'socal fluidity' over the past half century or so. (p. 225)

The second reason for advocating the importance of class in studies of rural social change relates to the *dynamism* of class and class analysis. Following the reasoning of Pahl (1984) and Pàhl and Wallace (1985, 1988) it should be stressed that the notion of class has been used in two distinct contexts. The first is *theoretical*, in which the concept is dynamic and historical and relates to divisions of labour that can be technical, sectoral and social. Whether Marxian or Weberian in origin, the theoretical treatment of class has continued to stress divisions of labour and the capital–labour relationship. The second context is *descriptive*, and here class is used as a static device relating to the statistical classification of occupational categories and often generating labels for different parts of an hierarchical social system.

It is in the tension between dynamic theory and static description that much of the recent debate on the apparent obsolescence of class has got bogged down. The use of static descriptive devices as the basis for the generation of dynamic theoretical models of class struggle will inevitably be problematic. Therefore, although conventional, static *descriptions* of working classes, middle classes and upper classes, of their corporate consciousness and identities, may be found wanting in the changing conditions of contemporary restructuring and recomposition, theoretical models of class struggle, class colonization and class power retain their value because of their essential dynamism and abstraction.

In order to substantiate this claim, we must discuss briefly how recent forms of economic restructuring have had impacts in the social order. These changes, resulting from radical and large-scale reorganizations of capital and labour, have particular significance for some rural localities, as we discuss later in this chapter. Capital has sought out more profitable technologies and sectors of operation, the ownership of capital has become more complex, and the control of investment and the organization of work practices have become stricter with the revisions to the legal arrangements between capital and labour and the resultant changes in the expectations of parts of the workforce with regard to their conditions of work. These changing facets of capital relations have led to widespread reorganization of labour, with shifts between employment sectors (for example, a decline in manufacturing and a growth of public sector and service employment in Britain), a reduction in job security, a rise in part-time employment, and the growth of informal employment. Conditions of labour have become sectorally uneven and diverse, and a widening gulf has emerged between those with no jobs or low job security, and those who are part of a secure company or occupational career structure.

Given these dynamic economic conditions, the existing static descriptions of class divisions have been strained to breaking point. As Crompton and Jones (1984) have stressed, the disappearance of traditional industries and therefore of 'traditional' workers has led some class analysts into a frantic search for replacement categories for the working class – proletarianized white-collar workers, low-paid women in service sector jobs, tenants of local authority housing and so on. But these new categories do not perform as the traditional ones did. If economic origins dictate class consciousness, and therefore class interests, these 'new' working classes might have been expected to align themselves politically with the labour movement against the ascendancy of the 'New Right' in the 1980s. Such alignments, and other expected regroupings of 'interests', have failed to materialize, so class analysts have sought to provide alternative attributes of social consciousness as part of their dynamic theoretical model of class. As Pahl and Wallace (1988: 129) succinctly suggest: 'The conventional model of structure–consciousness–action is a highly problematic notion: it needs to be carefully unpacked and each part scrutinized'.

Exploring class fractions

Of particular relevance to the contemporary study of rural social change are a number of new divisions that have been recognized as being important, besides the occupation of the male member of the household, as significant determinants of the ˙make-up of class and class consciousness. These divisions include: race; religion; gender; life-cycle factors; state sector dependency; consumption and production sector cleavages; and geographical distribution.

Thus employees of the new industries located in the booming towns of the south and south-east seem likely to differ, both in social consciousness and resultant action, from workers in declining manufacturing industries, for example in parts of northern Britain or South Wales. Equally, young black inner-city residents will probably display different attributes of consciousness and action from similarly unemployed rural workers, the like of whom in previous times have depended upon agriculture, forestry and other traditional employment in areas such as mid-Wales, the rural north of England or rural Scotland. Although such illustrations so easily fall prey to stereotyping, the underlying message is clear: people whose earnings, and relations with capital production are similar will *not* necessarily share a corporate consciousness, interest or inclination for action.

There is insufficient scope in this chapter to give full analysis to each of these, though several are illustrated in the section on the service class in rural Britain. However, it is clear that these and other factors can be recognized in the contemporary social divisions in rural localities. *Race*, for example, may immediately conjure up the stereotype of black, unemployed and inner city, but it, or at least ethnicity, is equally important as a sociocultural cleavage in localities such as those in rural Wales, where the in-migration in English groups, often affluent although sometimes not, is popularly perceived as usurping the customary opportunities for indigenous Welsh people in production and consumption relations. Similarly, *religious affiliation* can be important, although this may be less so in terms of the traditional pew-fillers of establishment religion than for those with genuine life-shaping conviction and faith (Cloke, 1988). Thus the type of community consciousness and action exhibited, for example, the Mennonite and Amish settler communities in North America is being reproduced to an extent in some rural communities where more contemporary religious movements have occurred. Examples of this phenomenon are offered by Richardson's (1988) account of the impact of ten rural churches on the local communities in which they are placed. Again, religious affiliation may be interlinked with racial and cultural factors, and will combine with other organizational interests over certain issues. Thus, recent debates over abortion and Sunday trading cannot be solely ascribed to 'new right' morality and trade union self-interest respectively. In both cases, a social trajectory relating to religious belief was an important element in the conflicting consciousness on display.

The influence of *gender* is felt not only through the increasing degree of workforce participation by women, but also via the life-cycle, and growing familism and domesticity (Little 1986, 1987). Although rates of female participation in employment have traditionally been lower in rural areas than elsewhere, many of the new manufacturing and service sector jobs in rural areas have been geared to female labour. Any such participation by women whether 'newcomer' of 'local' is likely to affect social consciousness both within households and within communities. Indeed the generally greater incidence of one-parent (more often a woman and children) households, will itself represent a changing balance of gender relations in many communities, leading to new cleavages in social consciousness.

There is fairly common agreement that the characterization of social relationships has also been influenced by the incidence of increasingly home-centric and family-centric life-styles. This idea of *cultural privatization* (Newby *et al.*, 1984) has been used to suggest that the private or home domain is as crucial an arena of the formation of social identity as is the public arena of the workplace, the organization or the community. Privatized lifestyles reflect not only the greater diffuseness of capitalism but also the expanding sphere of civil society and the development of a consumer society. Gorz (1982) has suggested that changes in non-work life may contribute to disillusionment with class politics and a further retreat into the world of the home where a greater perceived sense of control over circumstances can be maintained. Cultural privatization is particularly important in those rural areas that perform a dormitory function. Home-centric lifestyles will often denote the infusion of influence from beyond the locality and the further disruption and reduction of any traditional community-based consciousness, as has so frequently been ascribed to village life.

Given the importance ascribed to the home domain, familism and domesticity – although clearly present historically – may be assuming a new significance. *Familism* relates to the care and responsibility for children and their socialization within or by the family. It will vary considerably according to the employment regimes of parents; the broad cultural and specifically educational expectations, parental ambition, socialized norms and peer group pressure; the degree to which the daily care and education of children is subcontracted, for example to child minders or private schools; and so on. As rural areas, such as those in so many parts of south-east England, become colonized by different social fractions, they can be interpreted in some ways as a showcase for familistic trophies. This can lead to significant contrasts between these dominant groups and others (who may be relatively recent in-migrants rather than established local residents). This theme is taken up below in our discussion of service class colonization of some rural areas. The idea of *domesticity* suggests that a set of values arise from home-based relations. Genuflexion to Victorian family values has been widely described as a 'new right' or Thatcherite phenomenon. However, social historians such as Daunton (1983) have shown that domesticity has long been an important element of working-class life and should not, therefore, be viewed as a product of modern conservatism or consumerism:

> The working class turned away from dependence in their experience of work, towards a search for purpose in the life of the family and home, which came to be seen as a source of assertive dignity. The outcome might be a conservative retreat from wider issues, but it might also be a mechanism to assert independence and identity within a setting of sub-ordination. (p. 266)

Domesticity might thus be argued to represent an enduring set of values, although the nature of these values is dynamic and structured by the creation of a new social consciousness in the arena of *consumption*, for those who can afford to respond. As Pahl and Wallace (1988) suggest:

> ... it is a general part of capitalist marketing strategy to change the pattern or arrangement of objects ... so that each generation at different levels in the social structure to some extent defines itself by the way it comes to terms with this distinctive style of consumerism. (p. 142)

We will argue below that some groups will demand, rather than merely come to terms with, some forms of consumption by way of rural housing styles, interior decorations and furnishings, recreational activities, etc.

The nature of domesticity is also dynamic according to changing gender relations. Any stereotype of domesticity and familism, of a male bread-winner and dependent wife and two children, is quite inaccurate. Pahl (1984) found that it represented only 5 per cent of households on the Isle of Sheppey, whereas some 40 per cent of households had at least two earners. Social consciousness arising from domesticity represents a dynamic inter-linking of work and life-cycle experience. Research by Hakim (1979) and Dex (1985) suggests specific gender-linked attitudes to work and home, and that the varied commitment to employment by women does change the outlook of their partners. Contemporary reallocations between market and domestic labour seem likely to engender shifts in social consciousness towards the enduring arena of domesticity, which itself is being reinforced by the ability of multi-income families to buy in consumer items that have particular con-temporary status as social trophies.

In seeking to assess the structure–consciousness–action model, we should also appreciate that class action will be only partly a function of the determinants of social consiousness that we have mentioned here. Marshall *et al.* (1988), among others, strongly suggest that social consciousness will also depend on the attributes of the *organizations* that represent class interests. Interesting evidence to support this assertion comes from Elliot, McCrone and Bechhofer (1988) in their discussion of the role of associations representing small businesses. In charting the rise of a new bureaucratized, professionalized middle-class in the 1960s and 1970s, when 'degrees, certificates and technical qualifications' were the passport to influence, they also reveal the profound antipathy expressed by small business organizations to this new middle-class intelligentsia. The new right political agendum to reduce the power of this class was 'heavily endorsed' by entrepreneurs, and received active sponsorship from their organizations.

Thus, for researchers of rural social change, the geography of production, consumption and social consciousness must also embrace the organizational expression of class interests. In the last part of this chapter we explore the hows and whys of social reproduction in rural areas using the illustration of service-class colonization of particular rural locales in the south of England. It should be stressed, however, that this is but one example of the uneven social and economic change in rural localities. Here, the growth of financial and commercial capital in London, its satellite centres and radial motorway corridors, along with the outward migration of urban industrial capital have been associated with widespread recomposition in rural society. Not only are commuter and dormitory functions increasingly being imposed on rural localities at ever greater distances from London, but also economic changes have led to the growth of a new service class that has colonized particular rural locations.

Social recomposition in these rural localities has important implications for the underclasses, the agricultural sector and the environment. Some farmers, for example, have had the opportunity to cash in on the accumulated value of their land, either by selling for housing development or by diversifying their production to cater for the consumption requirements of the new classes or rural resident. Farming people in these places often play the contemporary role of *scenechangers* who create the ambience of the countryside for the benefit of the middle-class residents and urban visitors. At the same time, the booming house prices, aided and abetted by planning protection, are squeezing poorer residents out of local housing markets, and residual disadvantaged groups are being increasingly troubled by politics of service rationalization and privatization.

Elsewhere, in more peripheral rural localities, for example, there is equally important evidence of restructuring and recomposition. Many non-metropolitan areas now have dynamic labour markets, with the decentralization of manufacturing activity and the investment in services by both private and public sector organizations. Resultant job opportunities have been partly responsible for counter-urbanization in some peripheral areas. Also important in this respect, however, are responses to wider implications of restructuring such as early retirements, redundancy and the various forms of alternative lifestyle movements that are significant in many areas of remoter rural Britain (Cloke, 1985). Agriculture in these areas is also adapting to change, either through pluriactivity or by diversification of enterprise (particularly into tourism). Such diversification, however, is uneven due to the way in which wealth is distributed via agricultural support policies, and the variations in capital investment in other sectors in the rural localities concerned.

Thus different rural areas have attracted and responded to varying elements of the uneven nature of contemporary capitalist development. They have become favoured habitats both for adventitious and colonizing social groups seeking cultural privatization and domesticity within a valued rural environment. Also for many of the non-working class who are reliant on the state sector for their livelihood and who are seeking favoured alternative life-styles offered in some remoter rural areas, they represent the locus for many organizations of conventional political representation, as well as those pursuing contemporary modes of protest and sectional interests. In these and other cases, the traditional wisdoms of rural social change are insufficient analytical tools to match the needs of complex and dynamic class concepts.

The discussion and interpretation of rural change in class terms has been characterized by conceptual conflicts over the fundamental mechanisms that underlie class relations. In the broadly Weberian mould, researchers such as Newby *et al.* (1978) and Urry (1984) have argued that the organization of property relations is fundamental both to the definition of class and to the implementation of class-based analyses in rural society. An alternative, more structuralist view (see, for example, Barlow (1984) among others), criticizes this overriding focus on property relations and ownership. The changing spatial divisions of labour should be acknowledged as a powerful underlying force in the restructuring of property relations in rural localities.

Existing class-based analysis of rural social change has reflected these different viewpoints. The classic work by Newby (1977) outlined the apparatus used by farmers and landowners to ensure their hegemony over agrarian labour. This has been followed by further analysis relating property relations within capitalist agriculture to political power in local authorities and to wider strands of environmentalism within rural planning. Even the in-migration of new middle-class commuters did not disturb the dominance of property relations as the major element of class relations. Summarizing his work in East Anglia, Newby *et al.* (1978: 212) notes that:

> It was therefore possible to follow a chain of events which led from the continual reorganisation of property relations in agriculture ... through to changes in social recomposition in rural areas and on into an analysis of emergent social conflicts in the countryside, of which issues relating to environmental conservation, employment growth and housing may be regarded as emblematic.

Over the last decade, however, the size and structure of rural populations, and the local anatomy of political power and social control have undergone rapid transformation in many rural localities. Members of particular class fractions, already partially formed by capital–labour relations have captured and exploited many of the organizational and bureaucratic skills generated by increasingly complex divisions of labour. The fractions have thus been able to appropriate the means of consumption and create demand according to their own distinctive lifestyle.

We have argued elsewhere (Cloke and Thrift, 1987) that these new social relations require a new analysis of class relations that takes account of the complex conflicts and compromises that both shape and are shaped by the social circumstances of particular localities. Furthermore the growth of the middle classes has incorporated considerable internal diversity, and so intra-class conflict has become increasingly important. To illustrate the implications of these changes, we use the example of service-class colonization of some rural localities in Britain.

On the service class in rural Britain

As was noted above, recent writing on the middle class in rural areas has often lacked sufficient awareness of the multiplicity of different class fractions. However, this failing can be excused, to an extent, by a similar lack of differentiation found in the literature on the middle class. One contemporary attempt to overcome this problem has been the revival of the notion of a 'service class' of professional and managerial workers, in an attempt by authors like Urry to give the idea of an upper middle class some theoretical justification. For Urry and others, the service class is constructed via the relations of production (especially the class's function as non-productive wage labour, its bureaucratic advantages at work and its favourable position in the labour market); by its monopoly of the market in credentials, and by its ability (via its disposable income and taste) to influence the relations of consumption (Abercrombie and Urry, 1983; Lash and Urry, 1987; Thrift, 1987a). Clearly, the service class has to be separated out from other parts of the middle class, such as the 'clerical', white-collar middle class. Just as clearly, this is not always easy to do. (Certain occupations, such as teachers and others in the intermediate statistical group, are extremely hard to allocate satisfactorily.) Through the 1970s and 1980s the service class has been growing rapidly in Britain (Thrift, 1987b; Savage, Dickens and Fielding, 1988; Savage and Fielding, 1989). Between 1971 and 1981, the class expanded (as a workforce) by 17.76 per cent through a combination of the expansion of industrial sectors in which the class is chiefly represented (such as financial services) with a general move within the British economy towards employing more highly skilled workers.

At the same time, the economic situation of different parts of the service class has changed, and this is one of a number of obvious fault lines within it. The numbers of the service class based in the private sector have increased rapidly in the 1980s. This private sector fraction of the service class is paid more and has gradually gained more political, social and cultural influence than its public sector counterpart, especially via an individualist ideology and the 'disestablishment' of many of the old centres of influence in British society and their replacement by new ones formed around business (Lloyd, 1988). Concurrently, the service class based in the public sector has found itself losing influence as its numbers have slowly declined and as its collectivist ideology, and the state institutions to which this ideology relates, have both become less serviceable.

Another fault line is based on gender relations. The number of women in service-class occupations has increased rapidly in recent years (Crompton and Sanderson, 1986; Crompton, 1987) and this has led to a change in the class's nature. The service class now has more single-person households, more households made up of childless professional couples, and fewer households made up of a non-working wife and children than the national average. In line with the shift towards greater numbers of well-educated women occupying key posts in the labour force, members of the class cleave less strongly to stereotyping masculine values, to a traditional mode of familism or to a particular idea of domesticity than was the case. The restructuring of gender relations within the class has therefore led to the class becoming much more diverse insofar as the arrangements of 'reproductive work' are concerned. In turn, the high levels of choice of its members allow them to offset some of the problems of this restructuring of domestic work onto other classes (by hiring nannies, childminders, etc.) as well as allowing them to purchase more labour-saving and ready-to-consume goods.

A third fault line is created by position in the life cycle. The service class is currently a relatively young class. Large numbers of people were recruited into it in the 1980s as occupations in which it is based expanded more rapidly than did others. Thus, there are large numbers of younger people in the class, often with considerable disposable income and a degree of leisure time. This has led to a greater emphasis on the formation of particular 'lifestyles' because these people, less constrained by domestic arrangements, exercise very considerable choice over what patterns of living they adopt outside work.

A fourth fault line splits along different kinds of consumption practice. The service class is also keenly involved in using consumption of commodities as a way of interpreting and legitimizing its existence. Consumer goods are a vital part of the service class's self-production; an important way to communicate within the class and a vital means of converting economic capital into cultural capital (Bourdieu, 1984). Commodities that have particular value (economically and culturally) are those that are scarce (for example, houses with views), those that are old (for example, old houses) and those that can be associated with or are a part of activities that restrict the number of participants (because of cash or rules of entry), require considerable knowledge (and investment of time) to master and have a social cachet (for example, certain kinds of sport) (Hirsch, 1977).

Finally, there is a fault line based on place. The service class is concentrated into certain localities that provide appropriate sorts of jobs and housing. Clearly, within 'rural' Britain, many parts of the south of England already furnish appropriate service-class habitats. Other 'rural' locations that have appropriate economic structures nearby, which possess the right kinds of housing stock and are able to transmit the right cultural signals (such as particular kinds of countryside) are more and more able to attract members of the service class (see the chapters on Swindon and Cheltenham and their environs in Cooke, 1989). However, as has been shown, the service class is not a homogeneous entity. Certain locations will attract certain kinds of members of the service class. Other kinds of locality will attract other kinds of members. Thus, the gentrified inner city is more likely to be the preserve of younger, less well-off service-class people living in single-person households; the Solent seaside town, full of yachts and marinas, is more likely to be the preserve of wealthy service-class members nearing retirement, and so on.

These five fault lines – public/private sector, gender, life cycle, consumption practices and type of locality – provide the basis for many different service class fractions. Hence: 'What is being produced is not a single group . . . with homogeneous cultural practices and ways of using space, but several different, perhaps even divergent fractions' (Rose, 1989: 120). Conflict in rural areas can clearly erupt around these different class fractions in various interrelated ways, of which a number stand out. The first point of conflict is around an area's economic base. A shift of the kinds of job available in a locality – for example, from the public to the private sector – may produce conflict expressed through general campaigns to save local services, preserve local government, led by the local public-sector service class, and the efforts of the private-sector service class to extend its influence on local representation bodies of various kinds (management committees, training organizations, etc.).

A second point of conflict between service-class fractions concerns household composition. As this changes, so conflict can break out concerning the kind of amenities to be made available for new kinds of household, from local services through to types of housing. For example, developers may try to cater for new service-class household types wanting particular kinds of specialist housing (for example, apartments). Such developments may be blocked as inappropriate to the character of an area by coalitions of interests, often themselves having service-class involvement.

A third point of conflict is the life cycle. For example, a rural area may have filled up with older service-class members who then resist incursions by younger service-class members in the shape of opposition to development of housing estates and offices. Alternatively, conflict may be deferred by 'life-cycle leapfrog'. As younger service-class members are prevented from living in certain desirable service-class areas by house prices they may instead 'pioneer' another rural area previously relatively untouched by the service class, so founding a new service class area (Thrift, 1987b). This has happened, for example, in parts of Avon where rural areas once considered to be working class (because of coal-mining antecedents) have been invaded by younger service-class members who cannot afford the house prices of the Bristol and Bath conurbation.

A final conflict revolves around taste (Bourdieu, 1984). 'Taste' can be defined as the exercise of a specific cultural competence, learnt through general processes of family upbringing and education and reinforced or extended by producers of cultural value such as advertisers and designers. The exercise of this cultural competence requires the correct choice of commodities that display their owner's economic and cultural worth. Houses are a particular case in point. They are commodities with many facets – type of location, style, view, and so on – all of which can be chosen in order to elevate or depress the owner's cultural worth. The exercise of cultural competence also requires a more general commitment to particular types of locality in which to live and that need to be preserved or changed in certains ways so that they can reciprocate that commitment. This commitment is based on particular images of the countryside drawn from norms and conventions that have sedimented over the centuries and that are now reproduced daily in advertisements, and publications. Such choices are often deeply felt and transgressions against them are often sources of outrage (Thrift, 1989).

Tournaments of cultural value are a regular feature of life in rural areas. Opposing fractions of the service class draw on particular conceptions and images of the countryside to demonstrate both their own worth and the worth of their ideas on the countryside. These tournaments can erupt into quite vicious conflicts. Dry ski slopes provide an example here since they involve certain members of the service class who are willing to forego countryside in order to increase one kind of cultural capital, against other members of the service class who want to retain the store of cultural capital (to be found in the existing countryside). Of course, such tournaments and conflicts often have strong economic underpinnings. However, they cannot be reduced simply to the economic. For example, proposals for new housing are not fought out just because they may affect local service-class house prices, but also because they offend against particular images of what the countryside is. That is what can give these conflicts such intensity.

It is clear that there are numerous opportunities for conflict between service-class fractions and interests and that these conflicts can determine in which direction particular areas proceed, economically, socially and culturally.

Conclusions

Quite clearly, there is a pressing need to examine how different class fractions, and the clash between them, structures local rural change. That will require the adoption of five main strands of class-oriented research, each of them related to the other. First, more attention needs to be given to the identification of different class fractions and how these relate to broader conceptions of class (such as the service class, see Marshall *et al.*, 1988). What are the main axes of differentiation? Second, more attention needs to be given to the relative strengths of the internal organization of particular class fractions. How well organized are particular class fractions? What are the institutions through which they work? What social networks do they invade? To what extent is length of residence and important factor? Is there any connection between particular areas? Third, more attention needs to be given to the nature of conflicts and compromises between class fractions. Which conflicts are most common? Which class fractions are most likely to oppose each other in these conflicts? Which fractions are most likely to join in conflicts of interest with each other? In which kinds of rural area might we expect to find certain types of conflicts and compromise? Fourth, more attention needs to be given to how different class fractions may articulate with *other* classes and interest groups in rural areas (landed capital, petty bourgeoisie, farmers, developers) in pursuit of their interests. Such alliances can be expected to vary with the history of a locality and the particular issue. Finally, more attention needs to be paid to the aggregate effects of particular conflicts in changing the general class character of an area. Which trajectories of class development follow from the outcomes of particular conflicts?

What seems certain is that the importance and complexity of class needs to be recognized as well as its diversity of impacts. This need not be a surprising conclusion. This same point has been made many times before. For example, for Victorian Britain, Thompson (1988: 173–9) has described the great diversity of supposedly homogeneous middle-class neighbourhoods. It is a description that is just as relevant today:

> The homogeneity of these neighbourhoods ... was not the homogeneity of a single social class; it was the physical and cultural expression of the layer upon layer of subclasses, keenly aware of their subtle grades of distinction, which constituted the middle class. The range of ... these layers stretched all the way from the bare competence of the clerks, small shopkeepers and school teachers of the lower middle class ... up to key wealthy families. ... In between lay groups and social sets finely tuned to a sense of their own standing and their identity, which stemmed from occupational, income, educational, religious, and locational factors stirred in varying proportions, even if such groups have rarely been singled out and given distinct labels ...

This fractionated diversity is clearly not random or promiscuous and, as a result, it is open to study by researchers. There are three signs that such an enquiry in rural areas need not end in frustration. First, class fractions are structured, often highly, by the forces of the economy, state and civil society. The varying degree of structure renders an investigation plausible. Second, class fractions are often carefully calculated both by their members and by their non-members. People do not innocently or unconsciously fill class fractions. They often make a commitment to them that is born out of calculation and a conscious agreement to play by the rules of the game, even if this agreement sometimes masquerades as ironic detachment. Third, the urban based literature offers antecedents. For example, much of the literature on urban gentrification has become more concerned with identifying differing gentrifiers who will have different kinds of urban impacts (Mills, 1988; Rose, 1989).

It is no doubt the case that class will remain a difficult area of research, labouring under the weight of a tradition of work whose results are often obtuse or contradictory and also under the additional burden of the many problems of empirical operationalization. But we would claim that class is still an essential concept in understanding contemporary rural Britain, especially if the many fractions that go to make up class are recognized and accommodated into our analyses of rural change.

References

Abercrombie, N. and Urry, J. (1983) *Capital, Labour and the Middle Classes*, Allen and Unwin, London.

Ambrose, P. (1974) *The Quiet Revolution*, Chatto & Windus, London.

Barlow, J. (1984) Landowners, property ownership and the rural locality, *International Journal of Urban and Regional Research*, **10**, 309–29.

Bourdieu, P. (1984) *Distinction: a Social Critique of the Judgement of Taste*, Harvard University Press, Cambridge, Mass.

Cloke, P. (1985) Counterurbanisation: a rural perspective, *Geography*, **70**, 13–23.

Cloke, P. (1987) Rurality and change: some cautionary notes, *Journal of Rural Studies*, **3**, 71–6.

Cloke, P. (1988) Community development and political leadership in rural Britain, Paper presented to the Franco-British Association for Rural Studies conference on *Rural Diversification*, Paris, 1988.

Cloke, P. and Little, J. (1989) *The Rural State?*, Oxford University Press.

Cloke, P. and Thrift, N. (1987) Intra-class conflict in rural areas, *Journal of Rural Studies*, **3**, 321–33.

Cooke, P. (ed.) (1989) *Localities*, Unwin Hyman, London.

Crompton, R. (1987) Gender status and professionalism, *Sociology*, **21**, 413–28.

Crompton, R. and Jones, G. (1984) *White Collar Proletariat*, Macmillan, London.

Crompton, R. and Sanderson, K. (1986) Credentials and careers: some implications of the increase in professional qualifications amongst women, *Sociology*, **20**, 25–42.

Daunton, M. (1983) *House and Home in the Victorian City*, Edward Arnold, London.

Dex, S. (1985) *The Sexual Division of Work*, Wheatsheaf, Brighton.

Elliott, B., McCrone D. and Bechhofer, F. (1988) Anxieties and ambitions: the petit bourgeoisie and the New Right in Britain. In D. Rose, (ed.), *Social Stratification and Economic Change*, Hutchinson, London.

Gorz, A. (1982) *Farewell to the Working Class*, Pluto Press, London.

Hakim, C. (1979) *Occupational Segregation*, Department of Employment, Research Paper No. 9, London.

Hirsch, F. (1977) *The Social Limits to Growth*, Routledge & Kegan Paul, London.

Hobsbawm, E. (1981) The forward march of Labour halted? In M. Jacques and F. Mulhern (eds), *The Forward March of Labour Halted?*, New Left Books, London.

Lash, S. and Urry, J. (1987)*The End of Organised Capitalism*, Polity Press, Cambridge.

Little, J. (1986) Feminist perspectives in rural geography: an introduction, *Journal of Rural Studies*, **2**, 1–8.

Little, J. (1987) Gender relations in rural areas: the importance of women's domestic role, *Journal of Rural Studies*, **3**, 335–42.

180

Lloyd, J. (1988) The crumbling of the establishment; Preaching in the market place; Serving Thatcher's children, *Financial Times*, 16 July 6; 18 July 25; 20 July 20.

Lukes, S. (1984) The future of British Socialism? In B. Pimlott (ed.), *Fabian Essays in Socialist Thought*, Heinemann, London.

Mann, M. (1970) The social cohesion of liberal democracy, *American Sociological Review*, **35**, 423–38.

Marshall, G., Newby, H., Rose, D. and Vogler C. (1988) *Social Class in Modern Britain*, Hutchinson, London.

Mills, C.A. (1988) Life on the upslope: the post-modern landscape of gentrification, *Environment and Planning D: Society and Space*, **6**, 169–90.

Newby, H. (1977) *The Deferential Worker*, Allen Lane, London.

Newby, H., Bell, C., Rose, D. and Saunders, P. (1978) *Property, Paternalism and Power*, Hutchinson, London.

Newby, H. *et al.* (eds) (1984) *Restructuring Capital*, Macmillan, London.

Pahl, R. (1965) *Urbs in Rure*, Geographical Paper No. 2, London School of Economics.

Pahl, R. (1984) *Divisions of Labour*, Basil Blackwell, Oxford.

Pahl, R. and Wallace, C. (1985) Household work strategies in an economic recession. In N. Redclift and E. Mingione., *Beyond Employment*, Basil Blackwell, Oxford.

Pahl, R. and Wallace, C. (1988) Neither angels in marble nor rebels in red: privatization and working-class consciousness. In D. Rose (ed.), *Social Stratification and Economic Change*, Hutchinson, London.

Phillips, D. and Williams, A. (1984) *Rural Britain: a Social Geography*, Basil Blackwell, Oxford.

Radford, E. (1970) *The New Villagers*, Frank Cass, London.

Richardson, J. (ed.) (1988) *Ten Rural Churches*, Kingsway, Eastbourne.

Rose, D. (ed.) (1988) *Social Stratification and Economic Change*, Hutchinson, London.

Rose, D. (1989) A feminist perspective of employment, restructuring and gentrification: the case of Montreal. In J. Wolch and M. Dear (eds), *The Power of Geography*, Unwin Hyman, London, pp. 118–38.

Savage, M., Dickens, P. and Fielding, A. (1988) The social and political implications of the contemporary fragmentation of the service class in Britain, *International Journal of Urban and Regional Research*, **12**, 455–75.

Savage, M. and Fielding, A. (1989) Class formation and regional development: the service class in South East England, *Geoforum*, **20**, 203–18.

Thompson, F.M.L. (1988) *The Rise of Respectable Society: a Social History of Victorian Britain 1830–1900*, Fontana, London.

Thorns, D. (1968) The changing system of social stratification, *Sociologia Ruralis*, **8**, 161–77.

Thrift, N.J. (1987a) Manufacturing rural geography, *Journal of Rural Studies*, **3**, 77–81.

Thrift, N.J. (1987b) The geography of late twentieth century class formation. In N.J. Thrift and P. Williams (eds), *Class and Space: The Making of Urban Society*, Routledge & Kegan Paul, London, pp. 207–53.

Thrift, N.J. (1989) Images of social change. In C. Hamnett, L. McDowell and P. Sarre (eds), *The Changing Social Structure*, Sage, London.

Urry, J. (1984) Capitalist restructuring, recomposition and the regions. In T. Bradley and P. Lowe (eds), *Locality and Rurality*, GeoBooks, Norwich.

CHAPTER 7

Household, Consumption and Livelihood: Ideologies and Issues in Rural Research

Nanneke Redclift and Sarah Whatmore

Introduction

The erosion of agriculture as the determining feature of the economic and social relations of rural areas in Britain, as in many other advanced industrial countries, has precipitated a major shift in the concepts and concerns shaping research on these regions. Attention has focused on two dimensions of the pattern and process of rural change; first, the diversification of the economic and land-use role of rural areas within the wider restructuring of spatial divisions of capital and labour and, second, the multiplicity of strategies by which people resident in rural areas make a living. This process of rethinking categories and redefining agendas has been strongly influenced by the rise of Marxist analysis in rural sociology in the 1970s (Newby, 1980). Marxist work led first, and foremost, to the construction of a distinct sociology of agriculture unbounded by a specifically 'rural' focus (Buttel and Newby, 1980; Bradley, 1981). More recently, it has sought to redraw the wider rural canvas by challenging traditional property-based analyses of rural class structure with a labour-based approach, in the shape of the re-structuring thesis (see introduction to this volume; Urry, 1984; Barlow, 1986). Whereas such approaches have offered more convincing accounts of rural change than those that preceded them, they focus almost exclusively on the institutions and relations of capitalist production – agricultural or otherwise. A more elusive, but nonetheless important, thread that underlies these dominant themes is the recognition of the neglected significance of consumption, or more broadly, the processes of reproduction. It is here that the household is re-emerging as a key focus of analysis, representing the nexus of the livelihood practices and experiences of individuals, and changes in the wider relations of consumption and production structuring rural localities.

Two principle concerns within this largely Marxist-defined agenda can be identified as having given rise to the re-emergence of the household as an appropriate unit of analysis in British rural studies.

(1) Agricultural political economy and the persistence of domestic commodity forms of production in farming. Here attention is focused on household-based production at a time when non-corporate forms of economic activity are of growing significance in the wider economy with the rise of 'self-employment' and homeworking. Moreover, questions are raised about how such forms of production are reproduced and the significance of the social relations of kinship and the domestic group for their survival.

(2) Rural restructuring and class recomposition in the wake of population trends associated with counterurbanization. Here attention is focused on the growth of income and welfare disparities between households in rural areas with unequal access to the means of consumption during a period when state involvement in the provision of consumption services and goods has been systematically eroded by a government committed to the ideology of the free market.

Superficially these issues are unhappily reminiscent of the much criticized and effectively outmoded community studies tradition, characterized by a structural functionalist theory of the domestic group (Bouquet and de Haan, 1987) and local community (Stacey, 1969; Harper, 1989). However, their return to the research agenda is marked by a number of radical shifts in theoretical approach to the analysis of both localities and households as well as towards a qualitatively new understanding of their interdependence. Most importantly, the household itself has become an object of increasingly critical theoretical analysis, informed by a heightened awareness of the unevenness of people's experiences *within* the household, as much as between households. This more critical approach has, above all, been influenced by theoretical insights contributed by feminist scholarship, which has put gender firmly and irrevocably on the map in such key areas as family sociology (Harris, 1983) and development Studies (Young, Wolkowitz and McCullagh, 1981). However, with few exceptions, the diffusion of these ideas and concerns into rural studies lags some way behind their influence in other research arenas. Perhaps most interestingly, the negligible impact and fringe status of feminist-inspired analysis in rural research and policy agendas in many advanced industrial countries is in stark contrast to the extent of their impact and legitimacy on parallel agendas in developing countries.

In this chapter we trace some of the disparate ways in which concerns with households, consumption and livelihood have re-emerged as key issues in the analysis of rural restructuring. We draw predominantly on recent British literature but seek to stress the importance of research in the field of development studies for contemporary debates on the British rural scene, and for parallel debates in other advanced industrial countries. Three related themes are identified and examined in turn. These are, class recomposition, deprivation and household production. Each of these themes reflects the reciprocal influence of observed changes taking place at an empirical level and redefined concepts of what is analytically relevant. However, drawing on the very different research context of the rural south, we go on to argue that much research on these themes remains wedded to uncontested and mutually reinforcing ideologies of rurality and domesticity. In conclusion, we outline some pointers for future research concerning the complex and contradictory relationship between the material changes taking place in rural areas; the concepts that have come to inform their analysis; and the development of policy discourse.

Rediscovering the rural household

Economic restructuring and class recomposition

The 'restructuring thesis' has its roots in Marxist economic geography and industrial sociology and stresses the importance of local differences in the experience of industrial change within late capitalism. The idea of restructuring centres on the process of capital accumulation and the competitive transformation of the structure of industrial production through the adoption of new technologies and labour practices and its consequences for the spatial division of capital and labour (Massey, 1984; Newby et al., 1985). The way in which this process operates will be highly uneven because, it is argued, it is shaped by the geography of successive historical divisions of capital and labour and the peculiar social and economic features of particular localities. Most importantly, the restructuring process has heightened the sociopolitical salience of *local* systems of social stratification in contemporary capitalist societies. In consequence, despite the heavily urban bias of studies in this tradition, it has served to re-establish a more coherent sociological conception of the 'rural' as a particular structuring of local civil societies. Rural localities have been characterized as combining a specific historical legacy of an agriculturally dominated land-use and land-ownership pattern with low levels of public service provision, or collective consumption (Urry, 1984; see also Newby, 1985).

Cruder interpretations of this thesis suggest that local political, social and cultural change can be read off from the process of economic restructuring and the imposition of new spatial divisions of labour. The first impetus to devote attention to the household grew specifically from a dissatisfaction with this kind of analysis of local class politics and identity. It became clear that many contemporary forms of political action and conflict were being left unexplained and that the experience and representation of class membership could only be understood by exploring the processes of class reproduction, and thus the public and private institutions and social relations that shape them. From this perspective the significance of family and kinship systems, and hosuehold labour and resource practices embedded in local and community cultures, gained recognition (Pahl, 1985, see Cloke and Thrift, chapter 6).

Urry expressed this 'discovery' very clearly in stating that 'the analysis of the formal economy cannot provide an adequate understanding of the likely patterns of contemporary politics, and this is because such an analysis neglects an absolutely crucial dimension, namely, the characteristic social relations and social practices within and between households' (1985: 23). It is these relations and practices between households that are subsumed within his use of the term 'civil society' (1981).[1] A second focus of the restructuring literature (and still a subordinate one) has thus developed, centred on the impact of economic change on the processes of consumption and reproduction in the guise of 'civil society', a somewhat residual category of activities 'outside' the institutions of capitalist production. In particular, attention has focused on the erosion of state involvement, during a period of retrenchment in public welfare spending, in the provision of basic consumption goods and services and the privatization of these processes. This, it is suggested, promotes the diversification of household livelihood practices involving a far more flexible and varied combination of waged work, state welfare provision, self-provisioning and entrepreneurship using the collective resources of household and kinship networks.

As Pahl and Wallace found the privatization of consumption has had very varied social consequences; 'richer people may be spending more time in the domestic environment with their electronic gadgetry but poorer people may be privatized for opposite reasons. They cannot afford to buy services from the formal economy should they wish to do so' (1985: 195). Moreover, its effects are also spatially differentiated with the restructuring of service provision reflecting the particular combination of class relations, local state practices and gender relations in any given locality (Bowlby, Foord and McDowell, 1986). These arguments have surfaced in rural research in some of the more theoretically informed studies of the consequences of observed trends in the movement of people (Weekley, 1988; Kiernan, 1989) and manufacturing and service industries (Thrift, 1987) from cities to rural areas in the 1970s.

Rural deprivation

Whereas the complex processes underlying these trends have had highly differentiated impacts on rural localities, two aspects of the consequent restructuring of the social composition of rural regions have become particular concerns in the research literature – the *gentrification* and *geriatrification* of the rural population. Associated with changes in the household structure of rural communities have been studies concerned with the growing inequalities in 'household' resources and income-generating capacity particularly between elderly and unwaged, or low-waged, households and are more affluent, dual-income households (Bouquet, 1987). Thus, while initiated by demographic trends, the focus of concern has been with their consequences for social structure and conflict in rural localities associated with the analysis of rural deprivation (Shaw, 1979; Lowe, Bradley and Wright, 1987).

A particularly far-reaching study of these issues is provided by Bradley (1987), in many senses epitomizing the empirical concerns and welfare approach of the contemporary deprivation literature. Table 7.1 shows the results of his analysis of five contrasting rural localities in terms of changes in rural household structures and associated livelihood practices. These results emphasize the variability of the relationship between kinship and household in rural areas, with the nuclear family more dominant in lowland commuter belt areas (themselves expanding) and extended households and single person households more common in remoter rural areas. This research is important for a number of reasons. First, it demonstrates clearly that the close-knit kinship ties traditionally associated with rural areas are more important as a component of English ideologies of rurality – ideologies that inform both policy and research discourses (see below) – than as a con-

Table 7.1 Household structure in relation to kinship: Great Britain 1961 and 1979; survey by Bradley·(1981) (percentage of all households)

Household type	1961	1979	1981 E	D	SF	SP	N
					(*rural localities*)		
Filial kin-based all[1]	57	47	52	40	61	49	40
Parents & child/ren	37	32	38	25	38	31	21
Lone parent & child/ren	2.5	2.5	1	2	—	—	1
Parent & adult child/ren	10	8	9	4	14	13	10
Lone parent & adult child/ren	4.5	3.5	3	3	3	1	42
Extended families[2]	3	1	1	6	6	4	4
Non-family-based all[3]	17	26	16	27	12	21	30
Conjugal[4]	26	27					
pre-retirement			23	18	14	17	15
elderly			8	15	13	13	15

Notes: [1] Households based around blood relatives usually involving more than one generation; i.e. parent–child relations, but also sibling household.
     [2] Households incorporating blood relatives beyond the elementary kin-group.
     [3] Includes single persons and households comprised of more than one unrelated person.
     [4] Married couples without dependent children.

E = Essex; D = Yorkshire Dales, SF = Suffolk, SP = Shropshire; N = Northumberland.

Source: Adapted from Bradley (1987) after Harris (1983), using OPCS social trends data and the Bradley's own survey of five rural localities.

temporary feature of rural life. One in three households in village England in fact consists of two or fewer people, rising to an even higher proportion in the more isolated Northern rural localities. Second, it re-establishes the household as an important arena in defining close relations and class identity in rural society (see Cloke and Thrift, 1987 and in chapter 6 of this volume). Such themes have also been tackled through the extension of the restructuring thesis by examining the specificity of the class composition of rural localities, and in efforts to establish the gendered structure of the 'rural community' in terms of the physical and symbolic divisions of men's and women's space (Davidoff, Esperence and Newby, 1976; Middleton, 1987). These micro, cultural studies have succeeded in moving away from the functionalism of earlier ideas of community and towards an appreciation of the often conflictual process through which personal and local identities are constructed (Strathern, 1984; Cohen, 1986). However, they are susceptible to the criticism that the interrelations between different types of work, or economic activity, and local class and gender identities, are premised on a set of assumptions that place production and reproduction, work and home, men and women in analytically, and functionally, separate 'spheres' (Little, 1988). Such assumptions are confounded by the experience of family farming in Britain (Whatmore, 1990) and the rural household production systems characterizing many countries of the south (Redclift, 1985).

Households as enterprises

Interest in the organization of kinship and household associated with early analyses of the rural community and, more particularly the family farm, have re-emerged as key issues in contemporary analyses of the role of 'the family' in capitalist agriculture (Bouquet, 1982; Marsden, 1984; Gasson *et al.*, 1988). This re-emergence has been strongly coloured by the prism of Marxist political economy and its concern with simple commodity production (Winter, 1984; Scott, 1986). Family farming, based on 'family' ownership of the means of production and family labour, has attracted interest as a 'challenge to theory' in both Marxist and mainstream traditions. Firstly, it does not conform to the dominant pattern of corporate capitalism in terms of the separation of capital and labour and of home and work. Secondly, family enterprises have persisted despite corporate capital's domination of the wider economy. Nor is the significance of these arguments restricted to the specifics of agriculture. The contradictory class position of the petit bourgeoisie in modern capitalism has been a sustained interest in mainstream (Bechhoffer and Elliott, 1981) and Marxist (Bernstein, 1986) British sociology. Indeed, it has recently been argued that family farming as a form of petty production represents a model for the development of non-wage livelihood strategies in the wider economy associated with the rise of 'self-employment' and 'self-provisioning' (Benvenuti, 1985).[2] Right-wing political ideologies of the 'entrepreneur' and the 'small business' as pro-active forces in the economy, hold particular resonances in the rural context because of the strongly domestic idiom through which rural England has come to be represented as an idealized moral social (and economic) order (Davidoff and Hall, 1988).

Recent feminist work has drawn attention to the ways in which Marxist and mainstream analyses, as well as policy, are infused with familial ideology such that despite the long-standing interest in the family labour process very little critical attention has in fact been given to the nature of the social relations underlying it. Feminist research has argued instead that such forms of production cannot be understood without recourse to the concept and analysis of patriarchal gender relations as a fundamental feature of the inequitable division of property, labour and disposable income within the family household (Sachs, 1983; Barthez, 1983; Whatmore, 1990). There are strong parellels, and some dialogue, between this research and the development of feminist perspectives in the analysis of household production in the rural south (Redclift and Mingione, 1985; Moore, 1988). Such studies have emphasized that in rural societies labour activities associated with the reproduction of people on a daily and generational basis cannot be regarded as in any sense part of a 'reproductive sphere' separate from 'the economy' but are crucial to survival and fully 'economic' in themselves (Singh and Kelles-Viitanen, 1987).

The boundaries that had been drawn between household/family and economy are thus more accurately seen to reflect western assumptions deriving from the 19th century separation of home from work, and far from universal. In the literature on non-western societies these boundaries began to shift, revealing that households constructed livelihoods not only through the wage economy but also out of a multitude of self-provisioning strategies and interactions with the natural environment. Such arguments expose the explanatory limitations of earlier functionalist accounts of the family/household widespread in the British literature. In analysing the family household in terms of its functions for capitalism the contours of the nuclear family household were taken as given and gained the ideological status of a 'natural' unit of social organization (Barrett, 1980). Feminist work has focused attention on the internal relations of kinship and household systems that are interwoven into the fabric of familial ideology (Yanagisako, 1979).

Household, gender and differentiation

If recent studies of the household outlined so far have produced a broader view of the effects of macroeconomic changes in Britain and western Europe, it is arguably in studies of the South that major shifts in thinking have occurred. These have not simply incorporated a new level of analysis but have changed perceptions of problems and their solution. These seem, as yet, to have had relatively little impact outside the so-called 'women and development' literature. But in terms of our understanding of the consequences of technological change, transformation of land-use; patterns of labour allocation and, most importantly, the actual survival or rural populations into the 21st century their implications are far-reaching.

In the feminist literature the household represents a mediating institution between the individual and society, between the polarized concerns of wage and non-wage, use and exchange value (Schmink, 1984). It is only through understanding household structure and composition, relationships between earners and dependents, and the disparities between individual members that any sense can be made of the individual and collective activities in the processes of production or reproduction. In the research on 'developing' economies, a definition of the household as the site of material consumption forms an important focus emphasizing its role in the final redistribution of resources to individuals. Of key significance is the interaction between changing forms of production – in particular the development of capitalist production – and 'the domestic group formations through which the immediate material needs of most individuals are met' (Schmink, 1984).

The model initially developed to understand the intersection of internal characteristics and the position of particular households in the labour market and social structure was that of *household survival strategies*. This first emerged within the Latin American structural historical tradition and was later extended to British and European Sociology (Redclift, 1986). The study of survival strategies brought together a range of different components that had not previously been explored in relation to one another. These included demographic and life-cycle factors (Bryman *et al.*, 1987); monetary income; non-monetary income and self-provisioning through the production and exchange of goods and services between neighbour and kin; and additional employment-related benefits of various kinds, and across forms of collective consumption. It was also based on a more precise approach to the household as a variable structure that could take a number of different forms and fulfil very different functions in different times and places.

The concept of survival strategy has, however been roundly criticized in both 'third' (Schmink, 1984) and 'first' (Crow, 1989) world literature. As Schmink has put it 'like the concept of adaptation, that of strategy can lose its meaning to the extent that it becomes a mere functionalist label applied post-facto to whatever behaviour is found' (1984: 21). More seriously, its adequacy has been questioned, particularly as it has informed international policy making because 'it is taken as axiomatic that economic relations within the domestic group are based on pooling, sharing or distribution [and] defined in terms of a unified circuit of production and consumption into which exchange does not intrude' (Harris, 1982: 45).

Households, in fact, are constructed around various inequalities in terms of the division of property rights, labour and the products of labour by generation and, more particularly, gender. Whereas women hold a wide range of positions within these divisions in different times and places, their power and access is often considerably less than that of men, whether in terms of their control over property and the means of production; over disposable income or over the labour of other family members. Their participation may be coerced through physical violence or economic dependence within the institution of marriage (Young, Wolkowitz and McCullagh, 1981). This is not to argue that women are merely passive victims, nor that women share the same experiences of some universal set of domestic relations

(Redclift, 1985), but to emphasize that the household is rarely an equitable, harmonious and utility-maximizing unit. In studies of the rural South attempts to understand the kinds of restructuring produced by the development of capitalist relations in agrarian societies, resulted in a number of historical analyses that tried to explain and assess the ways in which households and family structures respond to economic change. Many of these set out to document the fact that economic processes affect men and women very differently, and argued for a much more careful disaggregation of information that could take gender divisions into account (Boserup, 1970). Similar issues have been taken up in Britain, but again with an urban focus, as the inequalities within households in terms of material resource allocation and the ideologies that sustain them have been put under scrutiny (Gray, 1979; Whitehead, 1981; Pahl, 1989). Few such studies in Britain have so far taken a rural focus (but see Bouquet, 1986; Whatmore, 1990).

Nevertheless, recent critiques of such studies in the 'development' context have exposed the more or less explicit value judgement that lay behind much of this work. Generalizations were often drawn from specific cases, and processes that appeared to be superficially similar seemed to give rise to very different assessments of whether women were better or worse off than before. The explanation for this lay partly in the underlying assumptions of individual researchers about the relative merits of different courses of action. For example, if the family was regarded as the site of subordination, the decline of unremunerated family labour obligations that had given rise to forms of female proletarianization in some rural economies was often taken to imply increased autonomy for women, particularly in terms of control over cash income. Many authors have regarded the generation of income as the key determinant of women's domestic power. If, on the other hand, the family was seen to offer some measure of support against oppressive class relations and forms of labour contract, and also perhaps to afford women some measure of independence as artisan or petty commodity producers, changes that undermined this took on a more negative interpretation. It was far from clear what the criteria for comparison and evaluation might be. For example, was the maintenance of a relatively rigid gender division of labour that nevertheless granted women some rights of decision-making over the use of their labour time and disposal of the product a 'preferable' outcome? Or, was a flexible allocation of tasks that might appear more egalitarian, but in which women's labour time had markedly increased, to be seen as a more positive change? Whose position was ultimately 'better', the women whose material circumstances were comfortable but whose social relations were circumscribed, or the woman who had greater freedom of movement but existed in poverty.

The contradictory nature of these assessments suggest that the problem lay in the underlying framework itself. First, in its tendency to look for a universal relationship between gender and capitalism. Second, as Wilson (1985) has pointed out, in its recourse to an 'impact' model, in which 'capitalism' as a unitary and *exogenous* entity intervened to transform gender relations that were seen as 'internal' and timeless (Beneria, 1982).

This could only produce a number of competing hypotheses. For example, the so-called 'female marginalization' thesis implied that a general outcome of capitalist development was the exclusion of women from previous sources of productive work. Conversely, drawing on different kinds of data and other historical experiences, the 'superexploitation' thesis showed women becoming increasingly incorporated into particular moments of a cash-cropping cycle, or into sexually segregated sectors of agribusiness production. Comparing these processes the relevance of analysing the selective use of different kinds of female labour became clearer. The significance of some important differences *between* women had, however, still to be drawn out in order to understand the local patterns that might result.

Among these differences between women are obviously those based on class, 'race' and 'ethnicity'. These affect women's relative bargaining position in the labour market. They also affect the trade-off between the wage women can command and the time they no longer have in which to carry out necessary reproductive labour. Such cross-cutting social divisions and identities would also influence the ideology of culturally appropriate practices in the sphere of reproduction, in other words the values and assumptions surrounding the material constitution of domestic lifestyles. What is regarded as 'necessary' labour at home varies by class and ethnic group and therefore influences the amount of time women feel they need to commit to this in order to maintain family status at a given level. Only women with some occupational advantage can afford to pay to substitute their labour at home. Paid domestic help and childcare accord with the domestic ideologies of specific social groups (Lowe and Gregson, 1989). However, for families at certain income levels it also results in restrictions in family budgets to compensate, with implicit consequences in terms of diet, health or children's education. In other class positions using kin or neighbours as caretakers is regarded as the appropriate solution and may be the only way in which women's labour time can be freed to earn necessary income. However, where mobility is high, among immigrant populations for example, this may no longer be an option and women may either not be able to earn at all or may have to leave their children in order to do so. The key point to emerge from studies such as these is that these patterned relationships between income-earning possibilities and reproductive choices are not simply 'outcomes' of change or 'effects' on women and households. They contribute to the overall process of stratification itself and the dynamic process by which households and individuals move up and down hierarchies of material access, and become relatively less or more impoverished.

An important distinction within this general set of arguments needs emphasizing – that is the difference between women at different points in the domestic and reproductive cycle, and in different kinship and family structures. In some rural contexts, for example, daughters are shed from the family unit in order to become urban domestic workers and remit small amounts of income. In others the labour of daughters increasingly replaces that of the mother as principal caretaker, as older women become sole heads of households and are forced to take on longer and longer hours of waged work to generate adequate family income. The effects of structural adjustment and the debt crisis in the South make these intergenerational patterns of mother /daughter substitution a particularly crucial area for further investigation because they significantly affect the subsistence and reproductive potential of future households. If daughters substitute for the domestic work of mothers their access to education and subsequent labour market options are weakened, lessening their chances of upward mobility and perhaps eventually condemning them to even poorer working conditions than those of their mothers.

A final area of consideration is the interrelationship between production systems themselves, with their specific organizational requirements in which tasks must be coordinated at particular moments, and the personal gendered relationships (of kinship or contract) that control the rights of the participants in each other's labour and in the product. Two points stand out here. First, the nature of the legitimate demands that members of a household can make of each other's physical capacities is not fixed but open to a certain amount of renegotiation. Some of the contradictory findings of earlier studies were the result of ignoring this diversity of household labour control, which was concealed by the rather more rigid idea of the gender division of labour as a simple allocation of tasks (Redclift, 1985). They were also the result of underplaying the diversity of the kinds of technological transformations that were taking place. Second, in many areas of the world a rigid rural–urban distinction is of little use in understanding household reproduction when it is built on the basis of multi-income sources, diversification of activities and remittances from migrant family members who may be widely geographically dispersed. More attention has now been paid to the limitations of abstracting production systems from the totality of household reproductive needs of food, fuel and water, the provision of which forms a significant proportion of most women's time use. Changes in one area of labour allocation have been found to have hidden effects on others with often disastrous consequences in terms of nutrition and health.

From the literature on the South it becomes clear that rather than simply being influenced by economic restructuring, divisions by gender are central to the way in which the economic system works. An interactive and historically specific view of the relationships between relations of gender, class and technological change based on a *reproductive* rather than an impact model is now emerging as a more relevant way of understanding the transformation of rural livelihoods. As Sen and Grown point out, 'what has been called a generalised reproduction crisis in the provision of "basic needs" has poor women at its centre, as the principal providers of those needs' (1987: 21).

Conclusions

An important aspect of the feminist critique of orthodox analyses of household and family, North and South, has been concerned with their ideological rather than economic status, as powerful representations of moral and social order and gender identity (Collins, 1985). The gap between dominant ideological representations and reality is a large one. We can compare, for instance, the nuclear family form denoted by the term 'the family' with the diverse experience of countries of the South and, as Bradley's study showed, in Britain too. Yet, such ideologies lie at the core of much of the state's involvement in the post-war provision of collective consumption through the welfare state system based on the idea of the 'family wage' (Barrett, 1980). They also underpin, in Britain, the retreat from welfarism into 'community care' which is premised on assumptions about women's nurturing domestic role even as this role is made increasingly untenable by the increasing economic need for households to command two incomes from waged-work. This contradiction endorses the maintenance of a patriarchal domestic social order thus legitimizing both state policy and family household values at the same time.

Policy debates remain largely uninformed by the considerable rethinking by social theorists of the processes reshaping the economy and society of rural regions of advanced societies, as do many of the empirical studies that inform them (Lowe, Bradley and Wright, 1987). Thus, for example, whereas the diversification of agricultural land-use and farm incomes has become a central part of the rhetoric of agricultural and rural development policies (Rural Voice, 1985), the issue is still couched in terms of individual farmers and farm businesses. The existence of the farm household and its composite nature, let alone the research showing the interdependence and inequalities structuring the roles of its individual members, remains unacknowledged. The contrast between the policy discourses of institutions such as the EEC and those of international aid agencies operating in the rural South with respect to these issues represent an important area for future comparative research.

As the previous sections have suggested, policy debates in Britain remain bound up in a complex web of nostalgia and wishful thinking in which representations of rural society feed upon domestic ideologies that support a bourgeoise social order as a 'natural' social order. The legitimation crisis in rural policy in Britain and, arguably in Europe more widely, results precisely from deep-rooted contradictions between the ideologies informing policy rhetoric, and the outcomes of policy instruments designed to extend the principles of market competition into the realms of both consumption and production. The 'family farmer' as an icon of policy rhetoric has been relentlessly corroded in the name of agricultural efficiency (see Peterson, chapter 3, and Lawrence, in chapter 4 of this volume). The 'rural community', populated by role models for the Tory 'active citizen', gives way to a picture of poverty and isolation in the real world of privatized consumption. The current bifurcation in the language and concepts informing academic and policy debates is an important measure of the gulf to have emerged between social science and Government agendas.

It is always a risk in seeking to synthesize the development of a research field, however defined, to project too uniform and linear a pattern. We have attempted here to indicate the centrality of the issues covered by the household/consumption/livelihood matrix to a range of contemporary concerns in rural research (class recomposition, deprivation, and household production), while acknowledging the dispersed, and sometimes patchy, nature of the feminist literature on these issues. This matrix links longstanding concerns in British rural studies with recent developments in social theory, particularly regarding gender relations and the significance of areas of social life and forms of economic activity 'outside' the purview of corporate industrial capital. What is important is that these issues are now given more priority on the research agendas of advanced industrial countries so that, as research on the rural South has already shown, old problems are brought under a new light.

Notes

1. Although Urry did not originate the term civil society, his influential book (1981) has played a large part in resurrecting it.
2. Although there has been a revival of research interest in the informal economy in Britain, this work has been notably urban in focus (see, for example, Pahl, 1985; Morris, 1985).

References

Barlow, J. (1986) Landowners, property ownership and the rural locality, *International Journal of Urban and Regional Research*, **10**, 309–29.

Barrett, M. (1980), *Women's Oppression Today*, Verso, London.

Barthez, A. (1983) *Famille et Travail Agriculture*, Economica, Paris.

Bechhoffer, F. and Elliott, B. (1981) *The Petite Bourgoisie*, Macmillan, London.

Beneria, L. (1982) *Women and Development: the Sexual Division of Labour in Rural Societies*, Praeger, New York.

Benvenuti, B. (1985) On the dualism between sociology and rural sociology: some hints for the case of modernisation, *Sociologica Ruralis*, **25**, 214–30.

Bernstein, H. (1986) Capitalism and petty commodity production, *Social Analysis*, **20**, 11–28.

Boserup, E. (1970) *Womens' Role in Economic Development*, St Martin's Press, New York.

Bouquet, M. (1982) Production and reproduction on family farms in rural south west England, *Sociologica Ruralis*, **xx**, 227–44.

Bouquet, M. (1986) *Family, Servants and Visitors*, Geobooks, Norwich.

Bouquet, M. (1987) Domestic economy and welfare. In Lowe, *et al*. (1987) *Deprivation and Welfare in Rural Areas*, pp. 85–98.

Bouquet, M. and de Haan, H. (1987) Kinship as an analytical category in rural sociology: an introduction, *Sociologia Ruralis*, **27**, 243–62.

Bowlby, S., Foord, J. and McDowell, L. (1986) The place of gender in locality studies, *Area*, **18** (4), 327–31.

Bradley, T. (1981) Capitalism and the countryside: rural sociology or political economy?, *International Journal of Urban and Regional Research*, **5**, 581–7.

Bradley, T. (1987) Poverty and dependency in village England. In Lowe *et al*. (1987) *Deprivation and Welfare in Rural Areas*, pp. 85–98.

Bryman, A. *et al*. (1987) *The Sociology of the Life-cycle*. Macmillan, London.

Buttel, F. and Newby, H. (1980) Introduction to *The Rural Sociology of Advanced Societies*, Allenheld, Osmun Co., Montclair, NJ.

Cloke, P. and Thrift, N. (1987) Intra-class conflict in rural areas, *Journal of Rural Studies*, **3**, 321–33.

Cohen, A. (ed.) (1986) *Symbolising Boundaries*, Manchester University Press.

Collins, R. (1985) 'Horses for courses': ideology and the division of domestic labour. In P. Close and R. Collins (eds), *Family and Economy in Modern Society*, Macmillan, London, pp. 64–83.

Crow, G. (1989) The use and concept of 'strategy' in recent sociological literature', *Sociology*, **23**, 1–24.

Davidoff, L., L'Esperence, J. and Newby, H. (1976) Landscape with figures. In J. Mitchell and A. Oakley (eds), *The Rights and Wrongs of Women*, Penguin, Harmondsworth.

Davidoff, L. and Hall, C. (1988) *Family Fortunes: Men and Women in the English Middle-class 1780–1850*, Hutchinson, London.

Gasson, R. *et al.* (1988) The farm as a family business, *Journal of Agricultural Economics*, **39**, 1–41.

Gray, A. (1979) The working class family as an economic unit. In C. Harris (ed.), *The Sociology of the family, Sociological Review Monograph*, **28**, 186–212.

Harper, S. (1989) The British rural community: an overview of perspectives, *Journal of Rural Studies*, **5**, 161–84.

Harris, C. (1983) *The Family and Industrial Society*, Allen & Unwin, London.

Harris, O. (1982) Households as natural units. In K. Young, *et al.* (1981) *Of Marriage and the Market*, pp. 136–56.

Kiernan, K. (1989) The family, formation and fission. In J. Heather (ed.), *The Changing Population of Britain*, Basil Blackwell, Oxford, pp. 27–41.

Little, J. (1988) Women's non-agricultural employment: constraints and opportunities within a rural development area. Paper presented to the World Congress on Rural Sociology, Bologna, July.

Lowe, M. and Gregson, N. (1989) Nannies, cooks, cleaners, au pairs . . . issues for feminist geography?, *Area*, **21**, 415–17.

Lowe, P., Bradley, T. and Wright, S. (eds) (1987) *Deprivation and Welfare in Rural Areas*, Geobooks, Norwich.

Marsden, T.K. (1984) Capitalist farming and the farm family: a case study, *Sociology*, **18**, 206–24.

Massey, D. (1984) *Spatial Divisions of Labour*, Macmillan, London.

Middleton, A. (1987) Marking boundaries: men's space and women's space in a Yorkshire village. In P. Lowe *et al.* (1987) *Deprivation and Welfare in Rural Areas*, pp. 121–34.

Moore, H. (1988) *Feminism and Anthropology*, Polity Press, Cambridge.

Morris, L. (1985) Renegotiation of the domestic division of labour in the context of male redundancy. In H. Newby *et al.* (1985) *Restructuring Capital*, pp. 221–44.

Newby, H. (1980) Rural Sociology: a trend report, *Current Sociology*, **28**, 125–66.

Newby, H. (1985) Locality and rurality: the restructuring of rural social relations, *Regional Studies*, **20**, 209–16.

Newby, H., Rose, C., Bujra, P., Littlewood, G. and Rees, T. (eds) (1985) *Restructuring Capital: Recession and Reorganisation in Industrial Society*, Hutchinson, London.

Pahl, J. (1989) *Money and Marriage*, Macmillan, London.

Pahl, R. (1985) *Divisions of Labour*, Basil Blackwell, Oxford.

Pahl, R. and Wallace, C. (1985) Household work strategies in economic recession. In N. Redclift and E. Mingione (1985) *Beyond Employment*, pp. 188-225.

Redclift, M. (1986) Survival strategies in rural Europe: and introduction, *Sociologia Ruralis*, **26**, 218-27.

Redclift, N. (1985) The contested domain: gender, accumulation and the labour process. In Redclift and Mingione (1985) *Beyond Employment*, pp. 92-125.

Redclift, N. and Mingione, E. (eds) (1985) *Beyond Employment: Household, Gender and Subsistence*, Basil Blackwell, Oxford.

Rural Voice (1985) *Agriculture and the Rural Economy*, Rural Voice, London.

Sachs, C. (1983) *Invisible Farmers*, Rhinehart & Allenheld, Totowa, NJ.

Schmink, M. (1984) Household economic strategies, *Latin American Research Review*, 29, 3.

Scott, A. (1986) Why rethink petty commodity production?, *Social Analysis*, **20**, 3-10.

Sen, G. and Grown, C. 1987, *Development, Crises and Alternative Visions: Third World Womens' Perspectives*, Monthly Review Press, New York.

Shaw, J. (ed.) (1979) *Rural Deprivation and Planning*, Geobooks, Norwich.

Singh, A.M. and Kelles-Viitanen, A. (eds) (1987) *Invisible Hands: Women and Home-based Production*, Sage, London.

Stacey, M. (1969) The Myth of Community Studies, *British Journal of Sociology*, **20**, 134-47.

Strathern, M. (1984) The social meaning of localism. In T. Bradley and P. Lowe (1984) *Locality and Rurality*, pp. 181-98.

Thrift, N. (1987) Manufactuuring rural geography, *Journal of Rural Studies*, **3**, 77-81.

Urry, J. (1981) *The Anatomy of Capitalist Society: the Economy, Civil Society and the State*, Pion, London.

Urry, J. (1984) Capitalist restructuring, recomposition and the regions. In T. Bradley and P. Lowe (eds) (1984) *Locality and Rurality*, pp. 45-64.

Urry, J. (1985) Deindustrialisation, households and politics. In Murgatroyd *et al.* (eds), *Localities, Class and Gender*, Macmillan, London, pp. 13-29.

Weekley, I. (1988) Rural depopulation and counterurbanisation, *Area*, **20**, 127-34.

Whatmore, S. (1990) *Farming Women: Gender, Work and Family Enterprise*, Macmillan, London.

Whitehead, A. (1981) "I'm hungry mum": the politics of domestic budgeting. In K. Young *et al.* (1981) *Of Marriage and the Market*, pp. 93-316.

Wilson, F. (1985) Women and agricultural change in Latin America: some concepts guiding research, *World Development*, **13/9**, pp. 1017-35.

Winter, M. (1984) Agrarian class structure and family farming. In T. Bradley and P. Lowe (1984), *Locality and Rurality*, pp. 115-28.

Yanagisako, S. (1979) Family and household: the analysis of domestic groups, *Annual Review of Anthropology*, **8**, 161–205.

Young, K., Wolkowitz, C. and McCullagh, R. (eds) (1981) *Of Marriage and the Market*, Routledge & Kegan Paul, London.

For Product Safety Concerns and Information please contact our EU
representative GPSR@taylorandfrancis.com
Taylor & Francis Verlag GmbH, Kaufingerstraße 24, 80331 München, Germany

www.ingramcontent.com/pod-product-compliance
Ingram Content Group UK Ltd.
Pitfield, Milton Keynes, MK11 3LW, UK
UKHW021828240425
457818UK00006B/115